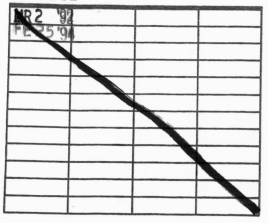
The

BY KARL A. LAMB

As Orange Goes: Twelve California Families and the Future of American Politics, 1974

The People, Maybe, 1971, 1974, 1978

Campaign Decision-Making: The Presidential Election of 1964 (with Paul A. Smith), 1968

Congress: Politics and Practice (with Norman C. Thomas), 1964

Apportionment and Representative Institutions: The Michigan Experience (with William J. Pierce and John P. White), 1963

KARL A. LAMB

The Guardians

Leadership Values and the American Tradition

W · W · NORTON & COMPANY
NEW YORK · LONDON

Copyright © 1982 by W. W. Norton & Company, Inc.

All rights reserved.

Published simultaneously in Canada by George J. McLeod Limited, Toronto.

Printed in the United States of America.

First Edition

The text of this book is composed in 10/12 Avanta, with display type set in Bodoni Bold.
Manufacturing by The Haddon Craftsmen, Inc.

Library of Congress Cataloging in Publication Data

Lamb, Karl A.
   The guardians.

   Includes bibliographical references and index.
   1. Political participation—United States.
2. Elite (Social sciences)—United States.
3.Values   I. Title
JK1764.L35   1982   323′.042′0973   82–8208

ISBN 0-393-01575-0

ISBN 0-393-95226-6 PBK

W. W. Norton & Company, Inc. 500 Fifth Avenue, New York, N.Y. 10110
W. W. Norton & Company Ltd. 37 Great Russell Street, London WC1B 3NU

1 2 3 4 5 6 7 8 9 0

To the memory of
V. O. Key, Jr.,
and
Daniel Lerner

Contents

Preface

Prefaces provide the author with space to acknowledge the aid he has received and absolve his helpers of responsibility for the product. In a work of this sort, the list of contributors is long, but the absolution must be fervent, for the interpretation is the author's alone.

My greatest debt is to the respondents. Their willingness to be interviewed made the book possible. I came to regard the 117 men and women I talked with as representatives of an American political class comparable to Plato's guardians. But this class has indeterminate boundaries, and not all its members are conscious of their membership and its apparent responsibilities. The Guardians are both private citizens and public officials; the interview itself constituted no small invasion of the privacy of private citizens. The publication of excerpts from those conversations is yet a further injury, for I now argue back—in many cases, after a lapse of several years.

In the book that follows, individuals are identified in one of three ways: by their real names—with their explicit permission in the case of private citizens and through recognition that the interview was on the record in the case of public officials; by fictional names, upon agreement with private citizens; and by occupation only, when the interview was explicitly off the record. Thus their mode of identification was specified by the individuals concerned.

The initial research was made possible by a Humanities Fellowship of the Rockefeller Foundation, which I held during the calendar year of 1977. Preparation of the manuscript was supported by a series of modest, but timely, grants from the Research Committee of the University of California, Santa Cruz, Faculty Senate. Neither agency attached conditions to their largesse, beyond standard accounting procedures. Neither can be blamed for the book; but I hope each will accept my gratitude.

As explained in the Introduction, I relied on consultants in each of the cities I visited for help in identifying appropriate respondents. I wish to thank them here. For Atlanta: Anna Grant, Susan Hadden, and Tobe Johnson. For Boston: Langley Keyes, Jackie (Mrs. Thomas III) O'Neil, Charles Page, and Robin Schmidt. For Chicago: Lou Masotti and Jim O'Callahan. For Houston: Ronnie Dugger, Kathleen Kemp, Mr. and Mrs. George Moore, Ted Schomburg, and Senator John Tower. For San Francisco: William K. Coblentz, Victor Jones, Dale Rogers Marshall, and Fred Wirt. In Washington I followed networks to which I gained entry with the help of two United States senators and a San Francisco feminist who are friends or classmates; and I consulted the late William Baroody, Sr., and Howard Penniman. At the end of three busy weeks in Washington, I felt nearly ready to go into business as a lobbyist.

The book owes much to my extraordinary research assistants. Pat Kolb helped during the early phases of research design and data gathering. Pat insisted that the interview guide include a question about the public interest; the answers became central to the analysis in chapter three. Rein Staal served during the months of indexing and cross-indexing, library searches, and preliminary writing. The book bears the marks of his keen intelligence and grasp of American political theory; among other matters, Rein suggested the title. On the quantitative side, Bob Marsh tamed the SPSS program and produced more cross-tabulations and indexes of correlation than I could ever use. We even developed some Guttman scales.

A number of colleagues lent a hand at various stages of the project. When the research design was being developed, I consulted Professors William K. Muir, Jr., Victor Jones, and Herbert McClosky, all of the University of California, Berkeley. I presented the data of chapter two in a paper for a special panel at the 1980 American Political Science Association Convention arranged by John Kessel of the Ohio State University. In addition to John Kessel's useful reactions, the paper received helpful comments from Lawrence Herson, Bernard Hennessy, and David Riesman of Ohio State, Hayward State, and Harvard, respectively. On my own campus, Grant McConnell and John Schaar have been helpful and supportive, Bruce Larkin made important suggestions concerning chapter five, and Bob Hawkinson read the entire manuscript at one stage or another, providing insightful suggestions far beyond the call of duty or even friendship. John Hummel, as usual, kept me alert to the importance of style.

The amused tolerance of my family made it possible to complete the manuscript. Cindy's birth on February 2, 1977, delayed my research travels by a few weeks; it now seems the fear that she would learn to read before the book was finished will go unrealized. I want to thank my wife, Sally, for her help on this and other projects and for more than two decades of collaboration.

Don Lamm of W. W. Norton has been my publisher and editor. I am grateful for his patience, for his integrity, and for his friendship. Everett Ladd of the University of Connecticut reviewed the initial manuscript for Norton and made important suggestions.

This book is dedicated to the memory of two giants of the social sciences. I knew V. O. Key only briefly, when he visited the University of Michigan in 1959–60. My intellectual debt is recorded in the following pages. Daniel Lerner came to Santa Cruz in 1979, upon retirement from M.I.T. Despite his terminal illness, he took an interest in this project. After reading early versions of two chapters, he persuaded me that I should be unblushingly normative in my treatment of these data. I should like to think that both scholars might have approved of the result.

KARL A. LAMB

Santa Cruz, California
June 2, 1982

The Guardians

Introduction

The American Guardians

In 1961 the late Professor V. O. Key wrote a paragraph which marks the beginning of this inquiry. Key was concluding a massive study of the role of public opinion in American government. His purpose was to assess the political relevance of the knowledge about public opinion gathered over the two preceding decades by scholars who did not always share the political scientist's concern for power and its influence on public policy. Finding that public opinion is formed by an interaction between political activists and the general public, Key wrote that opinion research focused upon mass publics cannot explain the relationship between public opinion and public policy, because the researchers' random samples do not include adequate data about the values, attitudes, and actions of the relatively small number of persons for whom politics is an all-consuming interest. Concentrated in the upper social and economic levels of American society, but present also at its middle and lower levels, these men and women are those whose voices count most in formulating policy decisions, once the electorate has determined which candidates will fill the offices of formal authority. Key concluded,

> [T]he critical element for the health of a democratic order consists in the beliefs, standards, and competence of those who constitute the influentials, the opinion-leaders, the political activists in the order. That group, as has been made plain, refuses to define itself with great clarity in the American system; yet analysis after analysis points to its existence. If a democracy tends toward indecision, decay, and disaster, the responsibility rests here, not in the mass of the people.

Key wrote at the beginning of a decade, the 1960s, that would be crowded with political turmoil, social change, and civil and military strife. After the 1970s, characterized at their mid-point by the revelations of malfeasance in high office symbolized by Watergate, America entered the 1980s with a list of problems that seemed outside the boundaries of American experience: inflation, the energy shortage, urban poverty, and environmental deterioration. Most domestic issues, and particularly economic problems, are affected by the uncertainties of a volatile international situation. The American citizenry expressed its lack of confidence in government efforts to resolve these and other problems by withdrawing from electoral participation and supporting revolts against taxation. Those who did vote elected both Jimmy Carter and Ronald Reagan upon promises to curb the growth and streamline the operations of the federal government.

The 1980s began as a period of indecision and decay, marked by widespread disaffection from the political process. The magnitude of Ronald Reagan's electoral victory obscured the fact that only a modest number of eligible voters bothered to decide whether Reagan might achieve some of the goals that Carter had been unable to implement. President Reagan's determination to limit or end federal involvement in several problem areas—such as environmental pollution and urban decay—did not automatically establish the marketplace as an arena certain to solve such problems in a socially acceptable manner.

V. O. Key suggested that the responsibility for political dilemmas in any era may be found in the beliefs and competence of our political activists. To follow Key's suggestion, a single assumption is necessary, and I take its truth to be self-evident: political influence in the United States is unequally distributed. The Supreme Court has decreed that each person shall have one vote, neither more nor less; and this is an important decree. But it does not tell us how policies are made (or fail to be made) by legislatures, or what determines the interpretation of policy by judges or its implementation by bureaucrats, or how any of these processes are influenced by private citizens, or for what reasons.

Locating the Activists and Learning of their Beliefs

Any attempt to assess the beliefs and standards of America's political leadership must begin with a theory about the distribution of political power that will locate the powerful. Those who write about the structure of power in America have debated for years the theories that undergird their research. One group of scholars may be called the elitists. They picture American society as a pyramid, with a small group of the wealthy, politically powerful, and socially distinguished occupying its pinnacle. They argue, logically, that the persons in that position must have achieved it, and certainly protect it, through their own actions. After a ritual bow to the shade of sociologist C. Wright Mills, the elitists describe the meeting- and eating-places of the rich and the pattern of multiple membership on boards of directors by the same powerful individuals. Older distinctions between inherited and *nouvelle richesse* disappear in the portrait of monolithic corporate power.

In its most extreme form, the elitist claim is that there is an upper social class in America which also, through its control of key institutions, constitutes a ruling class. This ruling class controls both political parties, making elections into fraudulent exercises designed to give the masses an illusion of political influence. In this view, the ruling class also controls the communications media, so it can manipulate public attitudes and create that public opinion upon which democracy theoretically rests. The elitist claim is simple: find out who benefits most from the social and economic structure, and you have an approximate notion of who wields political power.

The opposing view, mainly articulated by political scientists, is that of the pluralists. The pluralists share with elitists the perception that neither popular elections, nor any other democratic institution, give to the common man direct or continuing control over what government does. But pluralists see democratic values preserved by the ability of the common person to add his or her bit of labor or money to the efforts of one or more of the many organized groups that are politically active. It is thought to be a saving grace of the system that the same individual will adhere to, and be influenced by, several groups, because of his or her occupation, religious affiliation, or charitable impulse. The continuous conflict between these groups, and their combination and recombination into momentary majorities, produces public policy. Pluralists stipulate that the structure of power is understood only by studying the influences determining specific policy decisions. Power cannot be automatically ascribed to persons who occupy particular positions within institutions or in society as a whole. An upper social class exists, and many individuals influence the politics of particular issue areas. But wealth, social position, and political influence are not necessarily coterminous.

In its most extreme form, the pluralist argument holds that the political arena provides a neutral field for the contest between groups; that participation in the contest is open to all; and that the outcome of the contest assures the good of all, or at least of the majority. Something like the invisible hand of the classical economic marketplace takes over, and nobody need be praised or blamed for the outcome, which results from a momentary equilibrium of forces, and thus is morally neutral.

The attempt to portray the group contest as explaining the total reality of American politics reached an apex in the work of David B. Truman. To make the theory totally inclusive, Truman specified "unorganized" and "potential" groups made up of those whose attachment to the "rules of the game" would lead them to perceive an interest in defending proper procedures against attack. Nearly all political actors adhere to many groups, both organized and potential; Truman described this multiple membership as the principal guarantee of stability. Thus he avoided discussing such phenomena as beliefs or values.

> The group process will proceed in the usual fashion. Whether it eventuates in disaster will depend in the future as in the past basically upon the effects of overlapping membership, particularly the vitality of membership in those potential groups based on interests widely held throughout the society. These memberships are the means both of stability and of peaceful change. In the future as in the past, they will provide the answer to the ancient question: *quis custodiet ipsos custodes?* Guardianship will emerge out of the affiliations of the guardians.

The elitists draw their explanations of power distribution from the fact of position, while the pluralists draw theirs from the facts of behavior. The phenomena examined by each group are important, and the resulting explanations illuminate a complex reality. However, both theories are flawed, and for the same reason. Both assume that the predominant motive for political action, on the part of individuals and groups, is self-interest. And the conception of self-interest is fairly immediate and short-range in nature.

A number of political motives are barely acknowledged by the pluralist and elitist theories. Neither theory accounts for a Martin Luther King, Jr., who leaves a comfortable middle-class pastorate to lead a social revolution. Neither theory accounts for thousands of young men flocking to enlist in the armed forces on December 8, 1941. Neither theory explains why American labor organizations, while lacking the ideological orientation of their European counterparts, nonetheless take political action on a range of issues—social security and national health insurance, for example—that are not directly related to the essentially private practice of collective bargaining. In short, both pluralist and elitist theories help to identify the political influentials, but they do not tell us much about their values, if those values extend beyond self-interest.

While recognizing that the interests of individuals and groups are a primary motivating force in politics, my contention, following Key, is that the health of the democratic order depends on the values pursued by political activists that lie beyond self-interest. Such values provide long-range justification for the political actions of the moment and supply the standards by which political influentials judge proposed policies and the actions of others. The insights of both pluralists and elitists were used to designate the powerful and potentially powerful; but social science writings did not supply a critique of their values.

In the fall of 1977 and the summer of 1978, I traveled to six American cities—Atlanta, Boston, Chicago, Houston, San Francisco, and Washington, D.C.—to interview 117 men and women. I visited Washington during the presidential campaign in 1980 to reinterview several respondents. Then, when the Reagan administration had established its direction in 1981, I contacted other respondents yet again. The reinterviews suggested that changing political realities influence the connection between asserted values and policy preferences. In some cases, beliefs expressed in earlier conversations now have practical consequences.

The persons I sought out were defined as those who then had, or would have during the 1980s, a remarkable political voice. I was not attempting to designate an exclusive group who "run things" in any of the six cities. I was not concerned with the need to prove or disprove the existence of such a group. Instead, I sought persons of achieved or potential influence in leading institutions, including public officeholders; persons of the kind who can assert an effective veto power by resisting proposals for change in political institutions; the Guardians of the American tradition.

In the first five cities, that meant political influence on the local or state level and a concern for issues that are national in scope. I was careful to include persons from those groups that are known to give to each city much of its particular character—the established black middle class in Atlanta and the whites who have rebuilt the downtown; executives of high-technology industry near Boston and a covey of politicians; friends and enemies of the Democratic organization in Chicago; oilmen in Houston; bankers, builders, and the paragons of non-partisan politics in San Francisco. In Washington I spoke to senators, congressmen, a member of the Carter cabinet, and important civil servants, as well as attorneys, lobbyists, and journalists who work in Washington because the national government is headquartered there.

The persons I sought to interview were selected with the advice of local consultants—journalists and academics, usually political scientists or political sociologists. I asked these local experts to identify persons of achieved or growing stature in politics, law, business, and civic associations. Sometimes I asked respondents for references to colleagues in their own or other cities. Networks of the similarly educated and like-minded are a social reality, and I used whatever connections were useful to assure access to the targeted respondents, including the exploitation of my own status as a Yale alumnus and former Rhodes Scholar; there are "old boy networks."

This combination of approaches was used to locate persons of actual and potential influence in the politics of the 1980s. Only time will prove the success of my search for future leaders. What might be called "early returns" suggest that the result will be positive. This conclusion is reached by considering the later careers of some of the respondents I was led to believe would become influential. In Chicago, for example, I interviewed the seemingly obscure commissioner of consumer affairs. The commissioner, Jane Byrne, was elected mayor in 1979. An editor I interviewed in Washington in 1977 won the Pulitzer Prize in 1979. A United States senator I conversed with, Richard Lugar, was included in every list of potential running mates for Ronald Reagan in 1980, until Reagan selected George Bush. Boston's John Winthrop Sears was again elected to the City Council early in 1980. The staff economist of a Congressional committee has since been promoted into the hierarchy of the Council of Economic Advisers. Louis Martin, editor of Chicago's black newspaper, the *Defender,* was in 1979 called to the Democratic National Committee office in Washington to head the organizational effort among minorities for Jimmy Carter, as he had done for Lyndon Johnson. An attorney I interviewed in Houston became in 1981 the first Mexican-American member of the Houston Housing Authority. Barney Frank, a Massachusetts state legislator, was in 1980 elected to Congress from the Fourth District, which had been represented by Father Robert F. Drinan.

The respondents are well positioned by age to influence the politics of the 1980s. While I interviewed several persons in their sixties and one in his seventies who have achieved influential positions, along with Benjamin Mays, then eighty-three and president of the Atlanta school board, the respondents were largely in their mid-forties; the sample's median age in 1977 was just under forty-five. With three persons under thirty, and three-fourths of the entire group under fifty, they are comparable to the new wave of political leaders interviewed by David Broder. With a few exceptions, they are too young to bear the scars of the Great Depression or have personal memories of the battles and victories of World War II.

After locating the influential, the second requirement for pursuing V. O. Key's insight is to apply a technique that will reveal the values and standards of the persons one has found. I chose the well-developed technique of the open-ended depth interview. In such interviews, questions are not designed to yield responses that can be easily counted and compared. Instead, the questions are intended to stimulate candid reflections by the respondents that will reveal something of their most firmly held convictions.

The shortest interview lasted for fifteen minutes (with the secretary of the treasury, who was called away by pressing duties) and the longest ran for more than five hours, when I recorded a conversation with a Washington lobbyist and his wife at their home in Virginia. The usual interview lasted for well over an hour. These were busy people, but they found political conversation stimulating, and I usually over-stayed the allotted time.

Many interviews took place in a spacious, well-furnished office building, high above the mundane commerce of the city streets. The respondent was a senior partner in a law firm, or a high executive officer of a bank or industrial corporation. But others took place in restaurants and in private homes; in the office of a neighborhood organization in a devastated area of West Washington Boulevard in Chicago; in the cubbyhole space assigned to a Massachusetts state legislator; in the second-floor walkup office of a civil rights organization in San Francisco, and in an attorney's storefront office in a Mexican neighborhood in Houston. One interview was recorded in a private club, and two in very public bars.

At the end of the interview, I asked the respondents to sort thirty cards on a sort-board, according to the strength of their agreement or disagreement with each statement printed on a card. Eighty-four respondents (72 per cent) were willing to spend the extra minutes required to complete this task. Their responses added an extra dimension to the recorded interviews and supplied attitude data for analysis in the standard manner.

While over half the respondents admitted to a net worth of half a million dollars or more, several confessed that their debts were greater than their assets. Generally, these were the young people thrusting into the higher circles of political influence; one was a Catholic priest. Some of the respondents were government employees; a few were staff members in organizations dedicated to causes for which the respondents had at least temporarily renounced even comfort, much less wealth. Although neither wealth nor a particular kind of education are prerequisites for political influence in America, political influentials tend to be better educated and to have gained more wealth than the average citizen. The exceptions—political influentials of less than average education and wealth—are numerous enough to confound the application of socioeconomic determinism to American politics.

A Political Class, Not Quite Like Plato's Guardians

The actual and appropriate relationships between wealth, education, and political power have preoccupied political thinkers since the dawn of political speculation. On the basis of his disappointment with the *demos* of Athens, Plato formulated his conception of the ideal state, outlined in the dialogue called *The Republic.* Of the classic forms of government, Plato rejected tyranny because power corrupted the personality of the tyrant; oligarchy because the joining of wealth and power led to the oppression of the many by the few; and democracy because of the inability of citizens in the mass to understand their own best interest, much less the nature of the good. His ideal state was headed by a philosopher-king, who served as guide to understanding the good for a political class called the guardians, who ruled the government on a daily basis and defended the state against external enemies. For more than two thousand years, Plato's formulation has greatly attracted philosophers, but has won little support from kings, since much of *The Republic* is taken up by descriptions of the lengthy and difficult education needed to prepare philosopher-kings and guardians for their responsibilities.

This book is based on the perception that there is a fairly distinct class of political influentials—an elite—in America. In the usual terms of social science, they do not constitute either a social or an economic class, nor are they drawn exclusively from the highly educated persons skilled in communications that have been called "the new class" by a number of recent social commentators. "Guardian" is an appropriate label for a member of this class. Since the existence of such a class belies the democratic ideal of decisions affecting all being made by all, the antidemocratic connotations of Plato's term are intended. But the differences between the American Guardians and Plato's guardians are important. The American Guardians are not a military class; they are primarily civilians. Civilian control of the military is a principle adopted in America to prevent some of the disasters that befell the ancient Greek cities. The American Guardians do not serve under the direction of a philosopher-king. The founding American principle is that the people are sovereign, and the Guardians have absorbed this principle thoroughly. Very few express cynicism about the manipulation of public opinion. On the contrary, many more are so habituated to the popular influence upon politics that they tend to abdicate the responsibilities of guardianship.

Many paths lead Americans into the Guardian class; no particular education or apprenticeship is prescribed. (For Plato, full guardianship came only at the age of fifty.) But the American Guardians have ascended into their present status by working within established political institutions, often on the basis of knowledge gained through both education and experience in a particular field. Although they may criticize existing institutions and the results those institutions produce, they are chronic operators from "inside the system," and they perforce become the defenders of existing procedural arrangements. As practitioners, they become the conservators of the American political tradition.

The dimensions of this Guardian class would be hard to specify; the number of persons constituting it cannot be stated. V. O. Key wrote that it is a group that "refuses to define itself with great clarity." The persons I interviewed do not represent the Guardians in a statistically reliable manner; it is not possible to calculate a probable sampling error. (Demographic data concerning my 117 respondents will be found in the Appendix.) I have used what they told me as clues to the values and opinions held by the Guardians and as a body of data that can be used both to describe and to criticize the American class of political influentials.

The data were subjected to the standard techniques of quantitative analysis; these results are reported when they are both relevant and reliable. But the story to be told comes from the words of the individual respondents. The interviews were transcribed, and the resulting thirteen large volumes of typescript are the empirical base of this analysis.

As might be expected, these respondents were far more articulate and opinionated than those found in samples of the general electorate. Hardly ever did one of these political activists respond with an "I don't know." However, they frequently denigrated their own opinions by disclaiming expertise in a particular field. "I'm no economist" or "I don't have access to the information available in the Pentagon" were typical of the form that such disclaimers would take. This deference to experts, by persons who could themselves claim expertise in certain areas of politics or policy, has important consequences for the health of the democratic system.

The plan of the work is this. After a prologue highlighting Guardian worries about the loss of confidence in government, the first chapter is concerned with the staying power of traditional American political values and President Ronald Reagan's determination to use the past as a guide to the future. The second chapter examines the historic conflict between the values of liberty and equality as realized in the contemporary dilemmas of affirmative action. The third chapter reviews the Guardians' understanding of American political institutions, finding that Madison's prescription of the "public good" as the end sought by institutions has been forgotten. The fourth chapter shows the value conflicts described in chapters two and three as elements in the politics of the five cities I visited outside Washington. The fifth chapter concerns the difficulties of adapting past assumptions about natural abundance and international influence to present realities, while an epilogue returns to Washington to review Guardian values in the context of the substance of the public good for the balance of the 1980s. To restore public trust in American institutions is a challenge for the Guardians themselves.

Prologue

A Loss of Trust

To the effect of these changes, intellectual, moral, and social, the institutions and laws of the Country must be adapted, and it will require for the task all the wisdom of the wisest patriots.

—James Madison, 1829

Like Jimmy Carter four years earlier, Ronald Reagan ran for president in 1980 as an outsider assaulting the Washington establishment. Both candidates capitalized on the voters' loss of confidence in government and its operations. But Reagan's diagnosis of governmental ills was more severe. Carter had offered little more than the application of his engineering skills to the organization of the sprawling bureaucracy; a promise not to lie; and a hope (assuming election to a second term) to balance the budget by 1981. Reagan claimed that government itself had become the problem and promised to decrease the scope of government at home and strengthen it abroad while restoring prosperity by easing regulation and cutting taxes. He promised to balance the budget by 1984.

The Reagan administration brought a crusading spirit to the White House, and the partisan contest in Congress created a dramatic story. Commentators no longer raised the issue of soundness in the basic constitutional structure, as they had habitually done during the later years of Jimmy Carter's term. The question of the system's health dropped out of the columns. By late 1981, scandals clouded the effectiveness of such White House stalwarts as Richard Allen and David Stockman, international tensions mounted, and the administration confessed that it would be unable to balance the budget by the target date. As the recession gained momentum, the mood of confidence in the new administration faded. The question of the system's health again become paramount.

Where should one begin, to measure and understand the health of the American democratic order? The system's health must be related to the outlook of those responsible for operating it, so one's first impulse is to seek the contemporary center of that order, the District of Columbia. In Washington, men and women devote their waking hours to democratic politics; what for others may be only a spectator sport is for them the breath of life.

On a hot September afternoon, I visited the office of Senator Paul Sarbanes, Democrat of Maryland. Sarbanes was elected to the Senate in 1976, in the aftermath of Watergate. His service on the House Judiciary Committee during its consideration of impeachment articles against President Richard Nixon had made him a temporary national celebrity; this status translated into an easy victory in Maryland over Republican Senator J. Glenn Beall, Jr. Sarbanes told me that one of the most important national problems concerns the trustworthiness of government.

> [T]he integrity of our government covers a whole range of things, but that's an easy rubric for it. . . . It goes to the question of whether the government, in all of its working, is honest and open and responsive, and carries out its democratic principles and ideals.

Senator Sarbanes believes the American nation has remained remarkably true to its democratic and constitutional principles in the changing circumstances of the last two centuries, but he is not sure that the generation now assuming political responsibility appreciates those traditions.

> I don't think a very good job is being done in the educational system in transmitting this. We've tended to take it all for granted. We have a lot of people who just grew up with it and never had to think about it. . . . The understanding of the difference between acceptance of your substantive position, and commitment to a process by which conflicting substantive positions can be resolved, and the importance of the latter, is sort of a key to our society, and it is not fully understood.

There was in what Senator Sarbanes said a sense of impending loss. As the son of a Greek immigrant, he values American liberties and political processes. But he seems to wonder if the citizens who benefit from those freedoms and procedures can be counted on to guard and perpetuate them. His fear that the Watergate lesson about power and irresponsibility is being forgotten made him one of six senators to vote against confirmation of Alexander Haig, Richard Nixon's last chief of staff, as President Reagan's secretary of state. In 1981 Sarbanes was the first announced target of the National Conservative Political Action Committee, which claimed responsibility for the defeat of four of the six liberal senators it had marked for political extinction in 1980.

Elsewhere in Washington, I visited the comfortable regional editorial offices of the *Reader's Digest* for an appointment with Melvin Laird, the Washington editor, who served as a congressman from Wisconsin for eighteen years before he was appointed secretary of defense in Richard Nixon's cabinet. Laird's sense of something amiss with American politics was more emphatic.

> The biggest issue is whether we can make our system work. It is more and more difficult to get people to relate themselves to government. If we don't attract good people to government, all domestic and international issues take second position. Our system is being challenged, as it has never been challenged before, from the standpoint of confidence. If you look at Gallup, you look at Harris, you look at other surveys of public opinion, the Congress, the courts, the executive branch, all are subject to grave questioning on the part of the people.

The news stories about the vigor and convictions of President Reagan's cabinet members did not remind their readers that several of Reagan's initial cabinet choices declined appointment.

Back at the Capitol, I spoke with Senator Richard Lugar of Indiana. Like Sarbanes, Lugar was first elected to the Senate in 1976. Twenty-two years earlier, in the fall of 1954, Lugar and Sarbanes met on the transatlantic liner *Queen Elizabeth,* as both were traveling to England to enter upon their appointments as Rhodes Scholars. While Sarbanes was elected to the House of Representatives as a Democrat after service in the Maryland legislature, Lugar had been mayor of Indianapolis. His Republican ties to Richard Nixon prevented a victory over Democratic Senator Birch Bayh in 1974 but were not a handicap by 1976, when Lugar defeated incumbent Democrat Vance Hartke. In 1980 Lugar was prominent on all the published lists of candidates considered by Ronald Reagan for the Republican vice-presidential nomination. I found that problems of representation were very much on Lugar's mind.

> You know, hundreds of things float through here. I guess from week to week I can hardly remember what issue we disposed of the week before. . . . We've had 346 roll call-votes thus far this year, and I would guess that

there are not more than a tenth of those on which there would have been substantial reaction pro or con in Indiana, largely because people were not even aware that such an issue had arisen. On the so-called high profile issues, everybody who has something to say can be heard. . . . I'm always fascinated by any sort of poll, anywhere in Indiana. . . . It's very helpful, and often very surprising, but sometimes all you gather is that most people have not thought about the issue and therefore either their support or antipathy is very soft. . . . I think that is true of a broad gamut of issues, unless you get into something that is high profile enough, that's gone on long enough, that public opinion is crystallized in any way. . . . I would hope that most of my votes were based on what I believed was genuinely in the public interest.

Earlier in the conversation, Senator Lugar expressed a concern for the preservation of American liberties by the citizens who benefit from them.

One of the most important issues is the age-old issue of how powerful the state ought to be in relationship to individuals and families. It's a sophisticated issue in that most people are ambivalent on the question. I think there's a general feeling in the country that the people feel over-controlled and they would like less government interference in their lives; but it's also a fact that many people want more governmental services and see the federal government frequently as a superior provider.

A second major issue that I see is sort of an age-old quest for whether freedom of initiative and ambition to succeed or push ahead the wheels of individual invention and progress are more important than a quest for equity, and what people perceive as justice, or fairness.

Thus Senators Lugar and Sarbanes, who vote on different sides of many issues in the Senate, share a concern for the future of American values. I spoke with Congressman Elliott Levitas, who represents the suburbs adjacent to Atlanta, Georgia. Like Sarbanes, he was worried about the loss of trust in government; like Lugar, he was concerned by the growth of the federal establishment and by the problems of representation.

I would define the long-range issue as being public confidence in government, and, as a major sub-issue of that, a growing concern that government has gotten away from the people. It's not just a Watergate problem of mistrust of government, but that the government has become dehumanized, impersonal. . . . I think most of the members of Congress who were elected when I was perceive that the role of the Congress is, to a large extent, [to be] the people's representative. The Congress is really the only human link between people and the government.

Congressman Levitas described his crusade for wider usage of the "legislative veto," a provision that delays implementation of the rules promulgated by administrative agencies until they have been reviewed by Congress. It is one of the latest devices developed to assure Congress the ability to oversee the operations of the administrative state. Although it would give Congress an additional means of countering arbitrary bureaucratic power, it was opposed during the Carter administration by liberal congressmen who felt that the more extreme regulations of private behavior, such as the enforcement of affirmative action in education and employment, would never be approved by the full Congress.

I found Congressman Levitas's doubts about the efficacy of government shared by some high-level bureaucrats. The deputy undersecretary of a cabinet department told me that the greatest change in his political attitudes in the last twenty-five years was the realization that government is not able to solve all problems.

> I had the hope of someone who grew up in fairly poor circumstances during the New Deal that government programs could make things better. Very important in building that up in our generation was the Second World War, in which the U.S. government did put together an enormously productive enterprise, really, to successfully prosecute the war. . . . So we grew up in a time of faith in the power of government to solve problems. What we see now is that the government surely was solving them, but it was solving the easy ones, the superficial ones. When, during the 1960s, we attempted to extend the mechanisms that had worked in solving some problems to the purpose of solving all problems, it began to break down. And that's what we're living with now.

W. Michael Blumenthal, Jimmy Carter's first secretary of the treasury, told me that one of the most important problems facing the nation is the growth of bureaucratic authority.

> An overarching problem that affects everything . . . is that, as we get to be an older society, and perhaps a more democratic one in some ways, but more and more characterized by large organizations with large bundles of power, that we don't become too bureaucratized. . . . That process, as it continues, will make growth and the continued dynamism that has been the hallmark of this country increasingly difficult.

I spoke to a high official of the Justice Department who had not lost faith in government problem solving ("I was raised a liberal Democrat, believing in big government and the duty of government to intervene and improve the lives of everybody") but had grown concerned with the tendency of government lawyers to serve narrow interests.

> I would like to create a tone where every lawyer here believes that they have a dual function: that they represent not only their client agency but they also represent the people of the United States. . . . The traditional lawyer has a very narrow role, to seek the best interest of his client, whether that's good for the society or not. . . . When the public interest arises in a particular case, you can see it.

These assessments by members and former members of the legislative and executive branches do not support an optimistic view of the American governmental system's health. They lament the loss of public confidence in government; at the same time, they cite valid reasons why such confidence may not be justified. Their comments do not indicate whether the lost trust should be regained through the reform of government institutions and policies, or through some change in the consciousness of the people.

Opinions in the Constituencies

The Congressional district which neighbors that represented by Elliott Levitas includes central Atlanta; it was represented by Andrew Young before Young was appointed ambassador to the United Nations by Jimmy Carter. The central portion of the district is represented in the Georgia Senate by civil rights leader Julian Bond, perhaps the best-known state legislator in the United States. I talked to Julian Bond in his sparsely furnished basement office across the street from the campus of Morehouse College. At thirty-seven, Bond seemed much like the television images I remembered from the 1968 Democratic national convention, when he deserted the forces seeking his nomination as vice-president, since he was constitutionally ineligible because of youth. Although his civil rights activism made him a national celebrity, Bond decried the increasing tendency for celebrities to capture party nominations and through them, public office.

> You get people who may be at least publicly more intelligent, more articulate, more smooth than the typical officeholder has been, but who know absolutely nothing about government, and what's involved. . . . You have to have some knowledge of budgets. You have to have some sense about you

of what the whole purpose of the thing is. I think one of Ronald Reagan's difficulties was that he got elected governor of California, and had no real idea of what a governor does. The same thing was true of Lester Maddox here. This man was in effect a created celebrity. He ran for office a couple of times, and finally ran for an office he won. And had not the slightest idea of what government did or how it worked.

Bond saw the decline of the party institution as part of a general decline in the authority of social institutions; his version of the loss of trust in government placed the blame, at least in part, on the people.

I think we—by we I mean Americans—are becoming extremely selfish people, interested in self as opposed to the group. . . . I think it's a result of the trend away from public-mindedness, as is the interest in the Eastern religions. This introspection into oneself. As is the interest in drugs among certain people, dilettantes who sniff cocaine and smoke large quantities of marijuana. Aside from whatever pleasure may be derived from it, I think it's part and parcel of this seeking of personal enjoyment, as opposed to improvements for the group of us, the mass of us.

Elsewhere in Atlanta, I spoke to Benjamin Mays, a son of former slaves. Then eighty-three, Dr. Mays was in the midst of a successful campaign for reelection as president of the Atlanta school board. As president of Morehouse, the black men's college, from 1940 to 1967, Mays saw the civil rights revolution at first hand. Like Senator Sarbanes, Mays worried about the political future and emphasized the importance of education.

The most important issue facing the nation today is to make democracy function. It's the most difficult kind of government in the world. It requires an educated citizenry. People who can debate and argue, and run for public offic. . . . We must keep on talking about 1776, and never forget our roots and our past. But we ought to be looking forward to 2076. What must we do now? Our forefathers laid a foundation that enabled this country to last for a couple of centuries. What are we going to do with that, to see that we are alive in the years to come? Because civilizations do rise and fall. There's no guarantee that we'll be here two hundred years from now.

When we discussed the most fundamental American values, Mays said that they are found in the Declaration of Independence, and that the function of black Americans has been to remind the white majority of the promises made in that document.

It would have been a terrible thing if the American people didn't have Negroes to point out to them, "This is what you said; this is what this country

was founded on; this is what you fought for. We helped you do it. So, you must remember that we're part of this thing. Every war, our blood has been meshed with your blood." I think its still the function of the American Negro.

In Houston I heard a strait-laced version of Julian Bond's theme of individual selfishness from a lady who could be expected to agree with him on little else. She is an officer of the Republican Central Committee; I have called her Elizabeth Ladd. When I asked Mrs. Ladd to identify the most important issues confronting America, she replied,

> I would say the limitation of government and a re-definition of our moral fiber. There's no question in my mind that unless we get some hold on the sexual revolution, the pornographic revolution, all the things that have the connotation of morality, that we are going to be in more and more severe trouble. . . . I would never have gotten into politics, since I was a Bible teacher, unless it had been for the fact that I felt that civil government should have a moral basis.

Other respondents reminded me that the American government is founded on distrust; the protection of liberty requires eternal vigilance. Notable among them was Albert Jenner, then seventy, who capped his career as a lawyer's lawyer by serving as minority counsel to the House Judiciary Committee when it considered the impeachment of President Nixon.

> Our government was not designed for the purpose of efficiency. It was designed primarily for the citizen, the protection of the citizen, and the enjoyment of individual rights and liberties. And when you have efficiency in that, the individual must subjugate himself and herself to the government authority. Under our government, you must continually police government. Because once you form government, then you have to protect yourself against the government you form.

Mr. Jenner felt that the impeachment hearings had a salutary effect in educating citizens to the need for vigilance. In San Francisco I talked with a woman civil rights attorney, then aged thirty-one, who pointed out that declarations supporting individual liberties by the courts mean little unless they are supported by public opinion.

> The question I have is, what the underpinnings for the establishment of those rights are. In other words, they are easily eroded over time. While we may feel terrific that we won this case, or won that case, we all know now what those things were worth. While I think that those cases were important in

terms of establishing at least on the law books a kind of public policy, there is still a lot of education that has to go on; the legislative underpinnings of the policy is vital to it becoming a permanent fixture of this country's world view.

Elsewhere in San Francisco, I talked to Vilma Martinez, an attorney who then headed the Mexican-American Legal Defense and Education Fund.

You know, the whole system of values—what is valued, what are the underpinnings—is very much in question. And it's surprising to me that that should be true now, because in a very real sense, we have given real value to a very important concept in this country, but also world-wide, in surviving Watergate. And constitutional democracy survived. We should have been very excited about it. That didn't last very long. People weren't sure what it meant. I thought it was fabulous and fantastic! But nobody seems to have understood that.

I heard variations on these themes from officeholders and politically influential private citizens in Washington, Atlanta, Houston, and Chicago: a lament for the failure of trust in government, yet a belief that government has grown less trustworthy; fear that the people may not understand governmental traditions well enough to preserve them, coupled with a belief that those traditions are being subverted by the very officials chosen to defend them.

Echoes in Boston

Similar opinions were articulated by persons I conversed with in Boston. As the city that lit the flames of the American Revolution, Boston labels itself "the cradle of liberty." In the twentieth century, Boston politics became so robustly corrupt that it was chosen as the location for a classic study of the alienated voter. Perhaps these historical factors combined to produce the intensity of the Bostonians I interviewed; perhaps their articulateness should be credited instead to Cambridge, across the river, where many of my Boston respondents, including all four introduced here, attended Harvard College, or Harvard Law School, or both. Since this book is about the impact of historic American values upon contemporary political dilemmas, it seems appropriate to highlight the attitudes of persons I talked to in Boston, which claims to have nurtured those values from their inception.

In September 1977, high in an office building on Franklin Street, I spoke to Roger Moore, partner in a leading Boston law firm. Moore was slow-spoken and intense; I learned that he had spent some months in a monastery but finally rejected the Catholic faith. In 1976 he had worked in the Reagan presidential campaign and would do so again in 1980. When I asked about America's basic values, Moore opened his desk drawer and took out a page of writing, which he said he had been working on as a statement for the twenty-fifth reunion book of his college class. He read the following:

> I worry that I have spent less time fighting for, rather than trying to channel into orderly processes, the means of achieving what I then regarded as more desirable, but not necessarily essential, political objectives. I worry about how long a system of government can continue to function, let alone command the respect of its constituents, when it responds to every real or fancied excess or shortcoming with an avalanche of frequently inconsistent laws, rules, and regulations, the better to save us from the greater danger of ourselves. I worry about a society founded upon achievement, which is morbidly set on eliminating incentives to achieve. I worry that the denigration of the relevance of the symbols of excellence will destroy excellence, which will not be irrelevant. I worry, and I pray.

By the summer of 1981, Roger Moore's outlook was far less gloomy. He had served as parliamentarian of the 1980 Republican national convention and was appointed as general counsel of the National Committee. He felt that the record of the Reagan administration's first six months was "just splendid," and that the Reagan economic policies marked a reversal of the trends he had deplored in 1977. When I asked what would happen to Republican unity when legislative attention should turn to social issues, his answer was curt: "The Moral Majority doesn't have many congressmen."

In the Boston suburb of Quincy, the seat of Suffolk County, I spoke to Richard Stearns, an assistant district attorney. Stearns had worked in the McGovern presidential campaign in 1972. After McGovern's loss, he completed law school and became a prosecutor. In 1980 he was a leading strategist of the Kennedy nomination campaign. These experiences made him particularly aware of the average citizen's distrust of politics.

> You know, Americans in a sense have been entranced with what Edmund Burke used to call the arithmetical ideal of government—that somehow efficiency can replace the necessity for squabbling. What that model of government fails to recognize is that there's too little to go around. And

politics is basically a fight over who gets what. And as long as that fight exists, people are going to incline to one or another interest group.

Stearns went on to say that the model of efficiency had never made much headway in Massachusetts, and that he could understand why Boston voters might become alienated.

> Politics is an industry in this state. I don't think there's any place you could go where politics consume as much of both public and private life as they do [in Massachusetts]. There are very few decisions made anywhere within the business or public communities that aren't essentially political decisions. Everyone in this state is in politics. You start at age eight putting up campaign posters. . . . And its a small enough state that everyone feels somehow intimately connected to the political life. . . . I suspect you'd find that although participation is very intense in politics, it's also very exclusive. For those who participate, it probably means more to them than it probably means anywhere else. But then there are a large number of people who have given up, who either refuse, or see no profit in, participating. We had a 25 per cent vote in the City Council elections last time.

Despite Reagan's victory, Rick Stearns did not despair for his party on the national scene.

> The Democratic party is healthy on the local level. In general, we're back to the 1970 pre-Watergate level in the state legislatures. . . . Reagan is a president in the Eisenhower mold, in that he is personally popular and trusted in a way that his program will never be. . . . The Republican party carries the seeds of its own self-destruction; once the economic questions are settled, and they turn to social issues, the trouble will start.

At his Acorn Street home on Beacon Hill, I interviewed John Winthrop Sears. As a descendant of the first governor of the Massachusetts Bay Colony, Sears is an authentic Boston Brahmin. He is a former city councilor, city commissioner, state Republican chairman, and unsuccessful candidate for mayor. In 1980 Sears was elected to the City Council seat once held by Louise Day Hicks, heroine of the forces opposed to school integration in Boston. In 1982 Sears sought the Republican nomination for governor.

> Our country was built to a very high level of performance and habitability on a set of fairly simple principles that were accepted, conveyed from generation to generation; understood in places like Europe and Asia so that people wanted to come here and be a part of it. And in the last thirty-five to forty years, they have first cracked and then crumbled, and now they're deteriorating like a Caribbean gravestone. . . . I would say it was 1933 that led to the

trouble. And 1963 accelerated it very much on its path. The assassination of Kennedy damaged the country tremendously. The Democrats decided to transfer as much power as possible into the seat of government. . . . At the same time, they assumed they could recruit the best and brightest people into government. Since 1963, government has been a pretty unbearable place for men and women of sensitivity. And that's a fairly devastating combination, if you have all the judgments made in one place, and the people making them are not your strongest.

John Winthrop Sears is a moderate Republican; he points out that he should not be confused with his cousin, the John Sears who was Ronald Reagan's chief political strategist in 1976 and for a time in 1980. But Sears agreed with Houston's conservative Elizabeth Ladd and Atlanta's radical Julian Bond that the eclipse of personal moral standards has precipitated a decline in the political culture.

I think people are feeling extremely rootless. We move around an awful lot. We move homes and businesses. The truisms about the family, I don't need to repeat. That means that there were only a few kinds of navigational stars—fixed principles—that people could go home to, and one of them was the accepted values as set forth in the church. All those now seem to be in tremendous disarray.

Sears had mixed reactions to the course established by the Reagan administration.

I think the emphasis on opposing the Soviets is good, as is the rehabilitation of national wounds suffered over Vietnam. And to talk about old-fashioned values again, to get a debate going, is fine. But the Reagan administration's approach to aiding the cities, by providing block grants to the states, will not work. And James Watt as secretary of the interior is the worst appointment he's made. The Republican party was at the core of the conservation movement in this country, with Theodore Roosevelt and Gifford Pinchot. Watt's policies can't be called conservatism.

In a building on Post Office Square, I visited law offices less lavishly furnished than those of Roger Moore to speak to Thomas Atkins, an attorney for the National Association for the Advancement of Colored People. Born in Indiana, the son of a Pentecostal minister, Atkins completed his Harvard law degree while serving on the Boston City Council. He later served a term as an appointed state official. When I asked him to identify the nation's major problems, he replied,

Lack of trust in the integrity of public officials and institutions I would probably put at the top of the list, because it permeates and makes more difficult to solve almost all the other problems which might be listed.

A second one I would point at would be the problems of how to maintain democratic institutions at a time when the basic economic system seems less capable than before of growing at a rate to provide the jobs and capital necessary to sustain the growth of the country.

And a third one I would point to is the increasing extent to which people are relying, or are forced to rely, on less complete information as the basis for making fundamental choices and decisions. . . . It is a problem relating to not just the fact that our government and our society generally are becoming very complex, but the problem of how to report on the options realistically available at any given moment. Governmental agencies do that very poorly. So you have them talking to each other with mountains and mountains of paper flowing back and forth. That means that for the most part, information is gotten out from one or the other of three sources: either the media, the spokesmen for special-interest groups, or the hucksters for policymakers in the public sector.

Mr. Atkins had a modest proposal for the restoration of trust in government.

There are some structural things that can be done to approach the question of restoring trust, but most of it is not structural. One of the structural things I think would be helpful would be if at every level of government—local, state, and federal—there would be a limit placed on the amount of time a person could consecutively serve in an elected position. I think that would work wonders in the Congress, the state legislatures, and the local legislatures. . . . So that the concept of a citizen government is restored. Government ought to be, the political arena ought to have, an open door.

At the conclusion of our interview, Mr. Atkins left for the Boston airport to catch a flight that would eventually carry him to Kalamazoo, Michigan, where the NAACP was supporting a suit to achieve the racial integration of the public schools.

Activist Values and the Need for Adaptation

This research was undertaken in the belief that the United States confronts, in the 1980s, political problems of a nature and magnitude that are new to the national experience. The adjustments needed in our institutions and practices must be at least as great as those undertaken in the third decade of the nineteenth century, when the last elements of a politics of deference were purged from our political habits, and a politics was established that centered upon the participation of a mass electorate. In 1829 and 1830 Virginia held a convention to adapt its Constitution to the new realities. James Madison appeared in that convention as an authentic founding father to suggest that the solutions of 1787 were not sacred, and that the efforts of the "wisest patriots" were needed to adapt institutions to the new era.

The purpose of my research was to assess the directions that are likely to be taken in response to current problems by the political activists who constitute the stratum of political leadership in the 1980s. The extent of their attachment to values that were articulated at the time of the national foundation, coupled with their determination to work within the existing political structure (although some would reform it) led me to regard them as the contemporary American equivalents of Plato's guardians. The guardians are the political class in Plato's ideal republic which rules under the supervision of the philosopher-king. The American Guardians realize that here the people are sovereign; their own political influence depends upon relationships with groups and constituencies among the people, although I found that their values are determined more by the individualist tradition than by their organizational affiliations. Furthermore, the American Guardians, in fact and in theory, have quite different origins than did Plato's guardians.

> [T]he United States, in dedicating itself to the proposition that all men are created equal, became the first nation in the history of the world to enter upon the stage of independent existence claiming independence not in virtue of its own particular qualities, but in virtue of a right that it shared with all men everywhere.
>
> How novel the idea was, of founding a particular political order upon the idea of universal rights, may be indicated by comparing the Declaration of Independence with the most famous of all political books, Plato's *Republic*. [Plato describes] the "noble lie" upon which the education of the guardian class is based. In one part of that myth is the story that the birth and nurture of the guardians, their entire lives until maturity, have been underground, within the very earth of their native land. This is Plato's retelling of the ancient Athenian myth of autocthony; that the first Athenians had sprung from the ground itself, [which] expresses the consciousness of a motherland with vivid literalness. . . . [P]aradoxical though it may seem, the very fact that the doctrine of the universal rights of man was the negation of the idea of patriotism as it had hitherto existed enabled that doctrine to act as the unifying and patriotic theme in American politics.

While the functions of the American Guardians may be compared with those of the political elite imagined by Plato, their functions are performed to achieve different ends. The American Guardians thus far have preserved the values articulated at the time of the national foundation: human rights and a constitution that protects them, and a complex political process designed to elicit the "cool and deliberate sense of the community."

Fully a third of the 117 politically influential men and women I interviewed in six American cities voluntarily mentioned the loss of trust in government as a major contemporary problem. Three-quarters responded in a similar vein to specific questions about the performance of the federal government. The persons with whom I raised the question in 1981, when the Reagan administration's course was established, found no reason to reverse their judgment. The twelve persons introduced here were particularly thoughtful and articulate in discussing the loss of trust. Apart from Elliott Levitas and Thomas Atkins, the persons I talked with did not have concrete suggestions for regaining the people's trust. Nor did I, when I began the quest for understanding. Yet, as the data I gathered was analyzed, the transcripts indexed and cross-indexed, the conviction grew that many flaws in American government are traceable, at least in part, to the outlook of just such persons as those I had interviewed. These were public-spirited citizens, and their intentions could only be described as benign, although several served the interests of groups or industries with special claims to make upon the political system. I began to realize, however, that their values, in many cases, were confused or contradictory, and that in the modern world, conceptions of what ought to be often lag behind the changes in what is.

This book is about that realization.

CHAPTER ONE

Ronald Reagan and American Values

[I]t is not my intention to do away with government. It is, rather, to make it work. Work with us, not over us. To stand by our side, not ride on our backs. . . . Here, in this land, we unleashed the energy and individual genius of men to a greater extent than has ever been done before. Freedom, and the dignity of the individual, have been more available and assured here than in any other place on earth. . . . Let us begin an era of national renewal.

—Ronald Reagan, Inaugural Address, 1981

American reactions to the American political process are volatile. Hopes fade, then surge again, as events unfold. The dreary 1980 season for electing a president began in 1979, when the Iowa precinct caucuses attracted unprecedented media attention. The long primary trail soon designated Ronald Reagan as the inevitable nominee of the Republican party; John Anderson declared an independent candidacy, but the Anderson Difference eventually appealed to a small and specialized segment of the electorate. Senator Edward Kennedy mounted a challenge to the reelection of the incumbent Democratic president, Jimmy Carter, but Kennedy's candidacy was plagued by difficulties from the beginning, while Carter remained in the Rose Garden to supervise assuring the safety of the Americans taken hostage in Iran—and to avoid the dangers of a confrontation with Kennedy. Kennedy called his party to return to the true New Deal faith; the suspicion grew that the policies he proposed (like national health insurance) would only bring more of the troubles (like federal deficits and inflation) that he blamed on Carter. Kennedy's hopes finally died when the Carter delegate majority to the Democratic national convention refused to amend its rules to release delegates from pledges to vote for the candidate victorious in the primary elections of their states.

Commentators regarded the ensuing campaign with apathy. The nation seemed locked into double digit inflation with rising unemployment. Carter was unable to retrieve the hostages from Iran, even with a commando raid that proved abortive. Rather than offering specifics of what might be changed in his second administration, Carter depicted the Republican nominee as a dangerous warmonger, bigot, and enemy of the poor. For his part, Ronald Reagan offered no new vision of the American purpose. Instead, he called for a return to principles that had made America "great" and would do so again. He asked for a weaker and smaller presence by the federal government at home, and a stronger stance abroad, with increased defense spending. To restore prosperity, he proposed tax cuts for individuals and businesses, deregulation of private enterprise, a balanced government budget, and tax incentives to stimulate the modernization of industry.

The campaign wound on to its conclusion without generating much excitement in all but the most intense partisans. Then, on the anniversary of the Iranian hostages' captivity, came the election. Only 53.9 per cent of the voting age population participated. This represented about a 1 per cent decline in voting, compared to the 1976 election—and nearly a 10 per cent decrease since 1960. But it was 1.5 per cent greater than the turnout of 1932 and within 3 per cent of the 1936 turnout, which established New Deal hegemony. Turnout figures do not prove that the people have given up in despair of the political process.

Excitement came with the ballot count. Early returns suggested the magnitude of the Republican sweep and led Jimmy Carter to concede defeat while the polls in the West were still open. Within hours, it became clear that the Republican party had captured a narrow but potentially workable majority in the U.S. Senate, along with substantial gains in the House of Representatives. The rejection of Carter rubbed off on his party.

The people had spoken. Without speculating upon the precise meaning of their message, Ronald Reagan selected staff and cabinet members prepared to implement his programs. His helpers acted on their determination to "hit the ground running"; the people had endorsed their purposes.

Any victory of the 1980 magnitude tempts the victors to toy with the will-o'-the-wisp of mandate. It also makes the opposition tread softly in the opening months of the new administration. While political scientists are best at explaining the significance of elections long after they have taken place, there were strong signs in 1980 that the result marked a rejection of Jimmy Carter more than an acceptance of Ronald Reagan's conservative ideas.

Public disapproval of Carter's presidential record was not changed by the campaign. Carter's imitation of Lyndon Johnson's 1964 strategy against Barry Goldwater—depicting his opponent as dangerously irresponsible—was frustrated by Reagan's geniality, which was displayed with particular effectiveness in the Reagan-Anderson and Carter-Reagan television debates. Reagan demonstrated his acceptability as a means of denying Carter a second term.

The Guardians tended to vote against Carter, more than they voted in favor of Reagan. Since I sought out the political influentials in six big cities, my respondents were preponderantly identified with the Democratic party; the active Democrats outnumbered the Republicans by a ratio of 1.7 to 1. Their lament for the loss of trust in government indicated that, in several cases, the Guardians did not find Reagan's questioning of the government's role uncongenial, but the predominant mood was to criticize Carter's performance.

By the fall of 1980, I found a bipartisan rejection of Jimmy Carter that affected all but the most intense Democrats. A Washington attorney, born in Florida and a lifelong Democrat, told me in September, 1980, that he contemplated voting for Ronald Reagan.

> Incompetence is one thing, but I really began to *hate* Jimmy Carter when I saw how he was exploiting the Iranian hostages for political purposes. I have several Jewish friends who feel that our policy toward Israel will be better under anybody but Carter. They plan to hold their noses and vote for Reagan.

The distribution of the November vote—a uniform increase of the Republican vote among all regions and voting groups—suggested a national response to events, rather than a change in the perceived connection between accepted values and policy preferences that would trigger a massive change in the partisan affiliation of groups or areas. The suggestion was supported by the polls, which indicated that the election was a referendum on Jimmy Carter's performance: the only Reagan mandate was to be different than Carter.

Where, in this description, is the noble picture of the electorate chosing between competing visions of the national future? It is, of course, absent. Jimmy Carter described the difficulties of the presidency for the voters, but he never described exactly how his second term would differ from his first. Reagan attacked Carter's failures and promised a return to a time when the nation had been internally vital and internationally strong. Neither offered visions of the national future based on adapting national practices to such newly important realities as resource scarcity and the breakup of the bipolar power balance that dominated international relations after the Second World War.

The history of American presidential elections reveals few instances of electoral choice between competing definitions of the national future. Elections are referenda on the performance of the incumbent administration or party. Usually, they either confirm that party's continuance in office or install the opposition for a term, without changing the underlying partisan affiliation of the electorate. On at least five occasions, however—in 1800, 1832, 1864, 1896, and 1932—elections have signaled the realignment of the parties and designated a new party as the normal national majority. V. O. Key labeled these events as "critical elections." While the Reagan vote in 1980 did not seem to indicate a basic partisan realignment, critical elections are not obvious when they occur. The new administration must somehow live up to the expectations of the electors. Critical elections can only be designated after the fact, when the electorate reaffirms its choice, convinced that its well-being is involved in continuing the new majority party in power. Franklin D. Roosevelt won the 1932 election comfortably; he won a landslide victory in 1936, when five million voters who had been indifferent about the electoral choice in 1932 turned out to express support for the New Deal.

Thus, while the 1980 results did not express an endorsement of Reagan's philosophy or policies, if those policies should, by mid-1984, control inflation and create prosperity that trickles down to the least affluent voters, his philosophy will be vindicated, and an attachment to conservatism could be created which would make the Republicans into the national majority party and severely cripple the liberal Democrats. If those policies fail, Reagan would follow Jimmy Carter into history as another one-term president, his conservatism recorded as a one-term guiding ideology.

There is one striking difference between Reagan's situation and that of FDR. The New Deal was perceived as their friend by the economically destitute, those for whom the American promise had become a betrayal. Those of lesser income, education, and social status are the elements of the voting-age population least likely to vote. They were the untapped reservoir that supplied the Roosevelt landslide of 1936. The Reagan policies, as a negative mirror image of the New Deal, serve voters at the upper end of the economic scale. But these are habitual voters. In 1984, any untapped reservoir of occasional voters is likely to be drained by the opposition.

The theory of critical elections consigns the voter—and popular sovereignty itself—to an infrequent role in the determination of the grand purposes to which the nation may dedicate itself. It states that, every thirty or forty years, the electorate has affirmed a new national direction by shifting the partisan allegiance of the majority and making the issue agenda of the majority party a public philosophy that is the benchmark against which all proposals are measured. Debate centered on this public philosophy defines, for a time, the content of what Madison called the public good. Whether 1980 constituted such a critical election will not be clear until at least 1984. In between critical elections, less sweeping changes are made in the national direction by the interaction between political activists and the institutions of government.

Reagan's Values: What Is to Be Conserved?

Ronald Reagan proclaimed himself a conservative in 1964, and his assertion was only challenged as a matter of degree, not of substance, when he formed his administration in 1981. What is it that a conservative in America seeks to preserve? Edmund Burke, the father of English conservatism, had a vision of society as an organic whole. Each of the elements of society, he held, is bound by ties of obligation to the other elements; governments preside over the social arrangements worked out over the centuries; and those arrangements embody a greater wisdom than that possessed by any single generation. Evolutionary social change is inevitable and should be welcomed, but the sudden rupture of social arrangements can bring only suffering and disaster.

Aside from calling upon religious faith as a support for the state (a Burkean insight shared by Jimmy Carter), Ronald Reagan's values were not those of Edmund Burke. What Reagan and other American conservatives seek to conserve are the values of classic liberalism, the political and economic faith articulated by Locke, Jefferson, Adam Smith, and

John Stuart Mill. Rather than seeing society as a structure of mutual obligations, liberalism focuses on the individual; its values are liberty and property. Reagan's call was the same as that of John Locke: a government that fails to assure individual freedoms must be replaced; get government off the backs of the people.

Yet the pure faith of classic liberalism has been compromised, and the Reagan administration accepts many of the compromises originated or affirmed by the New Deal. The administration moved at once to propose policies for managing the economy. That government must intervene to shield individuals from the worst effects of the operation of the marketplace was a presumption Reagan accepted with enthusiasm. The method could change, but intervention there would be. And Reagan issued assurances that he had no intention of abandoning the elderly and the unemployed to the doubtful resources of local charity; "safety net" programs would be supported, at least for the "truly needy."

The inaugural address delivered by President Reagan on January 20, 1981, was a shorter version of the acceptance speech he delivered to the Republican national convention the previous July 17, with thanks for cooperation during the transition substituted for the sharpest and most personal attacks on Jimmy Carter. In his acceptance speech, Reagan repeated the five words used to summarize the intentions of the 1980 Republican platform.

> This convention has shown to all America a party united . . . with all those across the land who share a community of values embodied in these words: family, work, neighborhood, peace, and freedom. . . .

Candidate Reagan did not elaborate the Republican meaning of the five values on that particular occasion; one found specific policies tied to them in the platform. Work is the most important. The Republicans promise to restore a sound economy through deregulation, tax cuts, and the control of federal expenditures to cure both inflation and unemployment. This outcome will be facilitated by lowering the minimum wage for teenagers and emphasizing work incentives to end "welfare dependency." Families will find their authority renewed by the provision of tax credits for paying school tuition; the deregulation of health provision systems, with renewed emphasis on home-based care; and an end to taxes on social security benefits. The vitality of neighborhoods is to be assured by the encouragement of voluntary activity; charitable contributions are to be tax deductible, whether or not the taxpayer itemizes deductions. The threat of crime to neighborhood safety is to be met by restoration of the death penalty for serious crime; but the Republicans oppose the registration of handguns or any other regulation of the traffic in private weapons. The continuation of free institutions at home and peace abroad is to be assured by a firm foreign policy backed by military strength, including nuclear arms.

Perhaps Reagan did not offer the details because they could only create controversy and threaten the impression of party unity leading to national unity that he wished to create.

> I want my candidacy to unify our country, to renew the American spirit and sense of purpose. I want to carry our message to every American, regardless of party affiliation, who is a member of this community of shared values. . . .
> [Our] economic system has helped us master a continent, create a previously undreamed-of prosperity for our people and has fed millions of others around the globe. That system will continue to serve us in the future if our government will stop ignoring the basic values on which it was built and stop betraying the trust and goodwill of the American workers who keep it going.
> . . . Tonight, let us dedicate ourselves to renewing the American compact. I ask you not simply to "trust *me*," but to trust your values—our values— and to hold me responsible for living up to them.

Reagan's rhetoric has been consistent. He does not offer a bold vision of a different future; he would seek a return to past verities; and this will be done by a renewed dedication to values that have been cherished in the past. Unlike James Madison, who in the 1830s called upon "wise patriots" to adapt institutions to changed social realities, Reagan calls for restoration, not adaptation; his guide for the future lies in the past.

The president is certainly not alone in this feeling; the electorate did not reject it; and it is shared more than they realize by the persons I have designated the Guardian class. Contemporary Americans who call them- selves "liberal," as well as those claiming the label of "conservative," draw upon the same sources in the American tradition for the values they cherish. Each group emphasizes opposite faces of the same demo- cratic coin. This fact must be recognized before the more important question can be answered: do traditional American political values pro- vide appropriate responses for the challenges of the 1980s?

Values in American Political Culture

At least since the age of Andrew Jackson, American political leaders have shared the fundamental values of the general political culture. Jacksonian democracy eliminated the last pretensions of the political aristocracy, tentatively developed in the colonial era, which had been fading since the people of the thirteen colonies united in firm opposition to the Stamp Act in 1765.

The theoretical justification of the American Revolution, summarized by Jefferson in an immortal paragraph of the Declaration of Independence, was developed by the English opposition party, the Whigs, to support claims of the rising middle class of city merchants and country gentry for an increased voice in government. This theory asserts an equality of rights and endorses the ambitions of those, regardless of the circumstances of their birth, who can achieve economic prominence because of superior industry and wit. As a political conviction, this creed emphasized the responsibility of the individual for his own material success in the contest of life; but it was powerfully reinforced by Protestant convictions about the responsibility of the individual to achieve his own spiritual salvation. Individualism became the centerpiece of the American middle-class ethos.

If ever a national character was established at the moment of national birth, it was in the United States: the first new nation, brought into being by a conscious act of will; founded by identifiable persons, rather than a King Arthur or a Romulus, lost in the mists of legend. Like a stalagmite thrusting up from the floor of a limestone cave, the national character grows and changes. But it contains within itself the materials of its foundation. In the American case, those beginnings have nourished hope and conviction in generation after generation of newcomers, immigrants flocking into the "land of opportunity." The expectation of individual dignity and opportunity now extends to ethnic minorities who have been here for many generations, consigned by discrimination to the lowest social and economic orders, who are now reaching for ever higher rungs on the ladder of affluence and acceptance.

Social mobility for individuals creates stability for society. The vaunted "classless society" distributes wealth, prestige, and other items of value quite unequally. But members of the lower orders live out their lives in the conviction that they themselves, or certainly their children, will be able, through the application of energy, to climb the heights to wealth. The situation has been succinctly described by Ted Morgan, the former Sanche de Gramont, who renounced a French title to become an American citizen in 1977.

> The basic assumptions shared by Americans are the consent of the governed and the promises in the Declaration of Independence. People want what they have been promised. But the Declaration of Independence is a

farce for the 20 percent of the population who missed the upward-mobility escalator. They are not in revolt against the system, they are waiting for their turn. . . . The belief in the success creed is shared by rich and poor. The rich believe in it in order to hang on to their advantages and the poor believe in it because it seems a better paved road to upward mobility than the class struggle. Americans prefer the slogan "deal me in" to the slogan "soak the rich." All they ask is to be dealt a fair hand (and who knows what that is with so many wild cards). How can you have a class struggle when the rich and the poor keep the same faith?

Thus do Americans reduce to somewhat crass economic terms the long tradition of liberal individualism. Liberty means the freedom to get ahead. Equality is then interpreted as "equal liberty"; any contradiction between liberty and equality is hidden by defining one concept in terms of the other. To believe that equal opportunity is possible requires a prior belief, despite contrary evidence, that the marketplace allows open competition unfettered by economic monopoly or social prejudice.

If equal opportunity has been achieved, those who fail have nobody to blame but themselves, and persons who climb the pinnacle of wealth and power deserve accolades. In their own minds, the elites of a meritocracy must have achieved their positions as a reward for merit. This conviction is likely to prevent them from perceiving clearly the social realities that deny opportunity to others. Such belief patterns, although more complex than described here, were characteristic of a number of the Guardians. These attitudes, and their political implications, will be examined in the next chapter.

A second conviction brought to American shores by the early English immigrants was the belief that the authority of government should be limited by strict constitutions. Like individualism, constitutionalism flourished in the new nation, taking a form that seems exotic, by comparison with the concept's career in Britain, where adherence to custom, tradition, and law seems even more determined, although the constitution does not exist as a separate document. Colonial charters had given the colonists a sense of certainty in an uncertain environment. Beginning in 1776, these charters were revised into written constitutions, emphasizing the rights of individuals and the limited nature of government, while placing most governmental authority in the legislative body. Twelve years' experience suggested that suspicions of executive power, which animated the state constitutions, were not totally justified, and the Articles of Confederation proved inadequate for the organization of a nation. The Philadelphia Convention in 1787 proposed a structure of national government based on a revised understanding of the best design of governments. State conventions ratified the document but insisted upon the addition of a bill of rights. The Constitution quickly assumed a central place in American political culture. Much of the political contest thereafter centered upon its proper construction.

James Madison was the acknowledged intellectual leader of the Philadelphia Convention. Madison collaborated with Alexander Hamilton and John Jay to explicate the Constitution's principles in *The Federalist Papers*. Decisions that resulted from compromise in Philadelphia were portrayed as the necessary conclusions of a "new science of politics," establishing an understanding of the Constitution that was not explicit in the document itself. There were three important principles. The first was that sovereignty (which is singular and indivisible) resides in the people; thus both state and federal legislatures can serve the people's will. The second principle held that governmental tyranny can be prevented by separating power between the legislative, executive, and judicial branches and arranging for each branch to check the dangerous ambitions of the other two. These two principles are summarized in a famous sentence of *Federalist* 51: "A Dependence on the people is, no doubt, the primary control on the government; but experience has taught mankind the necessity of auxiliary precautions." The third principle recognized the diversity of a "modern commercial republic" and, denying the conventional wisdom of the time, asserted that republican institutions will function better in the government of an extended territory than in that of a limited one.

Then, in the First Congress, Madison led in drafting the Bill of Rights and submitting it to the states for ratification. Whether the Constitution is regarded primarily as the blueprint of government structure or as the charter of individual liberties, Madison's paternity is clear. The rules of the American political game are Madison's rules. The structures of governmental institutions are Madisonian structures. The Guardians who master the rules and labor within the structures are the heirs, the political children, of James Madison. Yet, as I will argue in the third chapter, Madison's true legacy has been overlooked. In pouring their energies into a single branch of government that will only be restrained by the checks of the two other branches, both congressmen and bureaucrats come to overlook what Madison decreed as the true purpose of all democratic governments: to define and achieve the public good.

Throughout American history, the values of individualism and constitutionalism have marched with a companion: nationalism. Nationalism is here defined as the vaunting of the nation as the embodiment of an abstract idea, rather than that sense of patriotism that has roots in the soil and is manifested as an inarticulate defense of a particular place. In the words of Max Lerner,

> American nationalism during most of its growth had in it the self-assertiveness of a people who had won their freedom and were certain of the dimensions of their destiny. American nationalist loyalties clustered around the Constitution as a symbol, the "American mission" as an evocative myth, and American wealth and prosperity as the visible signs of Providential grace.

Americans are no longer certain of their worldly destiny. They have seen the Ayatollah Khoumeni proclaim quite a different idea of the plans of Providence for the careers of nations. The recognition quickly followed that hostile nations may threaten American prosperity through the monopoly of critical resources, including petroleum. Adaptation to the newly perceived limits of American power in the international sphere, without surrendering to the wave of self-accusing isolationism stimulated by the Vietnam disaster, is a major challenge confronting American political leaders. Yet Ronald Reagan's campaign rhetoric and initial policies suggested an attempt to restore a national psychological state in which a realization of limits was impossible.

Political values change slowly. Conceptions of the nature and destiny of a nation certainly change more slowly than do the circumstances in which they will be realized, or seem to fail of realization. The 1980s began with a sense of confusion in high places. The feeling grew that America's understanding of itself had grown outmoded. The 1980 presidential election campaign failed to provide any orderly reconsideration of the national purpose. The blame for this failure cannot be simply laid at the feet of the candidates of the major political parties. Part of the blame rests with the Guardians, that stratum of political activists whose adherence to values which have become increasingly out of harmony with each other, and with reality, inhibits the consideration of any revised concept of the national destiny.

The Role of the Guardians

In explaining the Constitution as a well-designed machine, Madison argued that the system of elections and representation would serve to progressively refine the opinions of the people until the U.S. Congress should become capable of defining "the cool and deliberate sense of the community." In Madison's model, the flow of opinion is upward, from citizens whose basic virtue may be compromised by their connection with the local interest, to the more comprehensive outlook of their representatives. The "refinement" of opinions in their upward movement results from the representatives' superior understanding of, and attachment to, the public good. Not only do the voters have the wit to select representatives of superior character; in the extended republic, the representative is not bound to uphold the views of narrow, local interests.

Modern students of the impact of public opinion have studied the phenomenon of "feedback"—how public opinion reaches the organs of government, and how governmental reaction, or governmental failure to respond, in turn reinforces or modifies public opinion. Contrary to Madison's prediction, there is a two-way relationship between public opinion and public policy.

The formulation of public opinion is also more complex than is assumed in the pages of *The Federalist.* According to Katz and Lazarsfeld, opinions are formed in two steps. In their view, the impact of mass communications is indirect, a "two-step flow" from the media, via attentive opinion leaders, to the less attentive citizens. Between elections, these same attentive elites speak on behalf of the less articulate citizens to the organs of government.

The Guardians are precisely the attentive elite depicted in the two-step model. However, the use of television has grown considerably since the research of Katz and Lazarsfeld was conducted. Politicians now appear personally in the living room, with instant critiques of their performances supplied by a super-attentive elite, the network news commentators. Presidents have pressured the networks to insure that the commentators will not negate the impact of a presidential presentation. The print media remain an important source of information for those who seek actively to be informed. One Guardian pointed out to me that there is a growing gulf: policymakers and the activists who influence policymaking get their information about the world from newspapers like the *New York Times* and the *Washington Post,* while the public receives its information in the guise of entertainment from the tube.

The authority of journalism in the modern world is undeniable, and I interviewed several journalists, from both print and electronic media, as authentic Guardians. The impact of television upon presidential nominations and elections is substantial; to the extent that journalistic images replace any deliberative process within the political parties, it is also deplorable. The conscious and unconscious values of journalists have a great impact upon the contemporary electoral process. But the values of the Guardians as a group—private citizens and public officials as well as journalists—are of even greater importance in the process of formulating public policy. The procedures established by the Constitution ensure that an election is only one stimulus—albeit a major one—to the development of policy.

The Guardian class has permeable boundaries. The ranks of the habitual activists can be swollen by thousands of outraged citizens who suddenly seek a voice. This happened when Richard Nixon's dismissal of his attorney general—the "Saturday night massacre"—seemed to admit guilty knowledge of the Watergate transgressions. United Guardian opinion has the potential power to destroy the pretensions and even the career of a chief executive elected by a landslide. The more usual Guardian role is to serve as mediators between the public and the leaders of government.

My initial interviews revealed attitudes held by a substantial number of Guardians that were consistent with Jimmy Carter's half-conservative stance, just as they were responsive to Ronald Reagan's invocation of traditional American values during the 1980 campaign. My later interviews opened a window of understanding upon the way in which Reagan's specific policies stimulated enthusiasm in some, and disillusionment in others, of the Guardians who had been inclined to support his candidacy.

Political solutions located within the broad boundaries of the American political tradition are the only ones acceptable to the Guardians. However, the American tradition contains resources that suggest resolutions for several dilemmas confronting American politics. Some of those resources are contained in the thought of James Madison.

Much of the public responded favorably to Reagan's call for a return to traditional values, as did many of the Guardians. In all his praise of liberty (and free enterprise), Reagan had little to say about the principle of equality. Abraham Lincoln was absent from his personal pantheon of Republican heroes. This denial of a central aspect of the American heritage is discussed in the next chapter.

Aside from liberty, the values candidate Reagan referred to are individual attributes, such as thrift and ambition, or community virtues ("neighborhood"), rather than those public values articulated by Madison and the other founders, which they sought to embody in American political institutions. Two central concepts of Madison's thought are his insistence upon the pursuit of the public good as the natural end of government and his belief that establishing an extensive republic would prevent the tyranny of special interests. I will argue that these two principles have been increasingly obscured by the operations of American government for the last half-century and that they have been explicitly denied by Ronald Reagan.

CHAPTER TWO

Liberty and Equality:
Values on a Collision Course

> *We hold these truths to be self-evident, that all men are created equal, that they are endowed by their Creator with certain unalienable Rights, that among these are Life, Liberty and the pursuit of Happiness.*
>
> —*Thomas Jefferson*

> *I love liberty, I hate equality.*
>
> —*John Randolph of Roanoke*

The American nation was born in the full bloom of the Age of Reason, which insisted on the value and virtue of the individual person and attacked the social authority wielded by the church, the family, and the aristocracy. The single most important political relationship was seen as that between the individual and government. Viewing the establishment of government as a social compact between individuals, theorists of the era declared that the purpose of government is to secure personal liberties; if a particular government fails in that purpose, it is the right of the society to rebel and replace it.

The classic statement of this theory was penned as part of the Declaration of Independence by Thomas Jefferson. Jefferson's statement became, and has remained, a force in history, because his clear statement of principle was followed by the actions of the American Revolution. A new nation was born beneath the banners of Liberty and Equality.

American practice in the eighteenth century contradicted Jefferson's principles, as Jefferson himself recognized. In 1776 chattel slavery existed in all thirteen colonies, although its use was concentrated in the South. Women were excluded from political participation and social equality. Such education as was available was privately organized and too expensive for many parents, except for township schools in the North. Commerce and communication were established more completely between each colony and the home country than between neighboring colonies, dividing the colonies among themselves because of mistrust arising from different climate, agriculture, religion, and social structure. Presbyterian farmers in Massachusetts could not accept the Anglican slaveholders of Virginia as their moral equals, while Virginia planters did not view subsistence farmers as their social equals.

In the agrarian society of the eighteenth century, with its widespread distribution of small landholdings, the contrast between rich and poor citizens was less marked than it is today. Nevertheless, the distance was very great between what we would now consider to be the meanings of "liberty" and "equality" and actual social practices. Forces soon gathered that were dedicated to assuring that the promises of the Declaration would remain unfulfilled. One leader of these forces was Jefferson's fellow Virginian, John Randolph of Roanoke, who sought to perpetuate the agrarian aristocracy. Randolph stated the matter simply. "I am an aristocrat; I love liberty, I hate equality."

The statement of principle in the Declaration of Independence did not settle political questions, but it defined boundaries for their debate. The central political question concerned the rights of individuals against the authority of government. Throughout American history, nearly every issue has been discussed, and frequently resolved, within this framework. Many of those resolutions now seem bizarre. Barely six decades ago, for example, the Supreme Court struck down a minimum-wage law for interfering in the worker's freedom to make contracts. But the habit of treating social dilemmas as problems of individual liberty is a powerful tradition, which has both positive and negative results. I found that the tradition remains in force.

The Two Faces of Individualism

The concept of the value of the individual human being did not originate in the United States, nor was it invented by Thomas Jefferson. But the American nation can claim the distinction of having founded a polity dedicated, at least rhetorically, to a concern for human rights. This positive aspect of American individualism is one modern embodiment of an idea nearly as old as Western history. I was reminded of this fact as I sat in a natural foods restaurant in Houston, Texas. In between bites of his salad, Federal Judge Woodrow B. Seals began our conversation with a restatement of the tradition that verged on the poetical.

The moral law defines a civilization. And each civilization makes its own moral law. Once that moral law is promulgated by a consensus of a civilization, then if the civilization fails to live up to that standard, by its own definition the civilization has fallen. The moral law that defines our civilization, which is called Christendom, or the West, or the Atlantic Community, or the United States, is that every person has great worth and value: that every person is unique. Our entire social, economic, and political structure, as well as our religious structure, is built in America around this idea that each personality is unique. That each person is, like Thornton Wilder said in *The Bridge of San Luis Rey,* that we are not like ants that are crushed beneath the feet of a small boy on a hot summer day, but we are like the sparrow—not one feather falls unknown to God.

This is the consequence of the Judaeo-Christian heritage; also the ancient thoughts of the Greeks; as well as Locke, who influenced Jefferson so much. Locke and the Greeks complemented the Judaeo-Christian tradition of the worth of the individual. In the United States and in Texas, the model is that every person has great value. We see that in the social system. We see it in our marriage laws. We see it growing in our economic laws.

Judge Seals is a lay leader in the Methodist Church. He finds in his faith a guide to the conduct of his daily business, to the extent of assuring that no defendants on his criminal docket will languish in jail, unarraigned, over the weekend. Judge Seals was one of the first prominent Houstonians to support the presidential candidacy of Jimmy Carter. At that time, he saw Carter as a potential force for moral regeneration in the White House, sharing some of the positive qualities of Woodrow Wilson.

Although few Guardians provided such an eloquent account of the origins of American individualism, most supported the concept of making a concern for human rights central to American foreign policy. The number of persons who take pride in the historical connection between the United States and the human rights tradition and want it to be a central element of the American stance in international affairs was double the number who expressed any doubt about the principle. Their approval had an undertone of relief that the United States had at last found the appropriate theme to counter communist blandishments directed to the Third World nations. If one lesson of American defeat in Vietnam was that Wilsonian idealism too readily degenerates into chauvinistic nationalism, most of the Guardians did not hold this lesson in the forefront of their thought about international relations.

It should not be necessary to invoke the Vietnam disaster to recall that historic American values have a darker side. The word "individualism" entered the English language directly from the French with the first translation of Count Alexis de Tocqueville's classic *Democracy in America*. To Tocqueville, *individualisme* was a label for the negative aspects of American society as it existed in the time of President Andrew Jackson. The concept summarized the tendency of democratic societies to destroy all the noble or spiritual attributes of a society ruled by a responsible aristocracy. Lacking any *noblesse* to *oblige*, the democratic society would progressively level social distinctions and turn its attention to the relentless pursuit of material gratification. Eventually, wrote Tocqueville,

> As social conditions become more equal, the number of persons increases who, although they are neither rich enough nor powerful enough to exercise any great influence over their fellow-creatures, have nevertheless acquired or retained sufficient education and fortune to satisfy their own wants. They owe nothing to any man, they expect nothing from any man; they acquire the habit of always considering themselves as standing alone, and they are apt to imagine that their whole destiny is in their own hands.
>
> Thus not only does democracy make every man forget his ancestors, but it hides his descendents, and separates his contemporaries, from him; it throws him back for ever upon himself alone, and threatens in the end to confine him entirely within the solitude of his own heart.

This poignant passage tells us that the liberties of an individualistic society may come at the cost of social fragmentation and individual loneliness. This aspect of Tocqueville's thought gives it contemporary relevance as an explanation for that insistence upon self-gratification which was decried by respondents as diverse as Julian Bond of Atlanta, Elizabeth Ladd of Houston, and Boston's John Winthrop Sears. When individualism has become so pronounced as to destroy a person's sense of historical continuity and membership in a community, an exclusive focus upon self-interest results, which may be manifested in individuals by a restless search for sensual gratification and in politics by fragmentation and disorder.

Individualism became even more pronounced as an American characteristic in the decades after Tocqueville wrote. Later in the century, it was reinforced by the cold logic of social Darwinism, which held that only the fittest should survive. William Graham Sumner wrote a book on the question of *What Social Classes Owe to Each Other*. Sumner's answer was "nothing." To tax the rich for the benefit of the poor would be contrary to the laws of nature. In a contemporary context, taxing anybody to support unwed mothers or supply foreign aid for impoverished nations would be anathema. One can imagine a kind of coercive individualist who is the modern proponent of a perverse form of social Darwinism.

The category "coercive individualist" was used in a study of the opinions of partisan activists (largely county party leaders) in 1972. The label was defined as applying to persons who "want the government to let them alone to conduct their business affairs but are willing to use the military abroad and the police at home to intervene in the lives of others." Six per cent of the studied Democratic political activists were assigned to this category; the category was not used in the analysis of Republican activist attitudes. I believe that only two of the persons I interviewed could fairly be placed in a "coercive individualist" category.

One reason why the individualism of so few of these respondents could be labeled "coercive" is obvious. There is an element of the American heritage contrary to social Darwinism's grim economic struggle, although it offers no escape from individual responsibility. This tradition was restated in his quiet office by Senator Richard Lugar, Republican from Indiana, during a Congressional recess.

> I would define the American creed as a recognition that an individual human being is responsible for his or her actions under God. By that I mean simply a recognition that we have a temporal existence and that it's very important, when people all recognize that they are in that status, that they think about what sort of conduct in community affairs is appropriate. If, to take the opposite case, were people to act on the assumption that this life is it and that the particular material factors that are part of our country were ours to use and dispose of as rapidly and as happily as we could, then of course you'd have a different sort of country from one in which it's anticipated that people are stewards of valuable resources. And this leads to the thought of passing along a better country to future generations, with the thought that we will be judged on how well we do this. Sometimes by our political contemporaries, but in a more ultimate sense, by God. This leads to a very sober feeling about . . . the human dilemmas of trying to be sensitive to suffering and to the needs of other people, appreciating that we are all marching with each other through an uncertain period.

Senator Lugar's invocation of Christian stewardship joined the statement of Judge Seals as remarkably clear and calm assertions of the importance of religious belief as a guide to political judgment. Religious and ethical beliefs are the predominant sources of values beyond self-interest; I found that religion is a meaningful presence for many of the Guardians.

Forty-one per cent of the Guardians belong to the same Protestant denomination in which they were brought up. Another 22 per cent were raised in one Protestant sect but have changed their church membership to be more congruent with a higher social status, as from Baptist to Episcopalean. Thus nearly two-thirds of the respondents are Protestant, while 23 per cent are Catholic, and 11 per cent are Jewish. Only three persons identified themselves as atheists or agnostics. Of course, neither formal church membership nor the acknowledgment of private faith constitute a measure of the influence of religion on political attitudes.

Content analysis of the transcripts suggests that, for twenty of the respondents, church membership is a ritualistic formality. This is nearly a third of the sixty-two transcripts which provide adequate data for appraising the importance of religion. But twenty-five of these transcripts, or 40 per cent of the total, show a clear influence of religious belief upon political attitudes. This finding is based on inference, rather than on responses to direct questions. Since persons of this social stratum would be unlikely to volunteer a description of their fundamental religious convictions, the proportion for whom religion is a significant influence may be even greater.

And the place of religion for those who take it seriously can be profound. A Washington attorney whom I have called Fletcher Bradley told me,

> The central core of what I believe to be valuable about our civilization is its origin in, and the degree to which it continues, or at least individuals in the society continue, to be committeed to the insights of the Christian religion. And it seems to me that we have entered some time ago, and are going to get much more deeply into, a period in which Christianity will be as much in eclipse as a dominant force in people's lives as it was in the first couple of centuries.

Fletcher Bradley's legal practice largely consists in representing indigent clients before government agencies; his pay comes from foundation grants for legal assistance. He has renounced the higher paying corporate practice because of a sense of duty to a law higher than that of material success.

The history of American religious enthusiasms indicates that religion can reinforce a variety of political attitudes. But the dominant American religious tradition, descended from Calvinism, is that of individualistic, radical Protestantism. The secular power of this tradition is pervasive; it influences the social perceptions of American Catholics and Jews, as well as Protestants. I found that most of the Guardians did not formulate elaborate or sophisticated conceptions of social justice. Partly due to the heritage of radical Protestantism, much of their thought about politics was dominated by the vocabulary of individualism.

Triumph of the Individualist Vocabulary

Conversing with 117 American political activists about their most fundamental values, I was able to ask 90 persons point-blank whether they feel that there is some "American creed" that has endured since the national foundation. Three-fourths of them replied by invoking the most enduring symbols of American political culture. Their language was usually similar to that in the Declaration of Independence, and several quoted Thomas Jefferson directly. Others mentioned the Declaration and the Constitution as documentary sources of an American creed. I heard nearly seventy different versions of the devotion of this nation to individualist values, including all the classic themes.

The dominant theme was liberty. In the sparsely furnished offices of the Georgia AFL-CIO, for example, I spoke with Martha True, the secretary-treasurer, who is responsible for the organization's day-to-day operations.

> The American creed really is that every man, woman, and child in this country is free to live their life as they see fit. To work where they want to work, and do with their money that they make from that, whatever they want to do with it. Freedom is it, in one word. Freedom to be yourself.

Elsewhere in Atlanta, in the lavish offices of one of the city's leading corporate law firms, a senior partner took up the same theme. After quoting Jefferson's famous sentence, he added,

> I think the concept of personal liberty—and the fact that the individual has rights that may be contrary to the rights of the majority and to the state —is a very important concept that has been with us for a long time.

When asked about the American creed, the Guardians tended to mention liberty, or freedom, first. Their understanding of the meaning of liberty was quite clear. They emphasized the individual's freedom from social restraint, particularly in the form of governmental interference. The smaller number who referred to equality either described it as a value yet to be achieved or suggested that its meaning must be carefully defined.

I learned of the frustration of political ideals by the political process as I sat among cluttered papers in a client-interview room in the second-floor walkup office of a San Francisco law firm that specializes in civil rights cases, particularly when they grow out of feminist causes. The young woman who founded the firm was troubled by the questions I raised.

> It's hard not to be cynical, right? At the ripe old age of thirty-one? But I, in my relatively short adult life, have seen an awful lot. With the promises of the '60s, the Vietnam war, the women's movement. . . . [As a result of the 1960s activism,] we had a lot of things on paper. A lot of promises, which as the war began to drag on, and then finally was resolved or ended, and the economy declined, we had less to go around. And all of a sudden—I mean, isn't equality a wonderful principle when we have a booming economy, and we're just willing to hand it out hand over fist. But the minute when things get tough, I see this country standing up and saying, "Hmmm, maybe that was too much too fast." And equality is a nice thing; human rights are *marvelous*.

Elsewhere in San Francisco, I talked with an attorney who had been an influential adviser to former Governor Edmund G. ("Pat") Brown, Sr. When I asked about fundamental American principles, he stared at the magnificent view of the Bay Bridge stretching through the mist toward Oakland.

> What's put on paper isn't necessarily so, in actuality. "A perfect union." "Promote equality." Egalitarianism. They're nice things to say, but they haven't been achieved yet. Is the American goal equality? I'm not saying economic equality. No, not economic equality.

The power of Jefferson's language was shown in its specific rejection by the few who expressed cynicism about the national purpose. A young Italian-American member of the Boston City Council told me that the meaning of America is that "a lot of the folks who are on top cheated and lied and stole to get ahead. In business as well as politics." As he continued, his working-class Bostonian voice spat out the words like a machine gun.

The fact is that this country is not as egalitarian as it's been made out to be. And stupid people who have important fathers become important. And people with connections get credit cards. And a lot of people from humble backgrounds end up digging up streets. And, as long as education is not the great equalizer that it should be, and the doors to equality are thereby shut, then all that the Declaration of Independence said is just a bunch of shit. I really mean that. If you become a partner in a law firm because your father was a partner in a law firm, then the Declaration of Independence just does not work. If you sit in public office because your grandfather sat in public office, it just doesn't work. If Jerry Brown becomes governor because his father was governor, it's wrong. Linda Ronstadt notwithstanding.

A few of the Guardians found the roots of an American creed more in the nineteenth century than the eighteenth. They talked of free enterprise, an economic system, instead of echoing the language of the long struggle against arbitrary authority in a hierarchical society. Without exception, however, their descriptions of the meaning of America centered upon the rights or the opportunities of individual persons.

The difference between individual rights and individual opportunities is a crucial question of emphasis within the American tradition. When respondents referred casually to liberty or equality, the connotations they attached to the terms were seldom spelled out. The concepts were simply invoked as symbols for positive aspects of the American tradition. But the broader meaning that the symbol encompasses can be found elsewhere in many of the transcripts, making it possible to define the detailed meaning for each respondent of such terms as liberty and equality.

There are two main differences in these meanings; both are related to policy preferences. The first is the extent to which the individual sees liberty or equality as an accomplished reality, rather than an ideal that remains to be achieved. The second is concerned with whether the individual invests primarily a legal significance in the concept (as in defining liberty exclusively as freedom of speech, press, and religion), or whether there is an economic content, as in the belief that this country provides (or should provide) every citizen an equal chance for economic success, or even the guarantee of a minimum level of comfort.

Those for whom the symbols of liberty and equality have an economic connotation talk of "equality of opportunity." Equality is defined in terms of liberty by insisting that all should have equal freedom to strive for wealth. Those who feel that equal opportunity has been achieved are likely to seek the cutback of welfare programs and the diminution of business regulation by government, both in the name of restoring economic incentives. Those who see equal economic opportunity as a yet unachieved goal favor affirmative action programs in employment and college admissions, and many of them support the concept of the federal government as the employer of the last resort.

Without undue loss of the subtleties contained in their actual words, the attitudes of the Guardians may be sorted into four "pure" types of conviction. The first two types emphasize formal legal equality as the essence of liberty. The second two types find economic connotations in the concept of equality:

1. *Legal equality exists.* Americans have equal access to the legal process and are free to participate in the political system.
2. *Legal equality is an ideal.* The rich have easier access to law and to justice; individual rights are threatened by both government authority and private power.
3. *Equal opportunity exists.* The material success of an individual is limited only by his or her ambition and talent. All may gain access to the opportunities of the economic system.
4. *Equal opportunity is an ideal.* Many persons are denied access to economic opportunity. The provision of such access should be a first priority of politics.

Of course, these attitudes are not mutually exclusive. The most common combination was of numbers 1 and 3, the feeling that both legal equality and equal opportunity exist. This complacent conviction extended to half the respondents. The second most likely combination was of numbers 2 and 4: we must strive to achieve these ideals. Fourteen per cent of the respondents feel that legal equality has been substantially achieved, but that equal opportunity remains an ideal. The relationships are shown in Table 2–1.

Table 2–1
Guardian Beliefs about Equality

	3. EQUAL OPPOR- TUNITY EXISTS	4. EQUAL OPPORTU- NITY IS AN IDEAL
1. LEGAL EQUALITY EXISTS	35 (50%)	10 (14%)
2. LEGAL EQUALITY IS AN IDEAL	1 (1%)	24 (34%)

[N = 70, the number of transcripts adequate for content analysis on this point.]

There was a further relationship between these types of conviction. Those who believe that both legal equality and equal opportunity exist were often people who spend their days reading corporate balance sheets and similar devices that represent a business reality through numbers. But they have little contact with numbers representing social reality (the unemployment figures of urban black youth or the wage scale for nonunionized farm workers); and they do not look to such measures to improve their understanding of social reality. Their social convictions were strongly influenced by the knowledge of individual life stories—friends, relatives, celebrities like Sammy Davis, Jr., or they themselves had risen to success from obscure backgrounds. Therefore, success remains open to all. Their social vocabulary is exclusively the vocabulary of individualism.

The clearest exemplar of this mode of thought was a Chicago investment analyst I have named Gordon Thomas. Mr. Thomas's independent consulting firm, which has made him a millionaire, consists of two rooms high in an office building in the heart of Chicago's financial district. Thomas is a forceful man in his mid-fifties; business numbers were on the tip of his tongue. Discussing inflation, he quoted the price of gold and its increases in each of the last several years. Mentioning the energy crisis, he cited the amount added to the monetary reserves of Saudi Arabia.

> It's incredible to realize that in 1974–75, Saudi Arabia alone, after buying billions of dollars of U.S. goods and equipment, was still able to add $25 billion to its official reserves. This is nearly double the official reserves of the U.S. and equals the total cost of the Vietnam war. In addition, Saudi oil revenues for 1976 came in at around $30 billion, so by the end of '76 they collected more funds than the cost of two Vietnam wars.

Later, Mr. Thomas mentioned the radical politics of the 1960s.

> Essentially, I'd like to see America feel like its America. And I know there's twenty-two million blacks that feel oppressed—or forty million—or something. But the basic fact remains that it's better for a black to live in America than any other country in the world.

Although we should not expect all citizens to be demographers, Mr. Thomas's conception of the proportion of the population that is black is quite vague, compared to his total recall of gold prices or Saudi Arabian monetary reserves. He realizes that blacks perceive reasons for discontent, but he discounts those perceptions. He feels that equal opportunity is a reality, concluding that the individual is strictly responsible for his success or failure in life's contest.

Equality of Opportunity: The Failing Synthesis

Few respondents stated explicitly that there is an inherent conflict between the values of liberty and equality. One who perceived that conflict clearly was Senator Richard Lugar, who spoke of the ". . . age-old quest for whether freedom of initiative and ambition to succeed or push ahead the wheels of individual invention and progress, are more important than a quest for equity, and what people perceive as justice, or fairness."

When equality suggests that all persons, because of their humanity, deserve some minimum level of material comfort, the clash must come. At stake is the distribution of scarce goods. Unless the total available resources increase dramatically, the poor must achieve comfort at the expense of the rich.

When the Guardians invoked the concept of equal opportunity, they merely adopted the American habit of synthesizing liberty and equality in a manner that obscures their inherent contradiction. If opportunity is equal, the individual is responsible for whatever share of society's scarce goods he is able to garner for himself. Historically, this conviction has been reinforced by the Protestant belief in the individual's responsibility for his own spiritual salvation. In his message to Congress of July 4, 1861, Abraham Lincoln provided a gloss on the values proclaimed by the Declaration of Independence. Lincoln defined the struggle of the Union as the battle to continue that form of government "whose leading object is, to elevate the condition of men—to lift artificial weights from all shoulders—to clear the paths of laudable pursuits for all—to afford all, an unfettered start, and a fair chance, in the race of life."

In this brief passage, Lincoln both legitimizes placing equality within an economic context and introduces the compelling metaphor of the race. The first of these themes has become a major element of American belief. It was echoed by Franklin D. Roosevelt in his second inaugural with the declaration, "If the average citizen is guaranteed equal opportunity in the polling place, he must have equal opportunity in the market place." The second sentiment—the metaphor of the race—has captured the American imagination. Garry Wills has chronicled the concept's use, while demonstrating its absurdity.

This has been the great agreed-on undebated premise of our politics. Left and Right, liberal and conservative, Democrat and Republican, all work from this basis. Here is Ronald Reagan on the subject: "We offer equal opportunity at the starting line of life, but no compulsory tie for everyone at the finish." Here is Nixon: "I see a day when every child in this land has . . . an equal chance to go just as high as his talents will take him." . . . Here is Humphrey: "I'll take my stand, as I always have, on equal opportunity."
    . . . [W]here, when one gets down to it, is the starting line? Does a man begin the race at birth? Or when he enters school? When he enters the work force? When he attempts to open a business of his own? . . . We never even get to surmise where, in this science-fiction world of continual starting and racing, the finish line might be. Or, rather, the staggered infinite finishing lines for each runner. The metaphor is a mess.

Because of its basis in the individualist vocabulary, the "equal start" metaphor cannot withstand logical scrutiny. The individualist vocabulary further requires that the rights of individuals be seen as the central issue, while the attributes of the individual which result from group membership are considered irrelevant. The evidence that persons are being denied equality, as groups, because of religion, race, and sex, has accumulated throughout American history. The conditions—abundant resources and a growing national product—that kept the belief in equal opportunity alive by allowing those on the top of the social ladder eventually to yield a share to those below, without losing much of their own, are fading rapidly. And the institutions—the public schools—that have promised that equal opportunity will be possible, have broken down under the many burdens we have asked them to bear. Goaded by the judiciary, the schools have attempted to redress the inequality between the races created by multiple forces within the economic and social systems. Caught in a cross-fire of conflicting purposes, the schools have lost the confidence of the taxpayers who support them.

But the loss of confidence in the schools is only a part of the rejection of the quest for equal opportunity. Claiming to enact a mandate provided by the 1980 election, the Reagan administration has decimated social programs intended to support that quest. According to Nobel laureate economist James Tobin,

> Wealth breeds wealth and poverty breeds poverty. Despite legendary examples of spectacular social mobility, the unequal outcomes of one generation are generally the unequal opportunities of the next. Here as in other democracies, governments have sought to arrest the momentum of inequality by free public education, social insurance, "war on poverty" measures and progressive taxation.

The U.S. budget and tax legislation of 1981 is an historic reversal of direction. Existing institutions, commitments, and "safety nets" can't be rapidly dismantled, but the message is clear enough; inequality of opportunity is no longer a concern of the Federal Government.

The claim of the Reagan economic policymakers is that incentives must be restored to the wealthy through tax cuts, rather than opportunity being fostered for the disadvantaged. This is sanctioned by public opinion only if a majority feel that their own economic freedom is threatened by the cost of social programs; having achieved "fair opportunity" themselves, government efforts to supply it to others can have only negative consequences.

While the impact of the faith in equal opportunity on marginally successful working people has been studied—with contrasting results—by such scholars as Robert Lane and Sennett and Cobb, there has been little explicit attention to that impact upon the rich. The logic of individualism would lead us to expect that persons of power and wealth have been as thoroughly socialized into the ethos of equal opportunity as have working people. Except for those with inherited wealth who have been taught a sense of social responsibility (or guilt), they will believe that their wealth was attained by making the best use of the opportunities available. As winners, they are likely to believe that the rules of the game are just fine. This might be called the Marie Antoinette syndrome.

Comparing the Guardians' reported annual incomes with their agreement or disagreement with a strongly worded statement on the achievement of equal opportunity confirms this expectation, but only in the most general way. (See Table 2–2.) Even those who agree do so with

Table 2–2
Guardian Incomes and Belief in Achieved Equal Opportunity

Statement: "Equality of opportunity is a reality, not a dream, in the United States."

	ANNUAL INCOME IN 1976				
	$19,999 OR LESS	$20,000– 59,999	$60,000– 99,999	$100,000– 149,999	$150,000 OR MORE
Agree strongly	0	0	0	0	0
Agree with reservations	1	20	6	10	3
Undecided or neutral	0	2	0	0	1
Disagree with reservations	5	14	3	4	1
Disagree strongly	0	8	3	3	0

[N = 84. Thirty-three respondents either did not complete the card-sort exercise, or reveal their incomes, or both.]

reservations. The very richest tend to see equal opportunity as achieved; the poorest do not think it has been accomplished. But persons in the middle ranges from $60,000 to $150,000—a 1976 income most would consider more than comfortable—are divided about equally on the matter. Close scrutiny of the data suggests that wealth alone does not determine one's outlook. Wealth is related to the matrix of values, or ideology, that one acquires during a lifetime, but does not solely determine that ideology. And it is that ideology which filters perceptions of social reality.

Closer reading of the full transcripts reveals that my wealthiest respondents were not necessarily the most callous, and some of them demonstrated genuine empathy for minorities and the poor. Conversely, some of the minority respondents do believe in the reality of economic opportunity for members of their own ethnic group. Furthermore, the wealthiest of the Guardians did not agree with a bald restatement of social Darwinism ("Only the strongest and fittest survive. This is a law of nature and a law of society."). Nor, generally, did the respondents with lower incomes. A more important inhibition than wealth in preventing their perception of important social realities was their limited ability, rooted in the individualist vocabulary, to recognize the political claims of minority groups as groups.

The Limited Visibility of Racial Minorities

The individualist vocabulary and tradition inhibits political leaders, who operate only through one or another kind of organization, from perceiving the full significance of groups in society. This tendency is reinforced by the effort to eliminate prejudice by making an individual's attributes that result from group membership irrelevant. In Quincy, Massachusetts, I spoke with Richard Stearns, who had been a member of the McGovern-Fraser Commission which adopted rules with the practical effect of requiring that delegations to the 1972 Democratic convention include quotas of minority members. Despite this experience of political operations based on building majorities through the coalition of minorities, Stearns told me,

> Part of the American creed for me is tolerance. I think a function of tolerance is respect for the rights of others. I think that that fundamental respect for other's rights and the dignity of each individual as a person rather than as a member of a race or a group is really at the root of our sort of sense

of what liberty and individual rights are. The less quotas and so on are justified, the better. Because. . . . I think they're contrary to the American spirit. They may be an evil necessity, but I don't think that we should indulge in attempting to rationalize quotas or affirmative action as being somehow natively part of the American spirit.

The attachment to the individualist view of the world is fully as pervasive as Stearns's evocation of the American spirit would indicate. The Guardians operate in systems dominated by the reality of organizations, but they do not keep their own identity and that of their organizations in separate mental compartments. A staff member of a Chicago-based organization of urban neighborhoods did not view "the neighborhoods" as an abstraction. The phrase represented real values to him, and he felt the anguish of neighborhood residents as if it were his own. Oil company executives in Houston frequently used the term "we." It often referred to their own corporation, but it could also refer to the entire petroleum industry. Lawyers referred to their firms as "we," although they kept a discrete psychological distance from their corporate clients. Lawyers operate in the climate created by the legal fiction that treats corporations as if they were individuals, with many of the rights guaranteed to persons by the Constitution. Thus lawyers can think of specific organizations as if they were individuals, but this facility may inhibit them from comprehending the problems of a less well defined group, such as a racial minority. And, as will be shown below, the language of the law has proven incapable of recognizing the claim of ethnic groups to enjoy the rights guaranteed to persons.

The facility for identifying the self with organizational purposes helps explain the survival of the individualist vocabulary. If the line between the self and the organization is hazy, the picture of politics as a contest between organizations may not remain at the foreground of political consciousness. A more important influence, I believe, is the surrounding political culture, as transmitted by schools, history books, and continuing political debate. This century's most dramatic change in the nature of American government took place without modifying the individualist vocabulary. Since the New Deal launched governmental interventions in the economy in the name of social justice, many considered its impulses to be collectivist, the antithesis of individualism. But social justice was defined as equal opportunity, and President Roosevelt emphasized continuities with traditional American values. References to the need to assure equal opportunity abound in his speeches. The security of the individual, protection for "the common man," is stressed again and again. In his 1932 Commonwealth Club speech, considered the most complete and coherent statement of his political philosophy, Roosevelt defined his goal as achieving a society in which "every individual may have a place if he will take it, in which every individual may find safety if he wishes it; in which every individual may attain such power as his ability permits, consistent with his assuming the accompanying responsibility."

Such New Deal attitudes reinforced the individualist vocabulary, even as the New Deal presided over the establishment of myriad groups that sought new advantages, or the protection of achieved advantages, resulting from government policy. The interest group, its lobbyist, the legislator, and the government agency formed a circle of communication that did not always operate within public view. The pervasiveness of this activity led political scientists to develop theories of pluralism in which the interest group replaced the individual as the primary actor in politics; groups, rather than individuals, were seen as competing in the familiar arena of liberalism.

My interviews suggest that prescriptive pluralism has not won the allegiance of political practitioners. They regard organizations, including their own, as necessary instruments. But the individualist tradition establishes their values.

The politics of the 1960s brought activism by much broader segments of the population: young people, racial minorities, and women. The boundaries of their membership were more difficult to define, since not all women were feminists, all young men did not oppose the draft, and some members of minorities had little desire to disturb the pattern of accommodation with white majority power. These movements were bound to seem like amorphous groups to persons habituated to the quieter political style of the '50s. These groups thrust forward no single spokespersons to negotiate with government representatives. Instead, various leaders competed for media attention. Their politics of confrontation and demonstration were very public.

In the 1980s the domestic political strife of the '60s is but a memory. Evidence abounds that the official end of legal discrimination on the basis of race has yet to yield equal treatment for minorities in employment, housing, and education. Yet the claim of black Americans upon the conscience of America has faded. Only 19 per cent of the Guardians volunteered any mention of discrimination on the basis of race or sex as among the most important national problems. Of those who completed the card-sort exercise after the interview, only half indicated that awareness of that claim is at the forefront of their political conscious-

Table 2–3
The Visibility of Minorities

Statement A: "Members of racial minorities and women should get special advantages when considered for employment or promotion."

Statement B: "A basic reason for black rioting in the cities is white racism."

	A	B
Agree strongly	9	11
Agree with minor reservations	22	16
Agree with major doubts	15	19
Neutral or undecided	5	4
Disagree with major doubts	13	12
Disagree with minor reservations	18	19
Disagree strongly	9	10

[N = 91]

ness. While one of the questions asked about the reality of white racism, and the other asked if members of racial minorities and women should get special advantages in employment, the responses were remarkably similar, as Table 2–3 demonstrates. I take that similarity to be a measure of the limited visibility of minorities to the Guardians.

Affirmative Action: Challenge to Individualism

President Lyndon Johnson's Great Society established a variety of programs aimed at ameliorating the condition of minorities. Based on a tenuous theory of the causes of poverty, most channeled money into the pockets of middle-class administrators, without redistributing incomes. Jobs and education were recognized as the compelling permanent needs of minority groups. Accepting the equalization of opportunity as the goal, the means adopted were programs of affirmative action, particularly in employment and college admissions. In a typical pattern, Congress provided a noble but vague mandate; executive agencies supplied the specific rules; and the Supreme Court had to determine whether the rules were within Congressional intent. The champions of equality relaxed, perhaps in the mistaken belief that the question had passed from the realm of politics to that of administration. Their relaxation meant that the value of equality no longer served as the banner for mass political action.

Affirmative action asked the dominant white males to accept a perceived disadvantage so that other groups might overcome the historic burdens of prejudice. One question for public policy was how the minority disadvantagement should be measured. If the minority representation in a college freshman class or a particular occupation were below that minority's proportion of the population from which potential students or employees were drawn, then a rough quota was determined. The number of students or employees should be made equal to that proportion. Jewish organizations, speaking for those who had experienced such quotas as a limitation upon opportunity, protested the concept. The word "goal" was substituted for "quota," to demonstrate a positive, rather than a negative, intention. But this semantic quibble did not change the practice.

I raised the question of affirmative action with the Guardians in the context of equal employment opportunities. The answers I received reflected their feelings about liberty and equality but were modified, in some cases, by experience with affirmative action programs in industry and education. Only nine of the sixty-three persons with whom I discussed the question announced unqualified opposition to the principle. Typical of these was Elizabeth Ladd of Houston.

> My basic premise would be that a person should rise on his ability alone. I really don't care much about his skin color, as long as he has got a brain and a willingness to work. I cannot see going back and making atonement for so-called past sins in employment. We would be going back to the time of Methuselah if we did. I definitely do not believe in a quota system, either for industry or for schools.

Gordon Thomas of Chicago was predictably outspoken on the subject.

> I favor performance as a prime requisite. I'm in sympathy with the idealistic proposition, but I don't think you build a strong society by weakening qualifications. . . . [To weaken qualifications] only creates more problems. It creates a situation in which we're paying people not to riot and to sit home and drink beer and have babies and live off the taxpayers.

A more common response was to approve the principle but question its implementation. Elsewhere in Chicago, over lunch at the University Club, a corporate attorney explained to me that he is conservative on economic matters, but "on human rights and all that, I'm all for it. When civil rights is involved, minorities and all of that, I don't really quibble too much with affirmative action programs, desegregating the schools and all of that. Here again, though, I think the process sometimes creates abuses. Maybe the pendulum swings too far in favor of the minorities in certain instances."

A reaction based on the nature of his own professional office was offered by a San Francisco architect who has served as mayor of a Marin County suburb.

> The government says, "We'll give you a contract, provided you have at least one minority employee." Well, that's a way of making us participate, but then we could go out and try to find a minority employee, and what if all we do is sit him in a corner to draw doodles. That satisfies the requirement but it isn't helping him.

A very personal reaction was offered by a civic organization leader in Chicago who is the granddaughter of an immigrant Jewish tailor.

> I'm uncomfortable with quotas all across the board. . . . On principle, I am for affirmative action. But I don't know how you do it unless you have quantitative targets. . . . I don't cotton much to this "For one hundred years you have oppressed me." I haven't oppressed anybody for a hundred years, and I've spent a whole lifetime in trying to help people. And I see a lot of other people who need help, too. I just don't cotton to quotas at all, anywhere.

Passions were also stimulated on the opposite side of the issue. I found Louis Martin, editor of Chicago's black newspaper, the *Defender*, distressed at the use of tax incentives to encourage minority employment.

> It's ridiculous to me to see that the corporations are given fabulous money for so-called phony jobs for blacks. . . . There's a certain amount of fraud in that operation, which when people wake up to the fact that we've been taken for a little ride here, creates a kind of resentment that I don't think is good for this society. It leaves people more anti-establishment than they should be. . . . Here's XQ Corporation claiming how they love us, and we should patronize them and buy their products because they're so friendly with blacks. It turns out that every damn thing they gave us they took from Uncle Sam's tax dollars to give us.

Mr. Martin strongly approved the principle of affirmative action; I found his approval matched in Houston by Billie Carr, an organizational leader of the liberal wing of the Texas Democratic party.

> Quotas are a dirty word. But I think we've got to have enforced quotas. It's just like telling people, "Please don't run a red light." If you have to pay

five dollars if you get caught, that makes you not run it. . . . You have to be required to fill so many positions, and I think you've got to have the numbers, and you've got to hold the companies to it. And the Democratic party ought to be held to it.

The passionate reactions of the Guardians to affirmative action policies were inevitable. Affirmative action lays bare the contradictions in the tradition of liberal individualism, which emphasizes the good of both liberty and equality. Individualism implies a utilitarian standard for the judgment of public policy: policies should implement the greatest good of the greatest number of persons. This implies a calculus of addition and subtraction. Affirmative action raises the possibility that efforts to achieve equality for some will result in the subtraction of liberty from others.

Only one of the Guardians established a distance between himself and the individualist tradition. Columnist George Will, who described himself as "a failed academic," pointed out that our nation was founded at a specific time on the basis of particular ideas. He said that the question remains unanswered whether an urban, metropolitan nation can base its existence on those individualistic ideas that include a utilitarian calculus of what is right, rather than perceiving a source of guidance in natural law.

This exception underscored the unanimity of the other Guardians. Their strong feelings must be attributed to the recognized or unrecognized conflict between deeply held values. Their opinions followed the classic division between the two aspects of the individualist tradition. Supporters of affirmative action seek to maximize equality. Its opponents argue that affirmative action threatens the liberty of all. Some claim that the minority person benefited by affirmative action is thereby stigmatized: marked as one unable to compete on equal terms, a person of lesser competence. Thus, in a perverse way, affirmative action interferes with the liberty of the very persons it benefits. Such apparently principled opposition could be only an elaborate mask for racist or sexist attitudes. In general, however, I believe that the persons I conversed with were simply unable to perceive justice in the claims made by minorities as groups. Affirmative action seemed to provide rewards on some basis other than individual merit, and this was intolerable.

Over a third of the people I asked about affirmative action in employment brought up the case of Alan Bakke, then pending before the U.S. Supreme Court, which dealt with affirmative action in education. The case posed the conflict between liberty and equality in stark terms, and it had received lavish attention in the press. Briefs were submitted as "friends of the Court" by 146 organizations, each urging their preferred understanding of "equality." An analysis of these arguments reveals that none made the radical claim that groups, as groups, should enjoy the rights guaranteed by the Constitution to persons. The law reasons by analogy, and corporations, labor unions, and trusteeships have been found to share some characteristics analogous to those of individuals, and thus to deserve the rights (of property and free speech) guaranteed to individuals. However, Timothy O'Neill concludes that the language of the law has developed in such a way as to make the concept of "group rights absurd in American law."

A few of the Guardians expressed relief that a landmark decision by the Court would resolve the issue. A more frequent attitude was one of watchful anticipation. Several were willing to state what the Court's finding should be. One such reaction came from a Chicago alderman and practicing attorney who was a staunch supporter of former Mayor Bilandic.

> Whenever you have discrimination, regardless of the goals that that discrimination is used to achieve, it's un-American, and it's, in my opinion, illegal. And I think in the final analysis it will be self-defeating. . . . I would hope and expect that the Supreme Court will ultimately do what's right, in my opinion, and what is the law of the land, and strike down these affirmative action programs once and for all and settle the issue.

When the *Bakke* decision was handed down, it was greeted with initial enthusiasm, since each side seemed to have made its point. Alan Bakke, a white engineer, was admitted to the University of California medical school at Davis, yet universities were told they could take race into consideration as one factor in the admissions decision; the Constitution need not be totally color blind. Closer inspection of the six separate opinions in the case—none were endorsed by a majority of the justices —revealed that no new synthesis had been achieved. The justices of the Supreme Court were as divided among themselves on the problems of affirmative action in 1978 as the Guardians had been in 1977.

That division continued in the two years following. In 1979 the Court considered the case of Brian Weber, a white laborer denied admission to a training program to which blacks with less seniority had been admitted. Weber claimed that he had been discriminated against on the basis of race, and that such discrimination is declared illegal by Title VII of the Civil Rights Act of 1964. With two justices not participating, the Court ruled by a five-to-two majority that Weber's contention was incorrect. Their opinion held that the literal prohibition against discrimination written in Title VII was not in accord with the "spirit" of the Act, which therefore must permit voluntary affirmative action programs of the kind established at Brian Weber's plant.

On July 2, 1980, the Court announced its opinion on the constitutionality of the law which provides that 10 per cent of federal funds for local public works projects be "set aside" for minority businessmen, defining minorities as "Negroes, Spanish-speaking, Orientals, Indians, Eskimos, and Aleuts." By a vote of six to three, the justices found that the law does not violate the equal protection guarantee. However, none of the three major opinions won the concurrence of a majority. Justices Stewart and Rehnquist wrote in dissent that the Constitution must be forever color-blind. In a separate concurrence, joined by Justices Brennan and Blackmun, Thurgood Marshall wrote,

> Today, by upholding this race-conscious remedy, the Court accords Congress the authority necessary to undertake the task of moving our society toward a state of meaningful equality of opportunity, not an abstract version of equality in which the effects of past discrimination would be forever frozen into our social fabric.

By returning once again to the formula "equality of opportunity," Justice Marshall signaled that the Court remains unable to achieve that synthesis between the values of liberty and equality that could help to initiate a new era of social harmony.

Needed: A New Synthesis

The American tradition of insistence upon the value of the individual has noble aspects, despite the gap between the ideal and its realization in practice. The national challenge is to preserve the nobility inherent in the concept, recognizing that any modern notion of equality has a material dimension, even while accepting the fact that this society can no longer presume a future of increasing prosperity. I found that political leaders are divided on the question of how to formulate national policies that will work toward equality without threatening liberty. A significant number choose to believe that equality has been achieved, in the strictly legal sense, and that the concept promises nothing more. President Reagan's version of this conviction is summed up in the sentence, "The greatest social program is a job."

But half of the Guardians are well aware that racism and prejudice prevent the achievement of equal opportunity. They favor programs of affirmative action as a kind of temporary expedient that may, in a decade or in a generation, succeed in supplying for all Lincoln's goal of "an equal start in the race of life." But several fear that such programs, when once established with rules and a bureaucracy, will become permanent, retaining power after their purpose has been fulfilled. And others raise the spectre of a procession of minorities forming a queue, awaiting government certification as being disadvantaged. The study of genealogy would then become a passion, as individuals sought to prove membership in the latest group claiming special treatment to equalize its opportunities.

The obvious need is for new concepts that do not depend on such a flawed metaphor as that of "the race of life." If the spirit of Lincoln is to be invoked, it should be the spirit of the Second Inaugural: "With malice toward none; with charity for all; with firmness in the right, as God gives us to see the right, let us strive on to finish the work we are in."

What is needed is no less than a major shift in emphasis within the American democratic tradition which preserves the positive features of individualism while it accommodates the recognition of group attributes. As a guide to the achievement of justice, the Constitution can no longer be color-blind. This phrase means, simply, that legal abstractions must not prevent the perception of social reality and the careful design of programs that respect both equality and liberty.

Values beyond self-interest that guide the actions and attitudes of political elites change slowly, but they do change. That our understanding of racial justice can change is shown by the fact that the conception of a color-blind Constitution was radical in 1896, liberal in 1954, and was embraced in 1980 by only two conservative justices of the Supreme Court. As I shall argue in the next chapter, the champions of equality must further that value through normal political channels, broadening the basis of support for its achievement. The dependence upon judicial and administrative bureaucracies for remedial action has resulted in the diminution of public (and Guardian) support for the equality principle.

A new understanding that would transcend individualist values can hardly be imposed by judges, nor can it be defined by presidential candidates in a position paper that becomes a campaign relic. To formulate such a new conception must be the work of many minds, the labor of many seasons. At the right time, a new synthesis of liberty and equality must be taken before the public by a political figure who commands respect. Eventually, it must be recognized as an idea whose time has come. The task is difficult, but it must be undertaken.

CHAPTER THREE

The Inclusive Republic:
Madison in Modern Dress

> *It is too early for politicians to presume on our forgetting that*
> *the public good, the real welfare of the great body of the people,*
> *is the supreme object to be pursued; and that no form of govern-*
> *ment whatever has any other value than as it may be fitted for*
> *the attainment of this object. . . .*
>
> *In the extended republic of the United States, and among the*
> *great variety of interests, parties, and sects which it embraces, a*
> *coalition of a majority of the whole society could seldom take*
> *place on any other principles than those of justice and the gen-*
> *eral good.*
>
> —*James Madison, 1788*

When American political leaders designed a truly national government
in response to the turmoil of the 1780s, they welcomed the chance to
establish an institution that might assure the well-being of posterity.
They were confident that rational structures, embedded in a written
document, could create a new social order. John Adams wrote that "the
best republics will be virtuous and have been so. But we may hazard a
conjecture, that the virtues have been the effect of the well ordered
constitution, rather than the cause." Reporting these two sentences, a
British scholar commented, "Constitutionalism thus raised to the level
of an ideology was . . . to become a lasting feature of American political
culture."

John Adams was not present at the Philadelphia Convention of 1787; he was serving as United States ambassador to England, as Thomas Jefferson was to France. The Convention's intellectual leadership devolved upon James Madison. Madison later co-authored the classic explication of the Constitution, *The Federalist Papers*.

Madison did not regard the handiwork of the founders as permanent; he urged the 1829 Virginia Constitutional Convention to apply its collective wisdom to the adaptation of laws and institutions to social change. By 1829 constitutionalism was becoming part of an American ideology; the negative aspect of such extreme constitutionalism is that it may impede the advance of political understanding. The Constitution is acclaimed as a sacred document that settles all major questions, placing them beyond debate or even consideration. Any minor details are resolved by the enactment of laws in accord with the Constitution, as interpreted by the high priests of the Supreme Court. The modern result, in the phrase of Louis Hartz, is that "law has flourished on the corpse of philosophy."

This chapter considers aspects of Madison's philosophy that are relevant to contemporary dilemmas and insists that Madisonian principles should not be placed beyond the reach of debate or reconsideration.

Checks and Balances: Madison's Institutional Morality

When Alexander Hamilton, James Madison, and John Jay collaborated as "Publius" to write *The Federalist Papers*, they worked in the midst of heated controversy. The need for replies to opposition arguments inspired them to elaborate a theory that justified the decisions that won majority approval, not always on theoretical grounds, in Philadelphia. Publius portrayed the arrangements of federalism, for example, not merely as the strongest national power the states were likely to accept; federalism was the necessary solution dictated by the discoveries of "the new science of politics." Although the *Papers* did not decide the immediate contest over ratification, the power of Publius' argument has been so great as to supply an understanding of the Constitution that transcends the document itself.

> The "Federalist Papers" . . . give us a new and different constitution, or, if you like, a special set of rules for operating the Philadelphia Constitution which most of us have taken to heart. . . . The idea that we have three

separate and coordinate branches comes to us not from the Constitution, which is a legislative supremacy constitution, but from *The Federalist,* which lays down for us a constitutional morality, a political ethos that is as natural to us as the air we breathe.

The truth of this passage was demonstrated by my interviews. I found that the separation of powers principle has become so central to our understanding of American government that the Guardians take it for granted. A dozen respondents mentioned the principle in passing. It received surprising emphasis in 1977 when I sat in the basement Capitol office of the majority whip of the United States Senate, California's Alan Cranston, as Cranston's chief legislative assistant told me what the Democratic senators hoped to achieve during the Ninety-fifth Congress.

In the aftermath of Watergate, the Senate leadership, and certainly Senator Cranston, is concerned with developing in Congress the independent, separate branch of government that the constitutional founders envisaged. They're reestablishing that independence when we now have a Democratic president. It's a little tough, but we don't want to go back to the situation that existed in Lyndon Johnson's day, when the Congressional majority was viewed as, in effect, a rubber stamp for the majority party leader in the White House. So we are in the process of making sure that that independence occurs, and Carter is the president to do it with, because he believes, I think, that Congress should be an independent branch, and is not attempting to do what Nixon did, and that is simply ignore Congress and try to run things without Congress.

This statement is notable for several reasons. The first is that the principle is quite separate from the substance of policy. It holds that Congress must insist upon its independence even if it eventually endorses the initiatives of a president who leads the majority party. Thus it was not Richard Nixon who threatened to unbalance the Constitution; Nixon merely continued Lyndon Johnson's practices. Second, the validity of the principle is taken for granted: there is no mention of any end to be achieved through the institutional design of separate branches; the separation of powers with its corollary, the system of checks and balances, is seen as good for its own sake.

Perhaps the most striking aspect of this statement is its source: the Madisonian principle was invoked, during Jimmy Carter's presidential term, in the office of the Senate Democratic leadership. The traditional role of the majority leadership, when the president is of the same party, has been to guide the president's program through the Senate, yielding only reluctantly to the pressures for compromise. I thought at the time that the insistence of these partisan leaders upon independence must mean that the president's major programs would not be passed; or, if passed, they would be amended beyond recognition. And so, for this and other reasons, it transpired.

Has the unquestioning acceptance of the checks and balances principle become a barrier to political understanding? In accepting this much of Madison's message, have the Guardians overlooked some more fundamental meaning? Both questions must be answered in the affirmative. Certainly Madison's attachment to the separation of powers principle was independent of the substance of any particular policy. But Madison was very clear in his insistence that "justice and the public good" supplied the standard by which any policy must be judged, as well as any form of government. To Madison, "the public good" was a phrase that represented a recognizable reality. I will argue later in this chapter that the concept retains its validity.

Madison was equally clear on the ends to be achieved by the system of checks and balances. The problem was to "enable the government to control the governed; and in the next place to oblige it to control itself." In the system proposed by the Federalists, sovereignty resided with the people. Through periodic elections, the people would assess the stewardship by government officials of those powers delegated to them under the Constitution. The electorate's judgment would be the primary control upon the actions of government; but "experience has shown the need for auxiliary precautions." The greatest of these auxiliary precautions was achieved through the interior design of the the government, by creating three branches selected independently of each other, and responding to somewhat different constituencies, but with the motive and means to check any tyrannical impulse on the part of the other branches. In a famous passage from *Federalist* 51, Madison wrote:

> The great security against a gradual concentration of the several powers in the same department, consists in giving to those who administer each department, the necessary constitutional means, and personal motives, to resist encroachments of the others. The provisions for defense must in this, as in all other cases, be made commensurate to the danger of attack. Ambition must be made to counteract ambition. The interest of the man must be connected with the constitutional rights of the place.

Thus, while the three branches are separate and balanced, their realms of authority are not strictly cordoned off from each other. The president can subject legislation to a veto, which Congress in turn may override; presidential appointments must be approved by the Senate; the Supreme Court has developed its authority, barely implicit in the Constitution, to invalidate actions of the president or of Congress on constitutional grounds. Ambition counteracts ambition.

For Madison, popular control ("dependence on the people") was joined with the "auxiliary precautions" in a single principle of sound government. That unity has since been shattered. From the 1930s through the 1970s, liberals emphasized the need for responsiveness to popular majorities and decried the potential for stalemate in the separation of powers. Conservatives have lauded the deliberation and delay occasioned by the auxiliary precautions, while expressing alarm about the power of a temporary popular will. After the Republican electoral victories of 1980, liberals discovered new virtues in the powers of the Democratic House of Representatives, while conservatives worried about those powers thwarting the "popular mandate."

In addition to the general principle, what did Madison see as the function of the Senate? Senators were to be selected by the legislatures of their respective states. Madison praised this arrangement in *The Federalist* as being "most congenial to the public opinion" as well as involving state governments in the establishment of the new national authority, while creating "a convenient link between the two systems." The six-year term, coupled with this mode of selection, would create a body of cool and deliberate citizens.

> . . . [T]here are particular moments in public affairs, when the people stimulated by some irregular passion, or some illicit advantage, or misled by the artful misrepresentation of interested men, may call for measures which they themselves will afterwards be most ready to lament and condemn. In these critical moments, how salutary will be interference of some temperate and respectable body of citizens, in order to check the misguided career, and to suspend the blow mediated by the people against themselves, until reason, justice, and truth, can regain their authority over the public mind?

The need for the concurrence of both houses in Congressional legislation certainly ensures deliberation and lengthens the legislative process; some would argue that only an outraged public opinion (forgetting reason or justice) can assure expeditious action by Congress. Since Madison wrote, the prestige and authority of the Senate has been greatly increased by the elimination of the state legislative role in its selection. Since Madison argued against the localism of the state legislatures in the

Constitutional Convention, and argued in favor of the popular election of the president, it seems reasonable to imagine that he would have welcomed the electoral process as an appropriate means of securing able and responsive senators.

The Contemporary Congress

Direct election assures the quality of the Senate as an institution. I was reminded of this interpretation when I sat among a clutter of dirty coffee cups in the Senate restaurant, talking with Brock Brower. Brower is a journalist and novelist who frequently writes on political topics; he admires the process that culminates in the election of a United States senator.

> Fulbright used to say to me that he would take the U. S. Senate as a body of professionals—meaning senators—over the first one hundred men of any category in the country. He said, you would get down on the list to the ninety-eighth, ninety-ninth, or hundredth man to a worse banker than you would as a senator. . . . These are pretty damned good men, who went through a hell of a lot to get where they are. I really think you could pit them against the first hundred golf pros or the first hundred doctors in the country.

The contemporary Senate is indeed professional, the modern equivalent of a "temperate and respectable body of citizens." There are aspects of professionalism, however, that must modify any claim that Madison's hopes for the Senate have been realized. Professionalism can denote a narrowness of purpose which was no part of Madison's design. Recalling Madison in *Federalist* 51, we must acknowledge that senators, like others achieving positions of power, are normally ambitious. As an institution, the Senate focuses its ambition on the mandate perceived in Madison's own writing, a mandate to become as independently powerful as possible, with only external checks to be concerned with. If senators are true professionals of political power, the Senate's contest for authority with the president or the House may become such an obsession as to obscure Madison's greater purpose, which is to define and achieve the public good.

The House of Representatives has also perceived a Madisonian mandate to become as strong and independent as possible. In the last two or three decades, by nearly every objective measure, the Congress has become a stronger institution. Its members are better paid; their labors are supported by a growing, professional staff; the committee structure has undergone cycles of reform. Yet who could argue that the performance of the total institution in the 1970s was superior to the results it produced in the 1950s, when Lyndon Johnson and Sam Rayburn guided institutional cooperation with the unambitious program of President Eisenhower? Or that recent Congressional performance has been superior to that of the mid-1960s, when Lyndon Johnson as president created the legislative framework of his Great Society? The idea that Congress is "good" when it follows the lead of a vigorous president and "bad" when it charts an independent course was a deserved victim of Watergate.

The life of the United States Congress can be practically autonomous. The Capitol is flanked by the Senate and House office buildings; all are connected by subterranean passages, and the senators have an electric railway to ease their underground travels. Congressmen are served by their own restaurants, barber shops, gymnasia, post offices, and security forces. As a result of violence directed against public figures during the last two decades, the casual visitor to the office building will have his briefcase or her purse inspected to prevent the importation of infernal devices. Gallery spectators of the House or Senate sessions must deposit all parcels at a checkstand and pass through metal detectors before entering the respective chambers. Members of the legislative branch of the United States government, charged with representing the interests and opinions of the people, control their contact with the people. Legislators need acknowledge or respond to the clamor of constituents only as much as they wish to do so. The advantages of incumbents who seek reelection are formidable, and recent studies of Congress suggest that its members have focused their lives upon the internal norms of the institution, rather than the external realities affecting the next election. Most of their actions can be explained as striving for power and prestige within Congress. Contact with, and even much interest in, constituents can be a secondary concern. The Madisonian mandate to let ambitions grow, subject only to external check, has become normal behavior among congressmen and women. Surrounded by expert staff members, the people's representatives are equipped to remain as aloof as they wish from contact with the public.

James Madison approved a degree of aloofness on the part of congressmen; and, in his scheme of things, a president (like George Washington) would be the most aloof of all. For Madison argued that the Constitution was designed to find men of virtue genuinely dedicated to the general good who would not merely articulate the partial or particular interest. As Garry Wills makes plain, Madison's conception of the virtue of the extended republic was precisely that it would reduce the claim of narrow, localized interests upon the representative.

Members of Congress do not learn aloofness directly from Madison, as a means of concentrating on the public welfare. Instead, in a perverse reading of Madison's prescription for balanced branches to limit ambition, they see a mandate to let ambitions grow. Any neglect of constituents comes from the pursuit of prestige and authority within the private world of Congress itself. They want to make a personal impact upon the actions of their house. The respect of their colleagues, with the resulting increased perquisites ranging from a parking place to an office with a view, depends upon establishing a reputation for effectiveness. The impact of the "reforms" of Congress in the past few decades has been to share power resources—staff personnel, funds for operation of the office, and other perquisites—more equally among all members. The more equal distribution of power resources means that Congress is increasingly difficult to lead from within. Congress has established an elaborate staff system intended to make Congress independent of the traditional information monopoly of the executive branch; individual members who control committee and subcommittee staffs have a power resource of great potential value, since the individual demonstrates effectiveness on the basis of expertise, and expertise is based upon information.

The demand of the reform-oriented "Watergate class" (elected in 1974) for positions from which they could make an immediate public impact led to a proliferation of subcommittees that are relatively independent of direction by the chairmen of their parent committees. Thus "government by committee," marked by every critic of Congress since Woodrow Wilson, has been replaced by subcommittee government. The resulting fragmentation of influence within Congress adds yet another balance to those designed by the founders. With all members seeking power, and with a more equal distribution of power resources, no single member can work his will upon the institution in the manner of Sam Rayburn as Speaker or of Lyndon Johnson as Senate majority leader. Power fragmentation also makes Congress a restless institution, as its members seek issues to claim as their own, the base for establishing a reputation for legislative effectiveness. One searches in vain among the subcommittees of Congress for any coherent vision of the public good, and the realization grows that the myriad power centers of Congress deal with each other not as much through compromise as through logrolling —"I'll back your pet project if you'll support mine."

Bureaucratic Ambition

It is not only members of Congress who have taken Madison's morality to heart. What are the consequences for the national health when Madisonian guidelines are followed by functionaries of the executive branch who are officially in a line of command extending through a cabinet officer to the president, but who wield independent authority? Raising this question underscores a reality. Neither the Constitution, nor its explication by Publius, contemplated a government as extensive as ours has become in the twentieth century. The number of federal employees, including the military, now exceeds the total United States population of 1787. The only foreshadowing of this growth in the Constitution is the phrase in Article II providing that the president "may require the Opinion in writing, of the principal Officer in each of the executive Departments, upon any subject relating to the Duties of their respective offices." In *Federalist* 74, Alexander Hamilton hastily dismissed the clause: "This I consider as a mere redundancy in the plan, as the right for which it provides would result of itself from the office."

The federal government is presently involved in complex ways in the lives of American citizens and the operation of the economy. These involvements are far greater than Madison or Hamilton could have imagined in their wildest dreams—or nightmares. Most federal employees are classified civil servants, beyond the direct political control of the administration. Of necessity in the administrative state, executive agencies exercise legislative and judicial powers when they formulate and interpret administrative rules. Combining the three powers of government in a single office, the executive agency is outside the scheme of separation and balance, as conceived by Montesquieu and Madison. There is no opposing branch to balance the bureaucracy.

The ambitions of federal agencies may be checked by constituency reactions, and their budgets may be trimmed by the Office of Management and Budget, which is part of the Executive Office of the President. Bureaucratic decisions may be reviewed by the courts, in limited circumstances. But the problem posed by the representation of narrow interests through unelected bureaucrats is essentially a legislative problem, either for Congress or for the relevant state legislature. The legislature creates executive agencies and is responsible for the oversight of their operations. Such surveillance of the bureaucracy to assure that its operations are in accord with legislative intent may be sporadic and disorganized, but the effort is an inevitable response to the development of the administrative state. It is a function not explicit in the Constitution that attempts to compensate for the lack of constitutional checks upon bureaucratic excesses. The traditional Congressional method for performing legislative oversight is the committee investigation; it has been used for both good and evil.

A device used increasingly to ensure that oversight is performed regularly is the inclusion of a "sunset provision" in enabling statues which provides that the agency will expire on a certain date, unless its authority is renewed by law. It is, in effect, a "tenure-of-statutes provision." Sunset provisions have been attached to several specific laws by Congress, and half a dozen state legislatures have enacted generally applicable sunset provisions. The idea is not that administrative agencies will be collectively axed; rather it is that, in the months prior to an agency's anticipated renewal, its purpose and procedures will be open to public, and to legislative, scrutiny.

A second legislative weapon for the oversight of administration is the legislative veto of administrative rules. This provision, championed by Georgia Congressman Elliott Levitas, was added to forty-eight pieces of legislation signed by President Carter. Its requirements are simple. Administrative regulations promulgated by the executive agency are delayed in taking effect. During this waiting period, the rules can be reviewed on the basis of legislative intent and negated or amended by either house of Congress, acting upon the recommendation of the relevant committee. During Carter's presidency, legislative veto provisions were opposed by liberals who felt that the more advanced egalitarian practices of federal agencies, such as affirmative action requirements in employment, would never win the approval of Congress. But there is no substitute for the widespread public support of governmental policies; the majority sooner or later reasserts its sovereignty. Both sunset provisions and the legislative veto give to Congress as a body the power to review bureaucratic operations and make them accountable to the public will as temporarily reflected in Congress.

In 1982 Congress moved toward the adoption of a legislative veto applicable to nearly all agency rules, with the notable exception of those promulgated by the Department of Defense and the Internal Revenue Service. Although he had endorsed the legislative veto during the 1980 campaign, President Reagan opposed the 1982 legislation. Perhaps, like Jimmy Carter, he felt it the duty of presidents to protect the powers of the executive branch. He may have imagined his thrust toward eliminating government regulation being blunted by new liberal majorities after the 1982 elections.

To the senior civil servant in a Washington agency, Madison's morality mandates the expansion of ambition to its outermost limits; restraints are external, not internal. The concept meshes nicely with notions of professionalism and specialization within the civil service: the expert at performing a particular task need not be concerned with the public welfare; that will be taken care of automatically. But the external checks assumed by Madison's morality are, for practical purposes, absent.

The Separation of Powers Applied to Society At Large

Reinforced by classical liberalism's suspicion of government power, the concern for separation and balance has captured the American imagination. In some schemes of government, like the mercantilist arrangements of eighteenth-century England, governmental authority is expected to settle disputes between contesting elements of the society and the economy. The American propensity has been to establish a balance between such elements and assign to government no greater role than that of referee in their contest. The undersecretary of a cabinet department told me,

> I think the very adversarial process of consumer groups on the one hand and business groups on the other hand, contending within our political framework, is a healthy process which will probably lead to better regulations and to better business in the long run.

The concept was applied even more broadly by a Boston industrialist who, among other enterprises, owns a professional athletic team.

> We need to be careful we don't overregulate ourselves, to get into the condition an England is in today. At the same time, we do need the checks and balances not to let monopolies exist or let some of the powerful financial groups in this country, like the big banks and big insurance companies and big energy-related companies, which I feel do wield too much power, and you do need checks and balances on what they're doing.

The error of applying the separation and balance principle to society at large derives from the fact the Madison viewed it as a structural device to prevent one branch of government from tyrannizing over the other two, and thus over the citizenry. Madison expected the problem of private interests that tyrannize the citizenry, with or without the collusion of government, to be dissolved by the large constituencies of an extended republic. Those who apply separation and balance to the society at large overlook the compelling Madisonian consideration of constituency size.

The error is a common one. In 1952 John Kenneth Galbraith wrote that the characteristic New Deal reform legislation sought to strengthen the power of a numerous but disadvantaged group (workers or investors) locked into market relationships with a smaller but more powerful group (employers or stock market manipulators). The result was to referee a contest between private groups, essentially the buyers and the sellers. This marked a recognition that unregulated market forces can produce a socially unacceptable outcome. This pattern was not really clear to the New Deal reformers; many years elapsed before Galbraith labeled the result: an economy of "countervailing power."

The assumption of the efficacy of government intervention to equalize power has been expanded since the New Deal from economic to social, educational, and environmental problems. Countervailing power is often created within the councils of government itself. A U. S. senator's legislative assistant told me that only in America would the federal government fund a Center for Social Welfare Policy and Law to assure adequate articulation of the opposition to its own policy.

Galbraith's concept of countervailing power dovetails neatly with the pluralist prescription for American politics. The pluralist sees government policy as the outcome of a contest between organized groups, Madison's familiar "factions." As each group seeks its private interests, the bargaining and compromise between groups produces something akin to the public interest; the outcome need only be ratified by Congress. Adam Smith's invisible hand is seen to operate in politics, as well as in economics, and Madison's stipulation that the political process should function to produce the cool and deliberate sense of the community can be forgotten. Thus the most extreme form of normative pluralism denigrates the functions of democratic representation and, in essence, substitutes private agreement for public law.

This seems a harsh charge to make against the pluralists, since they ritualistically quote Madison's *Federalist* 10 as a source of their understanding of American politics. In fact, because of Madison's prominent identification with the formulation of the Constitution, several authors have taken an understanding of the Constitution that originated outside Madison's writings, matched it with a passage from Madison, and labeled their understanding with Madison's name.

Madison defined a faction as "a number of citizens, whether amounting to a majority or minority of the whole, who are united and actuated by some common impulse of passion, or of interest, adverse to the rights of other citizens, or to the permanent and aggregate interests of the community." He wrote that the seeds of factionalism are sown in the nature of man; the phenomenon is the regrettable, but inevitable, result of liberty. The regulation of these "interfering interests forms the principle task of modern legislation."

The extreme pluralists invert Madison's emphasis by celebrating factionalism, and they see the role of government as one of accommodating, more than regulating, group activities. The role of citizens as voters who wisely choose their representatives fades into insignificance compared to citizens' roles as actual or potential adherents of one or more voluntary associations. Pluralism retreats from Madison's insistence upon popular sovereignty expressed through periodic elections by claiming that some minimal democratic standard is achieved if the citizen has access to an association that will defend his interests. Theodore Lowi describes the conceptual result of exalting the group role in the political process:

> The most important difference between liberals and conservatives, Republicans and Democrats, is to be found in the interest groups they identify with. Congressmen are guided in their votes, presidents in their programs, and administrators in their discretion by whatever organized interest they have taken for themselves as the most legitimate; and that is the measure of the legitimacy of demands and the only necessary guideline for the framing of the laws.

In this conception, all interest groups are of equal significance and moral stature; there is no standard beyond the interest group contest that designates the public good. When Interior Secretary James Watt describes environmentalists as "just another interest group," he is merely stating the logical conclusion of contemporary pluralist theory.

Theodore Lowi argues further that practitioners who conceptualize the political system in this manner have produced an ersatz public philosophy, which he calls "interest-group liberalism." The resulting outlook is liberal (in the modern American sense) because of its faith in the positive role of an expanded national government; it is interest-group liberalism, because it approves a policy agenda that is open to all organized groups and "makes no independent judgment of their claims." Yet, because of the legacy of classical liberalism, interest-group liberalism is afraid of clear government authority, even when legitimated through popular sovereignty; indeed, it is afraid of sovereignty per se. It substitutes a mélange of overlapping agencies and conflicting policies that are neither amenable to popular control through elections nor subject to the balances of the Madisonian Constitution.

Although this trend originated with the inception of government regulation during the Progressive era (when regulation was often initiated at the request of the industries to be regulated), it was accelerated by the New Deal, and its velocity was redoubled by the Great Society. Its cumulative impact is to make an increasing share of government activity in the service of narrow interests immune to control by the public or its elected representatives. Resentment of the benefits bestowed upon special interests, and the realization that the agencies bestowing them are beyond public control, bring about the loss of public trust in government.

Madison's Wisdom and the Danger of Professionalism

Specialization within complex social organizations is the hallmark of our age. Political specialization follows, as night follows day. Congressmen build reputations by knowing more than their colleagues about complicated sections of the U.S. Code, such as those governing the Internal Revenue Service. Regulatory agencies develop intimate relationships with the industries they are designed to regulate. Special interest groups maintain lobbies in Washington to follow the proceedings of specific Congressional committees and subcommittees and the activities of specific bureaus. The most effective lobbies are those with narrow and specific interests and mailing lists that can stimulate complaints from the greatest number of Congressional districts.

The result of specialization in politics is a growing inability of persons who spend so much of their waking hours in contact with special interests to perceive the public good, or even to believe that such a concept can have meaning. Madison and Hamilton argued that the genius of the well-ordered constitution would be to draw persons in authority away from overriding concern with the narrow, localized interest, the better to recognize the public good. But they realized that personal ambition can eclipse any dedication to the public good. The Constitution enabled other governmental branches to limit such ambition and to call its possessor to an accounting. This means, in Madison's theory, that all elements of the constitutional structure are involved in the quest for the public interest, subject to periodic review by the voters. The Constitution creates an organic institution of conflicting parts; the result of conflict is to create a greater national harmony in the pursuit of the public good. Although the constitutional structure does not function in exactly the manner foretold in the pages of *The Federalist*, the basic design has served the nation remarkably well and should not be tampered with.

In our era, the growth of specialization and professionalism in politics threatens the continuance of a popular sovereignty that is more than a formality. Publius claimed that the American people would be particularly capable of electing able representatives, of assessing their performance of the public trust, and of preserving the delicate balance between national and state authority. Interest-group liberalism replaces such public-spirited activity with citizen concentration upon narrow, personalized interests, served by a bureaucracy that reflects the limited horizons of its clientele.

It is disturbing to report that many of the Guardians retreated from declaring firm opinions on one or more topics by disclaiming expertise in that area. Twenty-seven respondents volunteered such a statement; no question was designed to elicit a response on the matter. Half (thirteen) of these specifically disclaimed knowledge of economics; the remainder were divided between other topics, of which the most frequent had to do with weapons systems and the needs of national defense. It is no requirement of Madisonian theory that the average voter be capable of deciding the same questions, in advance, that the representative is elected to decide. But the Guardians are that stratum of political activists from which representatives are normally selected. They are the attentive activists, Madison's "wise patriots," whose support, if not participation, must be won by any effort to adapt institutions and policies to the challenges of the 1980s.

Knowledge about political affairs is now supplied by the print and electronic media, independently of the party organizations. The emphasis of the media upon the "horse-race" aspects of elections and the political process itself—dramatic confrontations in Congressional hearings, political strategy, slips of the candidate's tongue, and the reactions of crowds—at the expense of examining the substance of candidate positions and incumbent performance make the task of assessing the actual and potential performance of the public trust ever more difficult.

The tendency of persons who may claim expertise in particular areas of political organization or policy to defer to "the experts" in other areas suggests that the tendency toward political fragmentation feeds upon itself, and that broadly based conceptions of the public good can only recede from view. The Guardians are tempted to abdicate the responsibilities of guardianship.

The Relevance of the Public Good

In common with the leading thinkers of his age, James Madison used abstract concepts in full confidence that the words denoted a reality that would be recognized and understood by his audience. A typical example is the concept of "the public good."

> [Madison's] was the world of the American Enlightenment—a world of the classical virtues reborn, of optimism about man's effort to order society rationally, of a new science of man. . . .
> In that world, the concept of public virtue had a hard and clear meaning, a heft and weightiness of the real, no longer apparent to us. We do not even pretend that we choose our politicians for their virtue. That kind of talk would look sappy or insincere in our political discourse.

Madison was not burdened by the contemporary insistence upon the separation of the normative from the empirical, which deforms social science scholarship and makes the Guardians reticent about discussing their religious values. Madison could, in the same phrase, assert that "the public good" was a recognizable substance and claim that its achievement ought to be the chief end of government. In modern discourse, the term joins its synonyms, "public interest" and "common welfare," as terms valued by politicians because their vague meanings are joined with positive connotations. The same terms are condemned by social scientists for lacking rigor. These concepts are used in at least three different ways:

1. As a conscious or unconscious mask for one's personal interest: to identify one's private interest with the public good is the first step toward persuading another of its desirability.

2. As a standard for judging public policy: its ideal goal.
3. As a description of the political process in a pluralistic society: the common denominator remaining after the accommodation and compromise of all private interests involved in an issue. "The public interest as means and procedure replaces the public interest as end and goal."

The first meaning is the most common current usage. The phrase "the public interest" is used by bureaucracies to justify actions (such as refusing to release documents under the Freedom of Information Act) that protect the agency's interest rather than serving the public, and it is used as a generic term by professional lobbyists. The term has become the banner of organizations opposing corporations in the name of consumers, or of the environment, to the extent that the transcendent meaning invoked by Madison has been all but lost.

The third meaning seems quite Madisonian to the modern eye, but Madison clearly intended the term to be understood in the second sense. For Madison, the outcome of the political process was not the lowest common denominator of compromise; rather, its result was to "refine and enlarge the public views." Madison certainly felt that the political process established by the Constitution would be the most likely institutional design for the accomplishment of the public good, but the public good was unquestionably a matter of substance, not procedure. Apart from the purposes (including the "general Welfare" or public good) listed in the Preamble, the Constitution is strictly structural and procedural; its genius is that it imposes no specific policies upon the government it creates. The public good is simply the highest ethical standard by which one may judge the outcome (public policy) of institutions and procedures.

Madison's concept retains its relevance today, although the political science literature is replete with assertions that it does not. Such assertions are made by pluralists who oppose the public interest and the private or particular interest as opposites. Madison argued that the concept of the public good transcends the reality of private interests; and he is joined in this claim by a number of contemporary philosophers.

As it is in the literature, so is it among the political influentials. In 1977 I asked Roger Moore, the Boston attorney, to reflect on the law firm's practice of working *pro bono publico* (literally, for the public good; actually, representing a client without a fee). He replied flatly, "There is no such thing as a public interest." But Moore is no libertarian; I suspect that the phrase made him think more of Ralph Nader than of

James Madison. In 1981 he believed rather passionately that the Reagan economic policies would further the public good.

> The policies the president is trying to replace have failed, no matter what special interests may be supporting them. It is in everybody's interest to control inflation and to increase capital formation.

About one in seven of the persons with whom I raised the question of a substantive public interest responded negatively. An outright rejection of the concept was unusual; most at least recognized its standing in political discourse. About a fifth offered some approximation of the statement that "the public interest is in the eye of the beholder." One respondent, a former political science graduate student, stated explicitly that the public interest resides in procedures, rather than in the substance of policy. The remainder felt that it is possible to define the term in such a manner that it is useful on a daily basis. Not surprisingly, most of those in the approving category were incumbent elected officials or had experienced elective office.

A typical statement of this kind came from Congressman Leon Panetta, a California Democrat.

> I think there is a public interest that we try to serve. Obviously, it may vary from member to member, from district to district, depending on what the particular needs of those constituents are. But we are guided by this general term of the public interest, meaning essentially, "What is the overall interest of the public, both now and in the future?"

When I mentioned the concept of the public interest to Republican Senator Richard Lugar of Indiana, he responded that the public interest is not identical to the policy recommendations of the self-identified "public interest lobbies," such as Common Cause and the Consumer Federation. He continued,

> I would hope that most of my votes were based on what I believed was genuinely in the public interest. I'm aware of what specific persons or corporations or labor unions or veterans' groups are likely to think about it, and often they're going to have very diverse opinions of it. In other words, I am aware of who is likely to write both in praise and anguish, but essentially I think I'm aware of the fact that I was elected on the basis that most people thought I had good judgment and was a person of some honesty and integrity.

The most complete account of the public interest was given to me in his Beacon Hill home by John Winthrop Sears, the Boston Brahmin. Sears wrote his college thesis on the obligation of a representative to his constituency. He concluded that the representative who disagrees with the opinion of his constituents, when all his efforts to educate them to his point of view have failed, must still vote in accord with their opinion on a clearly defined issue, or else make a mockery of representative government. But few issues are that clear, and, in most circumstances, a concept of the public interest is the appropriate guide.

> If a representative is any good, and has the time and resources, simply by going out and experiencing the life of the street or the life of the farm; by having plenty of time on the home front, there is a way of determining that there is one large consensus—we might call it a tapestry of ideas and values —which can be called the public interest. It is more important than the interests of the Mobil Oil Company, or of the Shoeworker's Union, or of the concerned mothers in Pro-Life. However estimable, in many cases, they're all *special* interests. And there's a public interest beyond them, I think, which the representative has to hear; which the Supreme Court Justice has to hear.

The elected officeholders among the Guardians found the concept of the public interest, however vague or warped by constituency pressures, to be valuable as an ethical guide. But this conviction was compartmentalized. The same officials accept Madisonian checks and balances without question. They do not apply concepts of the public good to support a critique of institutional practices.

Madison assigned to politicians (not his word!) the main responsibility for defining and achieving the public good. Madison's argument was that politicians would be most likely to seek the public good when operating within the framework of a well-ordered Constitution. Since I will argue that the concept of the public good is too often overlooked by contemporary political actors, because the conditions Madison prescribed to assure its pursuit are less and less in evidence, the next step is to consider the conditions Madison specified and the contemporary institutions that best fulfill those conditions.

The Benefits of an Inclusive Republic

At the time Publius wrote, the accepted wisdom held that republics must be small in extent, so that all citizens will be adequately acquainted with, and devoted to, those measures required by the public good. Rome had been a republic; but the growth of its empire made authoritarian government necessary. Both history and theory seemed to establish the principle that the energy needed to govern an extended territory came only from autocracy.

The question was a major point of contention between the Constitution's supporters and opponents, second in importance only to the complaint that the Constitution lacked a bill of rights. The Anti-Federalists argued that the attempt to apply republican institutions to such an extensive territory would lead to a national despotism and the eclipse of local liberties. Developing a point made by David Hume, the Scottish Enlightenment philosopher, Madison argued to the contrary.

The argument Madison sets himself to solve is the problem of faction. Since oppressive minorities will be outvoted in a republic, his primary concern is with intemperate or "factious" majorities: the temporary majorities, stirred in the populace by demagogues and organized temporarily in state legislatures, which threatened the stability of society and the security of property. Madison cites the example of Rhode Island: not even the smallest state was small enough to avoid the republican disease of factionalism.

Madison writes that factions result naturally from the liberty of citizens; nobody would snuff out liberty to control them. What, then, is the republican remedy for this republican disease? Given the possibility of establishing a "modern commercial republic," the solution is to supply it with ample boundaries, extending its territory and increasing the variety of enterprises it contains. There will be so many diverse interests, and so many sources of division between them, that a majority will be impeded from forming for improper purposes.

> The influence of factious leaders may kindle a flame within their particular States, but will be unable to spread a general conflagration through the other States: a religious sect, may degenerate into a political faction in a part of the Confederacy; but the variety of sects dispersed over the entire face of it, must secure the national Councils against any danger from that source. A rage for paper money, for an abolition of debts, for an equal division of property, or for any other improper or wicked project, will be less apt to pervade the whole body of the Union, than a particular member of it; in the same proportion as such a malady is more likely to taint a particular county or district, than an entire state.

Thus Madison confirms that political liberty is not expected to yield economic equality, while arguing that minority rights are more certain of protection in an extensive republic, which supplies a kind of filter that excludes majorities in pursuit of improper objects but encourages the formation of majorities dedicated to the public interest. Madison is urging a consideration of the natural benefits of large constituencies.

Size influences the purposes and modes of operation of both public and private organizations. If the organization is small, and the constituency it serves is correspondingly small, it is more certain to have a narrow point of view, to exert its influence through private rather than public means, and to perceive the public welfare through the lens of self-interest. The implications of Madison's recommendation of the extended republic have been examined by Grant McConnell and applied to contemporary American politics.

In a small community there will probably be fewer different interests— economic, religious, ethnic, or other—than in a large community. Thus it may happen that a single economic interest, such as a particular farm product or a particular industry, is overwhelmingly the largest in the community. In a state, the relative importance of the particular crop or industry will be diluted by the existence of other interests; in the nation, the relative importance of the one interest will be even less. Thus, for example, the importance of dairy farmers will be greater in a rural county than in the state of New York at large, and the power of an oil company will be greater in Baton Rouge than in Washington, D.C. If decisions relating to dairy farming be put in the hands of the counties and those relating to the oil industry in the hands of the states, the power of both interests will be much greater than if such decisions were put in the hands of the nation as a whole.

... The chance of effective opposition to the dominant interest developing is much less in a small than in a large community, and the majority will be much more cohesive. But the general principle will also tend to operate where the means of power are not exclusively democratic and here it may, indeed, be more effective. The efficiency of money or even violence (if these are the established means of power) will be greater where there are numerous small constituencies than where there is a single large one, for, generally speaking, the difficulties of using such methods are greater in a large than in a small community.

The dominant interests in small communities, McConnell continues, readily overpower the smaller number of persons devoted to "justice and the general good." In a system of many small, autonomous communities, while the dominant interests in each are different, all succeed in suppressing the champions of the general interest. Such persons, to have an impact, must be able to find collaborators—compatriots who have the energy and resources to devote to a cause providing benefits for all—

from the larger numbers of a big constituency. One conclusion McConnell draws is that the modern, popularly elected United States Senate "can be expected more often than the House of Representatives to serve general interests."

In his formulation of the argument, Madison enlisted the vastness of the land itself as a virtue of the new republic. The argument for an extended republic is based primarily upon simple geography and secondarily upon the federal division of powers between national and state governments. The argument must be revised in recognition of contemporary technological advances. In 1980 Congressman Elliott Levitas of Georgia told me that he delivers a speech based on Madison's thought that attacks the continued growth of single-issue politics.

> At some point, single-issue politics have to be submerged, or we'll get torn asunder. I take as my text *Federalist* 10. . . . [The reality of] factions is the tip of the spear, that portion of a society that moves it from here to there by prodding, pushing, and advocating. And you've got to have them. The problem comes when factions take over to the exclusion of some realization of the need for a common good. And Madison, as I view it, felt that a federal system was one which would properly contain factions. What Madison didn't know about was the automobile, the telegram, the telephone, the radio, and television. Because you don't contain factions at the state line any more; a faction is immediately national in scope. So federalism, in and of itself, is no constraint on factions in the modern world.

Therefore, the constituencies in a well-ordered republic need not be geographically extensive (think of the variety and population density of New York City) so much as they must be inclusive—containing a variety of interests. From the contention of these various interests, there is hope that a sense of purpose beyond self-interest may develop within the constituency. The public interest suffers or disappears when constituencies are established that are narrow in either the functional or geographic sense.

The Constitution established Congress as the institution providing representation on a geographical basis; agencies of the executive branch have developed which provide representation on the basis of function. Their operations are monitored by Congressional committees made up of the representatives of districts in which that function predominates; the classic example is agriculture.

Typically, Congress establishes an agency in the executive branch to serve regulatory or redistributive purposes related to some vision of the public good. Following the internal logic of bureaucracy, rather than the noble, but vague, purposes stated in the preamble of the act that established it, the agency carves out a jurisdiction and enlists a clientele. The size of the clientele is of less importance than its intensity: if the agency provides services seen as essential to interests with an audible voice in several Congressional districts, the agency's future is secure, and its contribution to the public good becomes irrelevant. As the constituency served becomes more narrow and specialized, the more certain are the agency's services to seem essential. Republican Senator Malcolm Wallop of Wyoming offered some examples.

> I think that I have discovered why big business, I mean really Big Business, gets advantages from sending its money to liberals and Democrats. It's because they are using the regulatory powers of the United states government to eliminate the competition from small business. And Republicans are always running out and falling on their swords and looking like champions of big business. The more I watch it, the more convinced I become, for several reasons. One is, major regulatory schemes of the government really are not that complicated. Big business has all kinds of assets, lawyers and so forth, to handle them, but they are extremely difficult for small businessmen. Then, you get to the nature of bureaucracy, which wants to see results, and results are statistical. The number of cases prosecuted are more important than the effects of the cases prosecuted. . . . You get [the Department of Health, Education, and Welfare] dealing with schools, for example. They would rather desegregate forty schools with forty minor problems that they would one major school district where it might affect three or four thousand kids.

This argument is not intended to assert that democratic institutions encompassing vast geographic areas and numerous interests are universally superior to smaller ones. The tradition of small, homogeneous assemblies (a Quaker meeting, or a New England township's annual gathering) that make decisions by consensus remains viable for particular purposes. And the ideal size of the political institution and the constituency will vary, depending on the scope of the issues to be resolved and the import of local variations. The code establishing the depth water pipes should be buried, to prevent their freezing in winter, is a matter for local determination. Economic relationships require a wider foundation; the Constitution established a national monetary system, since the thirteen different currency systems placed a burden on commerce. Modern issues reach beyond national boundaries. The prevention of nuclear warfare cannot be entrusted to nation-states acting unilaterally; the constituency is, and the political institution ought to be, global.

Despite these distinctions, Madison is correct: if there is likelihood of internal disagreement in a political system, the larger the territory, and the more diverse the interests included therein, the less likely that a single interest will dominate or tyrannize. From this it follows that the institutions most likely to pursue the public interest are those which are truly national in scope.

Unfortunately, Americans (including many Guardians) value smallness for its own sake. This conviction seems to include the last gasp of Jeffersonian agrarianism, a yearning for some lost era when human organizations were of smaller scale, and the unquestioned acceptance of the myth of the wholesomeness of small-town America. The conflict between the Madisonian truth and the attachment to smallness exacerbates the clash within metropolitan areas between the suburbs and the central cities.

The Limits of the Judicial Process

Many legislators consciously form a conception of the public interest as an ethical standard to judge issues at hand. But a congressman's vision of the public good is necessarily influenced by the nature and pressures of his constituency. John Sears points out that there is "a public interest beyond, which the representative has to hear; which the Supreme Court justice has to hear."

The Supreme Court articulates its understanding of the public good and attempts to teach its relevance in changing circumstances. But the Court is severely constrained in its ability to establish national policies. It is dependent upon others to enforce its decisions; their willingness to do so depends on public acceptance of the Court's role as keeper of the Constitution's meaning. When a Court decision is in severe conflict with public attitudes, its edict will be ignored. The *Dred Scott* decision was only the most dramatic example of this fact.

Apart from such obvious aspects of the nature of the Court, there are less obvious aspects of its procedures that hamper its effectiveness as a maker of policy. The Court only decides issues in which the parties have standing—conflicts in which the Court's decision will make a difference to the persons involved. Justice is expected to result from the contest between adversaries. In essence, the Court must decide in favor of either the plaintiff or the defendant. Although each side may represent significant social forces or organizations, the Court is not able to formulate the compromises, or construct the syntheses of opposing principles, which are the hallmark of enduring public policy. The need to take sides between litigants who often represent the extreme sides of a particular dispute can result in bizarre public policy. And the dispute may be defined in terms which prevent the Court from officially recognizing the social complexities that are involved. This is often the result when the dispute is couched ind in terms of individual rights for the specific purpose of allowing the disputant to make a claim for constitutional protection. Federal Judge Woodrow Seals of Houston spoke of the result.

> The adversary system does not allow as much as it could for compromise, and to decide issues in shades of gray. Most of our issues today are not right versus wrong, or white versus black, but in shades of gray. Now, the courts can draw lines in shades of gray. But the real problem we have is when right is pitted against right. For instance, there is a right to a free trial; but there is also a right to a free press. . . . The Constitution gives the states the right to provide for public education; it also gives the right to the federal government to promulgate laws to protect the rights of children. . . . So many of our great social issues of the day could be resolved better in an atmosphere not of confrontation, lawyer pitted against lawyer, but in an atmosphere of community, and common good and welfare, and compromise and give and take.

James Madison believed that an atmosphere devoted to compromise and the public good would be established by the Constitution. But the constitutional political process has shown itself unresponsive to the claims of racial minorities. One harvest of that unresponsiveness was the confrontation politics of the 1960s. Having discovered the limits of that political style, activists turned to the courts. But judges are not able to resolve social problems in a manner that will be permanent and acceptable to national constituencies, because of the nature of the judicial process. Meanwhile, the training of yet more lawyers and the elaboration of yet more legal claims to individual rights feeds the tendency of an already litigious society to carry a broader range of problems to the courts. Lawyers become increasingly necessary to the conduct of daily affairs.

Professor David Riesman, a student of the sociology of the legal profession, explained the impact of this trend over lunch at a Chinese restaurant in Cambridge.

So many of the questions which should be handled by people who know demography, or who understand cost-benefit tradeoffs, are cast into legal form, in which you get either-or answers, disproportionate remedies, and the over-application of local cases nation-wide. So that our governing class has seemed to be predominantly the lawyers and the courts, trained in the top law schools to filter the significant holding out of an already filtered appellate court opinion, but who emerge as highly intelligent graduates who often arrogantly believe that there is nothing so complicated that they cannot master it . . . in a few weeks of cramming.

Thus the habitual substitution of legal contests for the more usual democratic procedures not only fails to establish firm national policies, it thrusts upon judges responsibilities that they are ill prepared to bear; and the judges in turn create remedies that may have a social impact that was sought by none of the originally contesting parties. The judicial movement for school integration through busing provides one example of such an outcome. If judicial authority is to retain its legitimacy, the results of judicial decision-making must win the support of substantial segments of the political activists, the opinion-makers of the order. In 1977 I found that 40 per cent of the Guardians agreed with the statement, "The courts have gone too far in ordering busing to achieve racial balance in the schools."

The leading example of judicial policy that divides the Guardians, rather than uniting them, is the evolving judicial definition of affirmative action. On this issue, the nature of the judicial process prevents the Court from achieving the synthesis of values that might establish lasting new policy. It should be no surprise that the justices were, and are, as seriously divided among themselves on the question of affirmative action as were the Guardians.

We have now considered Congress and the Courts. Of the three great branches of government, only the presidency remains as the one capable of forming and serving a truly national constituency.

National Institutions: The Presidency and the Parties

James Madison left the seat of national government in New York to return to Virginia before the numbers of *The Federalist* dealing with the executive and judicial branches were written. That task fell to the energetic Hamilton. Opponents of the Constitution attacked the presidency as an incipient monarchy; the first of eleven papers on the executive branch pokes fun at such critics, reminding them that the formal powers of the president will be "in few instances greater, in some instances less, than those of a governor of New York." The remaining papers are devoted to demonstrating that the single executive will display the needed energy, yet combine that energy with conformity to the republican principle. Whatever Hamilton thought about the potential authority of the presidential office (and his later behavior suggests that he thought that potential was very great), his description of the office in *The Federalist* seems, in light of what the office has become, rather circumspect.

As Hamilton was circumspect in describing presidential powers, George Washington was circumspect in exercising them. Andrew Jackson first argued explicitly that he represented all the people in a manner superior to that of Congress: the representative of the whole people is greater (better able to perceive the public good) than the sum of the representatives of the parts of the people. Presidents appealing for support in times of national emergency have repeated Jackson's claim. In times of clear crisis, Congress has yielded to that claim. The claim was renewed by Ronald Reagan.

The president and his hand-picked running mate are the only officials elected by the nation at large. The presidency is the institution most certain to guide the formulation of, and be responsible to, a national constituency, majority, or consensus; and these, if we can believe Madison, will not be formulated on any principle other than "justice and the common good." However, in a diverse nation of 230 million citizens, is a national consensus possible? The debate over isolationism was ended by the Japanese attack upon Pearl Harbor, but any nation can be unified by a clear external threat. Absent such a threat, is the notion of a national constituency only a myth?

If "myth" is defined as that method, widespread in a particular culture, of imposing an intelligible pattern upon the random occurrences of everyday life, the American presidency became, in the twentieth century, the very center of a mythical understanding by the people of the forces that governed them. Franklin D. Roosevelt, with his golden-toned radio chats, firmly established the myth on the foundations laid by his cousin Theodore Roosevelt and by Woodrow Wilson. His obsession with Vietnam caused the myth to be seriously eroded by Lyndon Johnson. In the administration of Richard Nixon, history and personal psychology intersected to destroy it, at least for a time.

The ability of the president to claim status as representative of all the people is not based directly upon the Constitution. The method of selecting the president was one of the final decisions made by the Convention. It was a compromise between democratic and aristocratic elements: the people in each state would select a number of electors equal to the state's representation in Congress, for the special purpose of designating a president. The electoral college worked very well in designating George Washington. By the time John Adams stood for reelection against Thomas Jefferson, the electors were informally bound to their parties' choice, and the main functions of the electoral college were being performed by the party organizations. The leading strategist for the Federalist party was Alexander Hamilton, while James Madison was the Congressional leader of the Jeffersonian Republicans.

Thus the collaborators in writing *The Federalist* were, a decade later, involved on opposite sides in the invention of the modern political party, the single original American addition to the list of fundamental democratic institutions. The party leaders of the era hardly realized that they were inventing an essential institution. Americans had long practiced the arts of political combination (caucuses, committees of correspondence, and the like), but their conception of party, based on the British example of the time, was of politicians seeking places of preferment, apparently associated for no other purpose. Anti-party sentiment was pervasive. In 1794, John Taylor of Caroline, a leading exponent of Jeffersonianism, declared

> The situation of the public good, in the hands of two parties nearly poised as to numbers, must be extremely perilous. Truth is a thing, not of divisibility into conflicting parts, but of unity.

Taylor here displays his attachment to the medieval ideal of unity. Madison, on the other hand, saw the division into parties as inevitable in a free society, and he knew that reasoned opinions will differ. He wrote in *Federalist* 50 that "an extinction of parties necessarily implies either a universal alarm for the public safety, or an absolute extinction of liberty." But Madison did not differentiate very carefully between parties and other types of faction.

The election of the president by the whole nation, even with the electoral college intervening, made the nation a vast single-member district. The logic of the republican principle required some way of placing candidates and issues before that vast constituency for decision; this became the role of the political party. The president then joined with his fellow partisans in Congress to overcome the potential for frustration inherent in the separation of powers. Voters judged the performance of parties, as well as that of individual officeholders.

But the leaders of the Federalists and Jeffersonian Republican parties established highly tentative organizations, which many regarded as only temporary expedients. The ideal of unity had not lost its charm. The election of 1800 had many of the aspects of an election with a modern party system: national partisan organization, opposing stands on recognized issues, and party discipline that made the electoral college a formality. And, after a peaceful transition of power, the Republican party became an instrument of government, as Jefferson guided measures through Congress with the exertion of his quiet charm as party leader. But both Jefferson and his successor, James Madison, tempered their policies to attract elements of the disintegrating Federalists into the Republican ranks; the Federalists disappeared from the national scene, except for a few New England strongholds. The Republican party became a coalition of hostile factions, for there was no creditable opposition to demonstrate the utility of party coherence or presidential leadership.

Madison was soon faced with a vigorous group of young Western Congressmen, the War Hawks, who led him reluctantly to recommend war against England, although the nation was ill prepared for warfare, and the conflict was not supported by every region of the nation. In 1814 the British invaded and burned the capital, driving President Madison away from his own dinner table.

This "Era of Good Feelings," when the Jeffersonian Republicans governed with little opposition, was in fact a time of bitter factionalism and presidential impotence. Party institutions were so strikingly revitalized by President Andrew Jackson as to constitute the development of a new party system. Jackson's 1832 example instituted the practice of making presidential nominations by national party conventions. State party organizations gained power over the national party, but presidents were no longer constrained by political debts owed to the Congressial caucus for their nominations. Responsive to the broadest national constituency, they could speak independently of fellow partisans in Congress. Jackson used his newly centralized political authority to support the decentralization of administration. He supported the state banks against the Bank of the United States; and he left the financing of internal improvements to the states, rather than the federal government.

There is a moral in the contrast between Andrew Jackson and his predecessors, Madison, Monroe, and John Quincy Adams. It is that the fate of presidents is intimately connected with the fortunes of the parties they lead. The prestige, authority, and ability to change history of parties and presidents rise and fall together. The party is the unique institution, and the president is the unique individual, able to form, speak for, and serve a constituency that is national in scope.

An Abdication of Guardianship

The anti-party sentiment of the founding era has persisted for two centuries. It is reflected in the contemporary ambivalence toward parties and politicians. This distrust was expressed voluntarily by more than a dozen of the Guardians. It was stated succinctly by Gordon Thomas, the Chicago commodities analyst. "Generally, I'm not attracted to politicians," he said. "I feel that they're a necessary evil."

Disdain for the traditional conception of party responsibility was expressed in Houston by a bank economist who had once served as a staff assistant to a United States senator.

Hopefully, once a man was elected president, he would forget about party affiliation, and would go to Washington and pull people out of the Congress, out of business, out of universities, who were best qualified to run the departments they're put in charge of. . . . I don't see why it has to come up through a party.

The ambivalence toward parties and politics is an established reality, and candidates are likely to capitalize upon it. The undersecretary of a cabinet department told me, "Someone like Jimmy Carter spent a lot of time running against traditional politics; but that's been going on since time immemorial. Every successful politician is an anti-politician." Unfortunately, when the candidate, once elected, reveals himself as "just another politician," the voters' political cynicism is reinforced.

American national parties have always been loose and decentralized organizations, directed from the center by diplomacy, not command. Their awesome task has been to provide sporadic unity for the diverse elements of a sprawling continent. The sense of membership in a common enterprise—a realization that officials bearing the same party label will be judged, at least partially, by the total performance of the party —has permitted the assertion of leadership by presidents, with some hope of obtaining cooperation from Congress, and has made state officials think twice before embarking upon a course that totally contradicts the direction of the national party.

American parties no longer function in this textbook manner. That the party system is disintegrating has become part of the accepted wisdom of political science. Within the electorate, party divisions on the basis of income, occupation, religion, and region which were established by the politics of the New Deal era have been shattered, but firm new allegiances have not been formed. The concept of party has become less significant to voters, with an increase in declared independence and split-ticket voting.

On the institutional level, the traditional functions of the party have been increasingly usurped by other organizations. With the specialization of modern life, rival organizations challenged the parties' monopoly of political mobilization. The naming of candidates through primaries began with the Progressive era. Campaigning had been much influenced by public-relations professionals before television accelerated the process. Candidates' volunteer organizations (such as Citizens for Eisenhower) are more dependable sources of campaign labor, since the rise of civil service has robbed the parties of the patronage that was once the certain reward for faithful party service. Reforms in party rules intended to make the national conventions more representative resulted in many additional states establishing presidential primary elections as the best way to assure compliance with the rules. Usually, the main prize of the convention, the presidential nomination, has been awarded before the convention opens to the winner of the primaries. Media reports of the early primaries as the equivalents of sports events have developed an image of the victor which speeds him on to further victories. The seasoned judgment of party leaders has no role in the process.

The compelling reason to decry the influence of the media upon the nominating process is a simple one. A newspaper or television network, no matter how great its secondary concern for the public good, is primarily interested in increasing its audience and thus its profits. And the medium is not responsible for the decisions it influences; an intervention in some political crisis that creates disaster for the political actors involved, or even for the nation, may only increase the audience of the intervening news team.

The media replace the party organizations as intermediaries between the people and candidates or incumbent officials. The parties' symbolic importance as cues for the voting decision soon vanishes. Candidates no longer find campaign leaders in the ranks of the party regulars. The cumulative impact of these changes results in the divorce of the presidency from the party organization. The elections of Jimmy Carter and Ronald Reagan together demonstrated the ultimate centralization of the presidential election process. Carter, as an outsider, won the media contest and captured the Democratic convention majority in 1976. He then installed his campaign team —which had no experience in dealing with independent U.S. congressmen—in the White House, with disastrous results. Ronald Reagan, as a master of the electronic medium, won the glamor contest in 1980, and installed conservative Republicans—both pragmatic practitioners and pure ideologues—in the White House. It is possible for a celebrity to capture the presidential nomination on the basis of winning different primary elections, without the traditional effort at building a coalition of support among the regionally based interests of the established party. Thus the partisan process of deliberation is bypassed. But the parties have been the single institution capable of planning for the future, of seeing beyond the horizon of this year's election. Carter and Reagan proved that candidates can bypass whatever collective wisdom the established parties may be able to offer. Through such candidacies, narrow interests gain the ascendancy, damaging the responsiveness to the general public of both the parties and the presidency.

There is no substitute in view for the political party that would be capable of fulfilling its historic functions. But who is available for the lengthy, difficult, and unpaid partisan labors that are needed to begin a restoration of the party system? By and large, the Guardians are not likely recruits, and many of them do not even perceive the need to undertake the task. George Allison, the Washington lobbyist, for example, welcomed the media influence.

> I would rather have more television exposure of candidates than backroom decisions made by politicians. I have very little faith in smoke-filled, backroom decisions by political bosses as to what's good for me. I think I will take the chance of—what's his face—Walter Crankcase, exposing candidates to me, and hoping Walter will do it openly and fairly. I think I will, and I think the public believes that too. They think Walter Cronkite has got a higher level of integrity than most politicians.

A number of the Guardians lamented the decline of the parties, and they usually linked that decline to the growing power of the media. Mrs. Andrea Garguillo, head of the Boston Finance Committee (a state-appointed watchdog agency that reviews the city administration) stated at the beginning of our 1977 conversation that the failure of the party system is the most important national problem.

[The two-party system] is not fulfilling its role as it should, providing a viable critic of the party in power, because the Republican party is in such bad need of revitalization it isn't taken too seriously. In this city, we don't have any Republican party at all. We have non-partisan elections. And this is a problem, because you tend to get into the cult of personality and away from issues. . . . The press definitely tends to stress the personalities of individual candidates and to get away from issues.

Julian Bond, the Georgia state senator, also decried the focus on personalities resulting from the decline of parties. He cited the coalition of convenience made between the civil rights movement and the Democratic party, and pointed out that the movement insisted upon retaining its independence of the party. This led him to think of the interests then supporting Ronald Reagan as a presidential candidate. Reagan, he said, "is not really in the Republican party; he's in his own political party; they're Republicans by convenience." As for the future,

There's the hope that rather than having parties as we now think of them, in the future we are going to have rather broadly based interest groups, which can become parties at the proper time. . . . These groups are going to have to learn how to trade interests much more effectively than they do now—trade support, and and engage in coalitions. It's a slim hope. But that's the only hope, I think, for any kind of replacement of [the crucial functions performed by] parties.

A thoughtful analysis of the problem was given me by the Washington editorial writer I have called Daniel Randolph.

I see the parties as vehicles of order and organization in the political process. I see them as vehicles of accountability and responsibility in the political process. I see them as vehicles of leadership selection and, unfortunately, I think that function is increasingly being taken over by plebiscitary processes in political primaries and also, to a degree, by the influence of the press and particularly of television, in its capacity to expose or not to expose on a national basis. And I tend to think that old process, in which the parties tended to throw up the leadership, was a much sounder and more reliable process for the selection of political leadership than the current kind of mixed system.

Randolph's theme was echoed by Melvin Laird, the former secretary of defense.

With communication—television and everything else, including the radio —we're getting more and more into a position where parties don't mean too much. They're kind of abused. Whoever wins through the primary system gets the nomination. . . . I don't think the parties really have the responsible role they should have.

On the opposite side of the continent, the same theme was echoed by Abe Mellinkoff, a San Francisco newspaper editor-turned-columnist.

Loyalties to all institutions have decreased, and along with that is allegiance to the political party. This flows from the ability of, or the fact that, so much political life is done through the media. Television. And that kind of saps the power of the political party.

Comments of this kind came from several of the persons I conversed with, but they were a minority. While all were agreed that the parties are declining, a few were delighted, and several were distressed, but most had not thought much about the problem and were not about to dedicate themselves to its solution.

The significant exception was Rick Stearns of Boston, who has been involved in Democratic politics and rule revisions of the Democratic national convention since 1972. In 1981 Stearns was a member of the Technical Advisory Committee to the commission headed by North Carolina Governor James B. Hunt, which would consider yet again the process for selecting delegates to the national convention.

The Hunt Commission will meet in August to look at the party rules again. It will probably take a step backwards—not all the way back to 1968, but some way to make a better balance between the power of the states and the interests of the national organization. For example, they will allow some delegates to be chosen without regard to their presidential preference, however that preference is determined in the state. The provisions which bind a state delegation to vote throughout for the candidate winning their primary will probably be abolished—that rule was only adopted for the convenience of an incumbent president.

But the primary elections are now so imbedded in our practice that the party would really be loath to name somebody else, when one candidate wins a clear victory in the primaries.

Thus the one Guardian I interviewed who is most closely associated with the changes in party rules which have so weakened the authority of the permanent party organization neither sought nor supported a return to the former system, when primary results were advisory, but national conventions controlled the nomination. When in 1982 the

Hunt Commission recommendations were adopted by the Democratic National Committee, their substance was much as Stearns had predicted. Happily, the primary election season was shortened by five weeks, and a block of uncommitted delegate slots was created, to be filled by elected and party officials. As the only delegates unpledged to any candidate, these professionals could "exercise unique influence in a close contest for the nomination." The established party leaders would thus have a real voice only if there were no clear winner as a result of the primaries.

The parties may be beyond repair. In 1980 the presidential campaign landscape was scattered with narrow interest groups injecting very specific policy demands, often based on religious beliefs not shared by the general population, into the electoral process. These groups used computer-generated mailing lists to make direct appeals to geographically dispersed persons who can be united by conviction. One leader of the New Right claims that he learned his tactic of targeting individuals from the old Left; he points out that direct mail is the method of the anti-establishment candidate, regardless of ideology; and he insists that the New Right must persist in its tactics, since the liberal bias of the established media prevent the Right's message from receiving a fair hearing.

Most of the persons I interviewed revealed an ability to see beyond personal interests while perceiving the importance of a broad range of issues. With few exceptions, the Guardians are marked by their generosity of spirit, the ability to comprehend the validity in diverse points of view. This ability is as close as we can expect a contemporary political activist to approach the public virtue championed by Madison and Hamilton: the ability to perceive, and the will to pursue, the public good. To the extent that the Guardians neither labor to reconstruct the parties, nor work to combat the influence of single-issue interest groups, according to Madison's standards they are abdicating the duties of Guardianship.

The Restoration of Madisonian Purpose

A fragment of James Madison's wisdom, enshrined in *The Federalist Papers*, has become part of the value structure of American political activists, just as it has influenced American thought about all of society. This is the belief that ambition is natural to man, and that ambition which threatens social equanimity should be controlled by separating the individuals and organizations wielding power, yet arranging the relationships between them so that the ambition and authority of one will check and balance the authority and ambition of the other. A system of separation and balance is accepted as good for its own sake, without attention being paid to other aspects of Madison's thought. Yet Madison argued that the great goal of any governmental structure must be to define and implement the public good. The system of separated powers would prevent a single branch of government from becoming so powerful as to threaten the liberties of society. But there was an equal danger that one element of society would tyrannize over the other elements. Madison taught that this danger would be avoided in the extensive republic by the creation of constituencies with the most inclusive geographical boundaries and the greatest possible variety of interests. But the American ethos includes a fondness for small organizations and small constituencies.

In modern America, the two institutions capable of forming and representing national constituencies are the presidency and the political parties. When both these institutions are held in low public esteem, public policy is more likely to result from the vigorous representations of narrowly based, often very local, interests. Ronald Reagan won the presidency as a result of the ultimately centralized campaign. His candidacy was supported by narrowly defined but geographically dispersed interests. Ironically, to the extent that Reagan's presidency has restored faith in the office, he has used this restored prestige to preach the decentralization of administration into the states, where narrow interests are more likely to prevail. Like Andrew Jackson, he has combined the centralization of politics with the decentralization of government, disdaining the challenge of attempting to lead a united people in a response to problems that are national in scope.

The concept of the public good retains its validity as the highest ethical standard that can be applied to judge both institutions and policy. Public officials who accept Madison's institutional morality as a mandate to expand their ambitions, with only an external check to be concerned with, ignore Madison's definition of the purpose of government, even if the phrase "the public interest" springs readily to their lips. I found that elected officials are particularly aware of the public good as the label for an ethical standard needed to judge particular policies. It is no longer remembered as the end Madison specified for the means provided by constitutional structures. The consideration of that purpose—the public good—must be revived, if the flaws that have grown into the Madisonian structure are to be repaired.

CHAPTER FOUR

Five Cities:
The Battlegrounds of
Value Conflict

*The mobs of great cities add just so much to the support of pure
government, as sores do to the strength of the human body.*

—*Thomas Jefferson, 1784*

*Most great cities are magical from a distance, especially at night.
And most of us know all too well what they are like up close.
That is the attraction, sometimes fatal, of cities: the constant
tension between beauty and degradation, the wars of the market-
places, the daily dog-eat-dog battles that produce a few winners
and too many losers—with too many of those turning bitter, if
not violent. . . . Talk about compassion and jobs and spreading
the wealth of this rich, rich country (and rich city) and you are
the lowest of the low, the bleeding heart kneejerk liberal. We
keep buying more police cars as bandits leap the back fences and
climb into the rear windows. . . . Socialism for the poor and
desperate, with not all that much to lose. Freedom? What's that?*

—*Herb Caen, 1981*

Most Americans prefer to view city problems from a distance. We may
appreciate the vitality of urban commerce and culture; cities are fine to

visit or work in, but middle-class families choose to live in the suburbs. Only the wealthy reside in rich enclaves like Boston's Beacon Hill or Chicago's North Shore. And they do not seek intimate contact with Jefferson's "mobs of great cities."

Large American cities present stark contrasts between wealth and poverty. As the leading values of American democracy, liberty and equality, have taken on economic connotations, they have become associated with class differences. Liberty is the freedom of the affluent to invest, to profit, and to inherit; equality is the hope of the poor for a share in national abundance, whether "earned" or not. When, as at present, a national administration chooses to emphasize economic liberty at the expense of any interest in a more equitable distribution of abundance, the certain arena for tension between classes and races, between the champions of equality and the practitioners of economic liberty, is the city. The contrast between success and failure is permanent in the city. Only occasionally does the tension break into violence.

I visited five cities outside Washington, expecting to compare the attitudes of those who labor at the center of the federal government with the opinions expressed in major constituencies. Since I sought quite different people in each city—those associated with its character and reputation—and the number I talked to in each city was small, I may have confirmed stereotypes with which I began. Rather than discovering stark contrasts with the outlook of the Guardians who work in Washington, I formed an image of each city centered upon different aspects of the value confusion that operates in national politics.

Boston and San Francisco, the two great former seaports, seem engaged in the commercialization of their proud traditions, while their ethnic neighborhoods are buffeted by outside forces, and even the mode of urban representation is challenged. The contest between liberty and equality becomes an element in controversies over the scale of political action and the size of constituencies.

Ironically, Atlanta and Houston seem the new homes of that "Yankee enterprise" which characterized Boston a century ago. In these cities, the growth of commerce is striking, but the new prosperity is unevenly distributed. The established black middle class of Atlanta brings stability to the city; in Houston, the blacks and Chicanos gain strength to claim a larger share of prosperity and power. The disregard for urban planning in Houston, which booms anew with every OPEC oil price increase, seems symbolic of the national failure to plan for the development of alternative energy sources. Yet, in all four of these cities, political power is fragmented, elections are nonpartisan, and institutions are diffuse, so that it is hard to imagine concerted efforts by local Guardians, enlisting the aid of other voters, which could oppose or alter the forces that are determining those cities' destinies.

Chicago is different. The Democratic party organization has provided a degree of centralization for its institutions, as well as expertise in mobilizing citizen support, and one can at least imagine Chicago making a conscious choice between optional futures. But the value conflicts of the other four cities are just as visible, and Chicago has made little progress toward their resolution. It is only after considering Chicago, therefore, that one is able to conclude something about the viability of the American city as the crucible in which will be forged the American future.

Guardian Images of Urban Problems

The political activists I have called the Guardians volunteered a variety of explanations of the problems of their own cities and of cities in general. All they had to say can be found in the literature of urban sociology and political science, and many of them have read portions of that literature, but they made the familiar conclusions come alive with the intensity of their own experience. It is possible to sort the Guardians' attitudes toward urban problems into four general categories, although most of them cited several factors and pointed out that those factors are interrelated. Heading the list is racial division considered in its broadest sense, as influencing the crime rate, the nature of the public schools, white migration to the suburbs, and more. The cities are the arenas for testing the sincerity of our national attempt to create a successful multiracial society.

The second kind of consideration is economic: the flight of productive industry away from the central cities, the inability of tourist-oriented business (hotels, restaurants, curio shops) to provide other than low-level employment; and the fact that sustained unemployment exacerbates racial tensions. The values of liberty and equality are variously invoked in discussing racial and economic problems.

The remaining two categories are institutional, concerned with the ability of established political practices to deal with urban problems. Some of the Guardians focus on the flaws of local political institutions; others decry the incapacity of state or national political processes to respond to urban needs.

Leon Despres, an attorney who served the Hyde Park district containing the University of Chicago for twenty years as an anti-organization alderman, described the centrality of racial conflict.

> The greatest social problem that I see is the polarization of black and white and the failure to bridge that gap. Putting it another way, the persistence of discrimination, segregation, and some forms of oppression against blacks. This is very, very serious in the urban areas, and it applies to some extent to other groups: Hispanic-Americans, Indians. . . . It stands in the way of the solution of all urban problems. It's particularly exacerbated in Chicago, where the city administration has been committed to keeping the lid on blacks. . . . Every single problem that we have in the city here, that I'm personally and intimately familiar with: housing, the quality of schooling, police, crime, unemployment, community conditions—everything that you try to do, you find you're prevented or inhibited or the project is distorted by the black-white polarization. What makes it so serious is that this is common to most of the big cities, and therefore a problem of national importance; it creates detachment and disloyalty if a group is persistently shortchanged.

While Despres blamed former Mayor Daley's organization for the subjugation of the blacks, the Washington editor I have called Daniel Randolph sounded almost fatalistic when discussing racism.

> Dealing with it bluntly, you would have to say that ultimately it is a consequence of the failure to deal vigorously and in a timely fashion with the race problem. Because it has been a massive migration of poorly educated, dependent blacks to the cities that has to a very great degree created the problem. I see so many ramifications of this. . . . These squalid conditions build on themselves. . . . I am convinced that the mere application of vast sums of money and programs, in the fashion of the 1960s, while it may be necessary, is not a sufficient treatment for urban decay.

Guardian sensitivity to urban problems was not limited to the journalists and elected officials who are expected to define such issues. In Houston, an oil company president volunteered urban decay as a central national issue.

> I think the destruction of our cities is a very serious problem: the flight of the upper- and middle-class white, leaving the disadvantaged and those that cannot manage cities to try to manage them. They don't have the interest; they don't work at it like they should; they're not part of the tax base. New York City is a good example, Washington, Detroit—they're surrounded by political entities that could care less about the major core, yet they are parasites on the major core. . . . It will take us sixty years to resolve [these problems].

Significantly, this Houstonian did not include Houston in his list of problem cities. His conception of urban problems was echoed in Atlanta; but Atlantans recognized the involvement of their own city. A Georgia Democratic activist told me,

> [Urban problems are caused by] more demands on the local government, and not enough money to pay them. The people in the inner cities are the people that don't pay taxes—if you want to get basic about it.

In a comfortable residence on West Wesley Drive in Atlanta, I spoke to a former president of the Atlanta League of Women Voters. She felt that financial institutions are implicated in urban decay.

> Urban blight is pretty awful. Because people bring urban blight, people can remove it. I think what happens in most communities, and it happened here, is that when sections start going down, all kinds of financial interests come into play, and everybody lets it run down to a point where its imperative that you rebuild completely. . . . Urban blight is closely associated with poverty. And if we deal with the unemployment, if we deal with the welfare mess, I think at the same time [we should] clean up cities, improve, renovate, and go into programs which help people buy a house that's old and run down but replace parts and renovate, make it new and livable.

In Boston the same phenomenon was cited by the director of the Massachusetts Tax Court, Sean Dunphy; but Dunphy assigned principal responsibility for the outcome to the federal government.

> There's been a lack, at the national level particularly, of an urban policy. For example, we've never had a tax policy that encouraged rehabilitation of our urban centers. It was more advantageous tax-wise to have a traditional rip and tear and destroy urban renewal program, rather than identify the buildings that could be rehabilitated, restored, maintained, and thus not have a disruptive effect.

Discussions of urban problems sometimes verged on the apocalyptic. Louis Martin, publisher of Chicago's black newspaper, the *Defender*, vividly described the potential results of widespread unemployment of minority youth.

> You see, when the lifestyle is built on poverty, it becomes worse and worse and more and more anti-social. . . . The economists are short-sighted when they talk about balancing the budget, when we know that a social explosion can unbalance any budget in America. All we need to do is have ten cities blow up in flames, and I don't care what the budget is—it will be unbalanced. These young people are too vigorous and too frustrated.

But apocalypse can have economic origins. When I asked him to define the cause of the "urban crisis," Mr. Martin's answer was abrupt.

Well, I think unmitigated corporate greed, however you want to describe it. I know that Carter has lashed out at the oil companies, but I think we've got to sober up on what kind of society we want to create. Some people deny any social responsibility of the corporation. But the only way I can see the government can move is through taxing.

In Atlanta I interviewed James Hope, a black graduate of the Harvard Business School, who was a senior member of Mayor Maynard Jackson's staff. Hope saw urban problems as a kind of vicious circle.

Let's say it's kind of a spiraling effect, or a domino effect. It gets to a situation of large numbers of people in an urban area being affected by unemployment—there is a relationship with unemployment and crime. Then that makes it difficult for business to be in the same environment. When you have large numbers of people unemployed, and a high rate of crime, then business decides, "We've got to get out of business in this area." So, moving the business out increases the number of unemployed, which may effect a higher rate of crime. It's like a Catch-22 effect: it just keeps going, and it gets worse.

I conversed with (more accurately, listened to) Barney Frank, then a Massachusetts state legislator, who has since been elected to Congress. He initially designated a single factor as the cause of urban problems.

Money. We have systems in America whereby the city is the place where a lot of money is made, but because of federalism, et cetera, the money isn't allowed to stay there. Cities are subordinate units to states, and most states take much more out of big cities than they put back in, and that's the problem. . . . And you've got a situation where people can live outside the city, take all the economic benefit out of being near the city and then not bear the city's problems.

Almost immediately, Frank added race as the second cause of big-city problems. Frank's initial political position had been as the chief assistant of Boston's mayor, Kevin White, and he had seen the turmoil of the late 1960s at first hand. Several Guardians mentioned racial and economic factors only in passing, since they felt that such problems could be ameliorated, if only governmental institutions were better designed or more powerful, or the leadership more competent. I talked of urban problems with a Californian who had served the Nixon administration as an official of the Department of Health, Education, and Welfare and stayed on in Washington as a lobbyist.

[There has been] a lot of deception on the part of some city governments, where instead of biting the bullet—like New York, when they got the pressure from the unions, the municipal employees' unions, for salary increases, they gave them some, but then said, "OK, you know, we can't give you too much more this year, but we'll kick up your pension plan." Well, every mayor was able to defer it to the next mayor, and [then it] caught up with them.

Many Guardians mentioned public school failures as an aspect of the urban dilemma. Carol Bellows, an attorney active in the leadership of the Illinois Bar Association, saw broad social causes for the schools' shortcomings.

> The urbanization of society leads to a great deal of our social ills—poverty, mental illness, violence; and that is very disturbing. Our education system in the urban areas is in bad shape, possibly because of a breakdown in the family, where we bring people into educational institutions when they are really not sufficiently socialized, because of a lack of family structure, violence in the home. . . . I think we handle our children and our elderly very badly, and that's a reflection of why society isn't working today.

At his home in Newton, I talked with Stanley Masaryk, a junior executive with a Boston-based life insurance company. His interpretation was in line with the standard explanation that has almost become a cliché in political science: the fragmentation of metropolitan areas by the proliferation of municipal entities.

> The problem in Boston is partly that the whole area isn't envisioned as one urban area. We have the city of Boston, the city of Cambridge, the city of Newton—and we have fifty-five little communities. And because of that, there's no solution which can encompass the whole area. [There's a] fragmentation of government authority, and the local governments are used as a defensive set-up. . . . any kind of housing for low- and middle- income people has been fought tooth and nail [by the suburbs].

The image of the city as an enclave of unemployed minorities strangled by affluent suburbs uninterested in the welfare of the inner city was restated in more gentle language by Father Mike Groden, a priest who heads the tiny Urban Planning and Renewal office of the Boston diocese.

> It has to do with the kind of role that the inner city is called upon to play, both in terms of the poor who live in the inner city, and the kinds of cultural and business worlds that are supported by the city system. The pilings [which shakily support the structure] haven't changed. The pilings are still an an-

tiquated financial structure, with tremendous unwillingness of suburban areas or the state in general to anywhere near compensate the city for the kind of services and systems that the inner city holds together. Obviously, too, the question of racial prejudice and the kind of explosive interactions between minorities and whites in the cities have meant a more rapid move-out of people. It's probably an abdication of concern; there may be a growing number of middle- and upper-middle-class people who have forsaken the city.

The institutional context of urban problems was best summarized by Senator Paul Sarbanes, Democrat of Maryland.

You have a mismatch of responsibilities and resources, given the way our local, state and federal systems operate. And that really almost defies a logical resolution. It involves questions of state constitutions and city boundaries and how the property tax works and how the state budget works. . . . There's no direct linkage between the government level that deals with the problem and the government level with the resources. . . . You don't have a total community, in a demographic sense, simply because of the boundary lines which create this separation, [yet] in all our political philosophy there is a premise that at some point or another that we come together and organize ourselves to provide for our mutual security in a domestic society.

I saw that premise—that we eventually come together to assure mutual security—being acted upon somewhat differently in five different cities. And I saw that attempt being frustrated by the conflicts between values and within institutions that have been described in the preceding chapters.

Boston and San Francisco: The Question of Constituency Size

Describing the attractions of their city, two Bostonians told me separately that the only comparable city is San Francisco. No San Franciscans invoked the name of Boston to define the delights of the City by the Golden Gate. While San Francisco's insistence upon uniqueness exemplifies the civic chauvinism that irritates other Californians, the comparison may have come to mind for the Bostonians because it was made in detail a decade ago by a writer in the *Boston Globe*. Ian Menzies wrote that, particularly for young Americans, Boston and San Francisco are "the two most exciting cities." Both have water on three sides, similar skylines, nearly equal land areas (about forty-six square miles), and similar populations—each central city has less than seven hundred thousand in a metropolitan area of more than three million. The boundaries of both cities are fixed; their suburbs grow, while the number housed in the central cities declines. Wrote Menzies,

> People know each other in San Francisco and Boston. They talk to each other, eat with each other, banker and cultural entrepreneur, student and newspaper editor, professor and legislator, architect and community leader. They are walkable cities, centralized, physically compact, friendly.

Their thrusting skylines signal that both cities are the vital cultural and commercial centers of metropolitan areas. Middle class bedroom communities like Newton, Mass., are duplicated in Marin County, north of the Golden Gate. Black Roxbury has its counterpart in San Francisco's Hunter's Point. Sensitively rehabilitated areas like Boston's Quincy Market (across from Faneuil Hall) and San Francisco's Ghiradelli Square (near Fisherman's Wharf) attract tourists and suburbanites alike into the urban trade centers. Sprucing up for the bicentennial celebration, Boston painted yellow lines that guide the pedestrian tourist through narrow streets to visit historic locations. San Francisco clings to the cable car as the symbol of its identity: overloaded vehicles carry all comers across the city's hills at a steady seven miles per hour, a triumph of nineteenth century technology. The daily influx of office workers is facilitated by subways: Boston's venerable transit system and San Francisco's shiny new, trouble-plagued Bay Area Rapid Transit system (BART). The thriving electronics industry lining highway 128 outside Boston is matched by similar firms on the San Francisco peninsula. Both cities contain monuments to their respective maritime histories, while both decline in significance as seaports. Boston is too close to the New York City-New Jersey complex, while San Francisco has lost its tonnage to Oakland, which early installed the facilities for handling container cargoes.

Both cities have academic suburbs reached by bridges—Boston's Cambridge and San Francisco's Berkeley. Both achieved much of the land areas upon which high-rise office buildings are now constructed by filling in their respective bays, bodies of water recognized only in recent years for their aesthetic qualities. In 1970 Ian Menzies saw political similarities.

> [Both cities have] that mix of academe, of history and the arts. While one has a Puritan heritage, the other Spanish, both today are managed by a rambunctious Irish-Italian political culture sitting uneasily over new militant

minorities while a Waspish establishment watches on the sidelines with the ultimate weapon of money.

With Dianne Feinstein installed as mayor, and dynamic members of the Board of Supervisors like Carol Ruth Silver, one should acknowledge that Jews have contributed to the ethnic complexion of San Francisco's political culture from the beginning; Jewish families established many of its commercial enterprises during the Gold Rush (think of Levi Straus), and Mayor Abe Reuf was its flamboyant last party boss at the turn of the century.

There is a difference in the political ambience of the two cities, as well as a difference in their formal municipal institutions. Boston is the capital of Massachusetts, which makes the city more important in its state than is San Francisco. The presence of the state legislature makes a convenient target for the rage of Bostonians who see their city losing its battles in the legislative halls. While some of Boston's essential services (mainly the court system) are provided by Suffolk County, San Francisco is a consolidated city and county government. This accounts for peculiar terminology: its city council is called the Board of Supervisors, and the city jails are administered by a sheriff.

The partisan past of Boston politics lives on in the intensity of the political contest in its neighborhoods. Edgar Litt writes that "the politics of Boston glows with a radiance like that of the tubercular patients who lived in the sanatorium of Thomas Mann's *The Magic Mountain.*" The distant political past of San Francisco is no less striking than that of Boston. Irish immigrants were staffing its political machine before the Brahmins of Boston were well aware of an immigrant challenge. But the era of bossism was ended by the Progressive movement in the first decade of the century, while the "last hurrahs" of Boston's former Mayor James Michael Curley and his associates extended into the 1950s. In 1950, Boston changed from a ward system of representation to a nine-member City Council elected at large. The revitalization of downtown Boston (which resulted from persuading WASP financial interests to support renewal) is dated from the administration of Mayor John Collins, inaugurated in 1960.

Both cities are Democratic; municipal elections are non-partisan, since an opposition with a Republican label would be doomed from the start. The result is a politics of personal image and organization. Both cities vote on the liberal side of politics in their states and in the nation. Both are proud of their civility: welcoming diversity, encompassing a rich mix of ethnic elements. The most newsworthy growing minority in San Francisco is the homosexual community, which has become active in politics and commercially expansive. Boston's neighborhoods are well established and ethnically centered; so are those of San Francisco. John Winthrop Sears told me about Boston.

There is a distinctly tough problem in Boston that's unique, we think, posed by the nature of the cold-hearted Yankee Brahmins, one of whom you are looking at at this moment. Because the Yankees raised the drawbridge against the immigrating Irish and subsequently the Italians, and the Irish and Italians discovered the one way of making their places was through the political process, there is an ethnicity in Boston politics that's at least a strong as anywhere else. . . . There are a couple of intergrated neighborhoods. I'm not talking just of black-white, but something other than Irish or something other than Yankee. There are some very, very prominent, visible, enclaved communities here, like Irish Charlestown and South Boston, and Italian North End and East Boston. In those areas. . . . people have wanted their kids to grown up in the culture that they knew, plus assimilating the new one that they crossed the ocean to acquire.

Ethnic neighborhoods may seem confining to those outside, yet serve as places of refuge for their inhabitants. The problem for urban politics is to preserve for the ethnic enclave its sense of access and influence, while assuring that the greater civic good is not forgotten in the quest for neighborhood advantage. More specifically, in the words of Robert Wood, the problem is "how you decentralize some functions like police and welfare that touch people's lives so intimately and terrifyingly, and at the same time centralize and regionalize developmental programs like those in air, water, transportation, and pollution." The desires of urban residents are the same as those of suburbanites: to achieve some measure of local control over the aspects of government that matter the most.

San Francisco: The Progressive Civic Legacy

Both San Francisco and Boston remade their local political structures in the Progressive image decades ago, with the avowed purpose of curbing the perceived corruption of party machines. The Progressive prescription includes at least three elements. First, city legislators are paid little more than expenses, to attract candidates on the basis of civic duty, rather than financial reward. Second, elections are made nonpartisan, and city legislators are elected at large, to avoid the particularity of neighborhoods: the good of the city, not the pet project of one of its districts, shall prevail. Third, operating control of the city departments is assigned to an appointed city manager, who presumably replaces political favoritism with sound managerial practices. Two of these "reforms" were achieved in both San Francisco and Boston; the attempt to achieve the third produced a curiously divided executive in San Francisco. The provision of at-large elections is consistent with Madison's belief that the larger constituency, containing diverse interests, would prevent the domination of special interests. The result in American cities has been to favor established economic interests at the expense of geographically based neighborhood concerns. As happened in most cities adopting the plan, the result of at-large elections in San Francisco was to empower the "downtown interests," the leading businessmen of the city, who can afford city-wide campaigns, and may begin their campaigns with name recognition.

Downtown influence was crucial in the revision of the San Francisco city charter in the 1930s. Businessmen hungered for a city manager, cushioned from direct influence by the electorate; labor and city workers favored retention of the strong mayor. A compromise was effected, giving the mayor supervision of several departments, while placing others under the direction of an appointed chief administrative officer (CAO). The resulting hybrid executive increased the fragmentation and complexity of the city government. Ironically, when controversial projects are launched, their direction is often assigned to the CAO, who has achieved an image of being "above politics."

Over the following decades, the movement for increased local control gained momentum. As federal judges intervened in the assignment of pupils to schools, the school board, which had been appointed by the mayor, was made an elected body in 1971. Business domination of the supervisors continued; in 1975, seven of the eleven members of the San Francisco Board of Supervisors lived in the two wealthiest of its eleven districts. In 1976, San Francisco voters passed Proposition T in a referendum election. Branded "Proposition Turkey" by its opponents, the proposal called for the election of supervisors by district. Its supporters, headed by a group called Citizens for Representative Government, claimed that neighborhoods would be more directly represented, and that minorities would able to achieve representation by one of their own members, assuring a closer tie with city government. Opponents argued that supervisors could be elected by a relative handful of votes, without needing to build a city-wide coalition of support.

In 1977, when I first interviewed San Franciscans, only one election had been held under the district system; several incumbents, elected originally at large, had been reelected; some had moved into the districts they sought to represent. The system of district elections was so new that firm judgments of its effectiveness could not be made. In that year, however, the champions of city-wide elections attempted unsuccessfully to repeal the district system. The Guardians with whom I raised the issue were apprehensive about neighborhood representation. An attorney who has been very active in community affairs, including higher education, reacted vehemently.

> I'm against it. I just think it's going to be ward politics at its worst, and parochialism. . . . Now you're going to have pressures for real sectionalism in the city, and you'll not need very many votes to get elected. I'm fearful of what's going to happen.

In Chicago I would find many respondents who were quite pleased with "ward politics." The apprehensions of the San Francisco Guardians seemed to be based more on stereotypes of cities like Chicago than on their own experience. Abe Mellinkoff, former city editor of the *San Francisco Chronicle*, offered a more sophisticated analysis. It was a version of the argument made in the eighteenth and nineteenth centuries in favor of property qualifications for voting—that those with a "stake in the community" are best entrusted with the formulation of community policy.

> The problem of district elections is, during a campaign, for instance, you hear arguments like this, "We want every dollar that comes out of X district returned to us." The fact is, in a metropolitan city, at least, if you really followed that, all money would go downtown, because that's where two-thirds of the taxes are collected, right in this area. But they don't have any votes because they don't live here, they live out of town. And yet, without that core, there's no city left. In San Francisco, last time I checked, two-thirds of the local taxes are from commercial and nonresident privately owned property, which includes hotels, apartment houses, flats, not owned by the people who live in them. And one-third is from private residences, either rented or owned. Well, with that kind of situation, you need really some kind of overall view when you start spending money.

One result of district elections was that the homosexual community, centered in District Five, elected its first gay member of the Board of Supervisors, Harvey Milk. Elsewhere in the city, a former policeman and fireman named Dan White campaigned among the people he had grown up with, the neighbors he had known all his life, and won his first political office. He was tagged as the "most anti-gay" of the successful candidates.

Dan White had hardly been installed in office when he discovered that the $9,600 salary for supervisors, written into the city charter in 1967, was not adequate to support his family. He resigned from the position, but offers of support from relatives and neighbors persuaded him to seek appointment to the vacancy he had created. The appointment power rested with Mayor George Moscone. White called on Moscone, carrying his police pistol. Moscone had apparently been warned by Harvey Milk that the appointment of White would alienate the support of the gay constituency. In the heat of the argument, White drew the pistol and shot the mayor. He then walked down the corridor of City Hall, entered Milk's office, and shot Supervisor Milk. Both men died instantly. White confessed to his acts.

In the ensuing trial, Dan White's lawyer argued that White was suffering from "diminished mental capacity" at the time. Trying to make sense of a jumble of legal holdings, the jury found him guilty of unpremeditated manslaughter; White was sentenced to a seven-year prison term. The district attorney, Joseph Freitas, was accused of "throwing" the case. It was publicly charged that the jury merely expressed the resentment of traditional San Franciscans to the aggressiveness, growing influence and affluent lifestyle of the gay community. Wrote one columnist, "The smartest thing White ever did in his own defense . . . was to murder Harvey Milk, so that he was tried on a tandem charge." A meeting of gays outside City Hall to protest White's light sentence degenerated into a riot.

But the issue of constituency size was also involved in the tragedy. Dan White could only have been elected in a district system; and Harvey Milk was elected because he needed only the votes of District Five. In an indirect way, the district election system was responsible for the deaths of Mayor Moscone and of Harvey Milk himself. It enabled White and Milk to be elected as the symbolic representatives of neighborhood causes and resentments. Madison argued that small constituencies are less likely to select those who are dedicated to the public good. Madison would also have argued (and did, against Jefferson's contrary conviction) that elected representatives should be paid an adequate salary, in order to attract large-minded men away from alternative pursuits.

Supervisor Dianne Feinstein was selected by her colleagues to fill Moscone's term as mayor and then was elected in her own right. Harry Britt, appointed to complete Harvey Milk's term, was the only incumbent to survive the next election, in 1979, when six of the eleven seats on the board were on the ballot. A charter amendment to increase the supervisors' salary was defeated, although most of the candidates claimed their desire to serve their neighborhoods as full-time representatives. The voters also agreed to repeal the single-member district system and return to city-wide elections. A suit was filed raising legal objections to the referendum vote. In March of 1981, in the early morning hours after a tiring session, the Board of Supervisors voted to award themselves an annual expense account of $10,000 each.

The district election system was adopted on the claim that it would make city government newly responsive; but the executive authority remained divided between an elected mayor and an appointed manager; the city departments remained as devoted to bureaucratic habits as ever; the housing situation became more critical; and one critic of the district-based Board of Supervisors said it had been "trivialized. . . . Members and their staffs spend much of their time dealing with stop signs and red curbs instead of the massive problems that plague the whole city." Among others, those problems include a housing crunch for all but the very wealthy, urban crime, the collapse of order in overcrowded Chinatown, and budgetary pressures created by economic recession and vanishing federal support for urban programs. The voters of San Francisco had yearned for a simpler time, when political representation was personal, direct, and neighborhood-oriented; but they were not willing to pay a living wage to persons undertaking that responsibility.

Meanwhile, corporations continue to move their headquarters to San Francisco; office buildings thrust skyward but cannot fill the demand for space; professional San Franciscans like columnist Herb Caen write requiems for each view of the bay newly blocked by stone and steel.

Boston's Little City Halls

The eight years of Mayor John F. Collins's administration, beginning in 1961, brought impressive physical and economic changes to Boston. Scabrous old Scollay Square was replaced by the new Government Center district, including a monumental new City Hall. Tax legislation was rewritten to permit the construction of the Prudential Building and its followers. As if on signal, new high-rise office buildings rose to transform the Boston skyline.

While Collins's efforts revitalized downtown Boston and restored its historic function as a commercial center, the new allegiance of government and commerce left neighborhood residents wondering who would defend their interests; in fact, redevelopment destroyed one vital Italian neighborhood.

Increasing conflict between the commercial center and the residential neighborhoods served as the basis of Kevin White's mayoral campaign, when Collins declined to seek a third term. Promising new responsiveness to the neighborhoods, White narrowly defeated Louise Day Hicks, the heroine of Boston's bitter fight against school integration. White's promise was realized by the creation of an Office of Public Service (OPS), directly under his own control, consisting of a headquarters and fourteen district offices which soon became known as "Little City Halls." Designed with the aid of Harvard consultants, the plan was inspired by the call of the Kerner Commission's Report on Civil Disorders for city government offices in minority neighborhoods as a means of alleviating minority alienation from the city bureaucracy. However, the concept of the "alienated voter" had been a cliche of the mayoralty campaign, and it applied to all of Boston's citizens. The district offices were planned to serve all the city's neighborhoods.

The designated purposes of the Little City Halls (each staffed by half a dozen or more people) were threefold: to increase the responsiveness of city government by serving as communications channels and issue advocates; to reduce citizen alienation by facilitating community participation and serving as complaint referral centers; and to improve the level of city services as a result of performing the first two functions, along with providing certain services directly.

The OPS was criticized for becoming an adjunct to Mayor White's growing political organization. Some of the leading officials in the Office of Public Services had been recruited from the 1967 mayoral campaign; the standard departments of city government were filled with civil servants who had no particular reason to care about White's career. It was not surprising that the OPS, as a new agency directly answerable to the mayor, would house his political supporters. Thomas Atkins, who was then a city councilman, made a structural argument. He charged that, to the extent that the district office merely registered complaints, without supervising bureaucratic responses, the Little City Halls were simply an additional level of government interposed between the citizen and City Hall. But the OPS was more a political structure than a governmental one. Critics charged that, after about 1971, the Little City Halls were far more responsive to the needs of Mayor White's political supporters than to those of his opponents.

City councilors would indeed have reason to suspect an agency that replaced their own function as ombudspersons. A careful analysis showed that, while the OPS offices dealt with some eighty thousand service complaints annually, the number of such complaints taken to the departments and to the councilors themselves did not diminish. OPS was handling complaints that would otherwise not have been received; and they were able to focus the energies of the existing city departments, with no increase in the cost of departmental operations. An estimated $2,000,000 in additional city services were delivered, in a year when the OPS budget was around $800,000.

The argument that the Office of Public Service was too expensive for the results it produced was diminished when monies from the federal Model Cities program were allocated to its support; local taxpayers see money from Washington as free. In 1977 the voters of Boston narrowly rejected a charter amendment which would have provided for the district election of the City Council. While the success of the Little City Halls probably persuaded some voters that the change was not needed, the election results suggested a racist influence. Neighborhoods that most strongly opposed school integration also voted against district elections, which would have increased minority membership on the Council.

Meanwhile, Boston voters yearned to escape the burdens of city taxation, which several Guardians described as perhaps the heaviest in the nation, because of inadequate support by the state. Individuals and businesses, they said, were moving to New Hampshire to enjoy its governmental frugality. In 1980 "Proposition 2 1/2" was passed by the state's voters. It limited property taxes to 2.5 per cent of market value. City finances were further strained by a court-ordered repayment of nearly $60 million in property taxes that been collected as a result of overcharges levied by the Assessor's Office. In the spring of 1981, Mayor White announced with some fanfare the closure of the Little City Halls as an economy measure—but he transferred their personnel to other city jobs. (The OPS had always been a labor-intensive operation; the typical Little City Hall was a trailer parked on a city-owned lot.) In an effort to stimulate opposition to Proposition 2 1/2, Mayor White announced a layoff of policemen and firemen. Of course, the Proposition had not mandated cutbacks in provisions for public safety.

In 1981 the movement calling for district-based councilmanic elections was revived. Its strongest support came from the incumbent councilors, including John Sears, who had won the most votes on a city-wide basis.

The dilemma of balancing local responsiveness against assuring a vision of the general civic good has been handled in some cities by combining the election of some city legislators from districts with other seats elected at large. NAACP attorney Thomas Atkins recommended this plan for Boston.

My feeling is that a councilmanic or school board elected solely by districts would have problems on a scale equal to those we now have, with at-large bodies in each instance. I think that a combination of at-large and district elections are needed in both the school and the City Council spheres. The district-based officeholders are necessary to guarantee wall-to-wall coverage, and to usher in a greater measure of accountability. People have got to be able to get at somebody. . . . There is little accountability when every elected official is presumed accountable to everybody; it means they're not accountable to anybody. So the district election provides representation of particular points of view, and accountability. . . . The at-large component provides a way of offsetting the predictable parochialism of district election. Congressmen are parochial; they're more parochial than senators, who are more parochial than the president. District-elected people at the city level would be predictably parochial; and people elected at large are less parochial. You need to have in a city government the capacity simultaneously to know and articulate the particular point of view; but, when needed, to articulate a city point of view. A city is not just a sum of its parts. A city is organic, dynamic; an entity in and of itself. And you don't get the sum of a city's existence by taking all of its district councilors and adding them up. They end up weighing a lot less than the city is worth. The at-large component would go some way toward redressing that imbalance.

None of the Guardians gave a more moving description of the nature of the city; and Atkins would be the first to admit that the redesign of its system of representation cannot by itself resolve a city's problems; many are beyond the competence of any city legislature. In fact, both Boston and San Francisco have been torn by struggles over a process with which Mr. Atkins, in his professional capacity, has been intimately connected: the racial integration of the public schools.

School Busing: San Francisco and Boston

If the appeal of ethnic enclaves in urban areas lies in the ability to raise children who appreciate their parents' culture, as well as assimilating the standards of the larger society, the local schools become very important. The tradition of American public education is that of effort by the community; financed by local taxes, the schools have been managed by local school boards, and there have been at least formal efforts to bring teachers and parents together for mutual reinforcement. This pattern of cooperation has taken place more often between middle-class parents and educational professionals than it has, say, in the working-class neighborhoods of Boston. Nevertheless, the neighborhood school has been an important source of community identity.

Considerations of this kind played little part in the judicial movement toward school integration through busing. But such considerations, as much as conscious racism, probably motivated the resistance to court orders. Resistance was particularly strong in both Boston and San Francisco. Judge Weigle in San Francisco and Judge Garrity in Boston exercised judicial control over the school systems; Judge Garrity found it necessary to run the school system as a ward of the court.

Racial confrontations, including riots and the stoning of buses, which led to schools guarded by uniformed policemen, erupted in Boston beginning in 1974, when integration orders were first enforced. Violence had subsided by 1977, when I visited Boston, and I found the Guardians cautiously hopeful for the future. Barney Frank, then a state legislator, told me,

> You're not going to have a great depopulation of Boston, because there is a lot of white neighborhood ethnic pride. . . . The busing issue has quieted down substantially. The recent [school committee and city council] elections showed much less impact by busing. I think within three or four years it will have petered out substantially.

Frank's judgment was repeated by Lieutenant Governor Thomas P. O'Neill III, who said that candidates in Boston could no longer be defeated on the busing issue, as they had been two or three years earlier. But these hopes went unrealized. In the fall of 1979, antibusing demonstrations were renewed. A black athlete, Darryl Williams, was shot in the neck by a sniper during a scrimmage at Charlestown High School and left paralyzed from the neck down. This triggered violence by roving youth gangs of both races. By 1980 Boston religious leaders were circulating a "Covenant of Justice, Equity, and Harmony," with the signature drive launched at an ecumenical meeting on Boston Common. Speaking at this ceremony, John Winthrop Sears noted that blacks fear entering white neighborhoods, and vice versa. Declared Sears, "Hatred and violence make this city a nightmare."

The statistical outcome of the struggle over busing was that school enrollment plunged from over ninety thousand to sixty-seven thousand. Families that could afford the cost moved to the suburbs or placed their children in private, and particularly parochial, schools. By 1980, 38 per cent of the pupils in public schools were white, although the population of Boston is 75 per cent white. The withdrawal of community support from local schools is displayed in Irish South Boston, where the predominantly black student body is transported from outside the area to attend the local high school. According to a national newsmagazine, residents see the high school as "an enemy fortress atop a hill menacing their modest homes. Jerome Winegar, headmaster of the school, says that 'the community has written us off.'"

In San Francisco, Judge Weigle defined as "segregated" any school that had a higher proportion of blacks than the school district as a whole—47 per cent. The residents of black Hunter's Point demanded a new school, and the board acquiesced; when their children were ordered bused to white schools miles away, parents complained, just as white parents resisted the assignment of their children to the school in Hunter's Point. When the school board yielded to these complaints, Judge Weigle found it guilty of making decisions with a segregatory intent. He ordered that every elementary-school pupil in the city be allocated to one of four categories (white, black, Asian, or Spanish) and become subject to transportation, so that each school would have an average mix of the four. The immediate reaction was that enrollment in the elementary schools declined by 13 per cent; the high schools were not yet subjected to busing, and their enrollment remained stable.

Cooperation—and even contact—between teachers and parents has been inhibited by busing for integration. Activities such as the Parent Teacher Association diminish or vanish. Nathan Glazer cites a striking example of the phenomenon from San Francisco.

> In San Francisco's Mission District, owing to the effective work of the Mission Coalition (an Alinsky-style community organization), the local community had considerable influence on public programs. With a wide base of membership, this organization could help determine what was most effective in the local schools. But if it wanted to create an atmosphere in the school best suited to the education of Spanish-speaking children, what sense does this make when the local schools are filled with non-Spanish-speaking children from distant areas? And how could it influence the education the Mission children received in the distant schools to which many of them were now sent? In Boston, as in San Francisco, bilingual education has become more difficult owing to dispersion.

Earlier, Glazer forcefully made the point that there is a significant difference between the now ended *de jure* segregation (separate schools required for each race) of the South and Northern *de facto* (residential) segregation, but that this distinction has been progressively eroded by court decisions. In 1979 the voters of California approved an amendment to the state constitution which was based on the wording of a 1973 U.S. Supreme Court decision, requiring busing for integration only when school segregation had been created deliberately by the actions of public officials. Supporters of the busing program in Los Angeles challenged the California amendment before the California Supreme Court, which, in 1981, found it in accord with the national Constitution, and cleared the way for dismantling the Los Angeles busing program. Meanwhile, the Reagan Justice Department withdrew federal support from busing advocates, and only court action prevented the Internal Revenue Service from restoring the tax-exempt status of private schools that discriminate on the basis of race.

Abe Mellinkoff described the California outcome for readers of the *San Francisco Chronicle.*

> [The amendment] won overwhelmingly statewide by a 2-to-1 vote, and even easily by 3-to-2 in San Francisco. . . . It is hard to believe now that about a decade ago the courts were somehow convinced that deliberate segregation existed in S.F schools. . . . Currently there is not much busing remaining in San Francisco and what there is could be ended by new court action. Lawyers who fought such a reform would find little backing from the minority communities. Blacks derived little from busing beyond the natural satisfaction for old wrongs finally recognized. Polls show it no longer has their overwhelming approval. . . . Neither Assembly Speaker Willie Brown, of San Francisco, nor Los Angeles Mayor Tom Bradley, the two leading black politicians in California, any longer favor it. Busing is a dying political issue and the time for burial is at hand.

Neither Boston nor San Francisco is a city in decline. Both are growing, attractive commercial and cultural centers. Downtown Boston has been substantially reborn in the last two decades, while the San Francisco boom in constructing high-rise office buildings continues unabated. In both cities, scattered revitalization is occurring in residential areas as middle-class individuals or couples, usually without children, occupy restored homes or purchase apartments in buildings converted to condominiums. As a long-term trend, this return of managerial talent and increase in the tax base bode well for the two cities. But the returnees from suburbia displace the poor and the elderly, often from homes they have occupied for many years. The process has been tagged as "gentrification," a mildly derisive term, which hardly describes the agony that the process may bring to the aging residents of an ethnic neighborhood.

Both cities display the clash of values that characterizes the American attitude toward government and its goals. The contest between liberty and equality is exemplified in the shifting racial makeup of residential areas and the attempts to achieve racial balance, and hence equal opportunity, within the public schools. And the effort to achieve a balance between responsiveness to local needs and the pursuit of the civic good have caused both cities to question the very form of their civic governments.

Atlanta and Houston: Affluence and Inequality

I found that, although they are separated by a continent, the similarities between Boston and San Francisco are striking. While they are much closer in distance, the contrasts between Houston and Atlanta are more noteworthy. Atlanta was the home city of Martin Luther King, Jr.; the black community was well established there, with its own colleges and other institutions, before the civil rights revolution made black political power possible. Atlanta proclaims itself "the city too busy to hate," and the reelection of Mayor Maynard Jackson signaled the acceptance by white economic elites of the realities of black political power. Houston seems too busy to invent slogans, and its race relations are more burdened by Southern history than are those of Atlanta. The whites of Houston have not had to adapt their political attitudes to a black political majority.

Throughout its history, Atlanta has been a transportation hub; its airport is the second busiest in the nation. Its skyline is dominated by the stunning new hotels designed by John Portman, and it is working to increase its already formidable position as a convention center. Houston's prosperity is based on oil and chemicals; its boast of being "the oil capital of the world" is more fact than slogan. Oil-company headquarters dominate the skyline downtown; but high-rise commercial centers spring up along the circular freeway beyond.

The development of downtown Atlanta has been planned and accomplished by a semiprivate authority called Central Atlanta Progress. By contrast, Houston is proud of lacking a zoning ordinance, and the city's planning effort is minimal. The Metropolitan Atlanta Rapid Transit Authority (MARTA) is well developed, with more than seven hundred buses. Its subway system, serving suburban DeKalb County, opened in 1980. Public transportation barely exists in Houston, and blacks from the downtown slum find it nearly impossible to get to industrial jobs on the city's periphery.

Despite these differences, a common reality underlies the civic life of both Atlanta and Houston. Both cities are growing, constantly attracting newcomers. The frantic pace of physical growth and commercial development in both cities creates a marked contrast with Boston and San Francisco, which continually lose residential population to the suburbs. Yet, as Houston and Atlanta create new affluence, inequalities grow—inequalities between races, and inequalities between the poor and affluent within each race.

A New Politics for Atlanta

In the Atlanta mayor's office, I conversed with a senior staff member whom I have called James Hope. Hope was born in New York, lived in the Bedford-Stuyvesant section ("It seemed like a paradise, growing up there, until I looked back on it"), was an undergraduate at Ohio's black Central State University, and earned a graduate degree from the Harvard Business School. At the end of the interview, Hope explained why a black trained in administration would build a career in Atlanta.

> The South is where it's at. It will be, for some time. The South is like a child, being born again in a sense. There is opportunity to mold the personality of this child. Given the right influence, the right direction, you can't completely change it, but you can try to weed out some of the bad habits before they are created. And I think that some of the cities in the South are very open to that.

It would be hard to imagine a young, black professional making such an idealistic statement twenty or twenty-five years ago. That it could be made in all seriousness in 1977 can be taken as a measure of national, and particularly Southern, progress toward achieving equal opportunity for all races. However, to accentuate the distance yet untraveled, one might point to the special circumstances of Atlanta and declare that James Hope was simply emphasizing that Atlanta is no longer a Southern city. Atlanta's black and white citizens have largely concluded that the interests of each race are best pursued in a context of harmony. This is not a universal Southern attitude. One could also point to the slaying of black youths which began in 1980 (and apparently ended with the conviction of Wayne B. Williams in 1982) as proof that racial harmony is fragile and that Atlanta, like any American city, lives with daily violence. Nevertheless, what James Hope said was far more encouraging, since it did not merely emphasize economic factors, than anything I had read about the growth of the sunbelt at the expense of the tired cities of the Northeast.

Atlanta was perhaps the inevitable place for the civil rights revolution to bear fruit. With six black colleges, including some founded in the aftermath of the Civil War, the black middle class has been solidly anchored. It also has a long history of coexistence with white elites. By the 1970s, Atlanta had a population that was 55 per cent black; in 1973, 49 per cent of the registered voters were black. In that year, Maynard H. Jackson was elected as Atlanta's first black mayor, and the first to serve under the new city charter, which took effect in 1974.

The charter was developed by a commission; unlike practices in the "home rule" states of the West, it was voted into existence, not by the citizens of Atlanta, but by the Georgia legislature. The most important change of the new charter was the shift from a weak mayor, with semiautonomous city departments, to a strong mayor, who was given the crucial authority of appointment and removal of the department heads. The mayor in turn is assisted by a chief administrative officer who exerts close supervision over the departments, but is directly responsible to the mayor. The legislature did not wish to inspire a big-city-style organization; the mayor was limited to two terms.

The charter commission had recommended the election of twelve councilmen from districts. The legislature added six seats elected at large from the entire city, resulting in the form of mixed representation recommended for Boston by William Atkins. However, the legislature was not moved by Madisonian considerations. District elections were needed to satisfy requirements of the Civil Rights Act of 1965, so that the black population would be able to elect blacks to the Council. The legislature added the at-large seats in an attempt to retain some aspects of the former system. When I visited Atlanta, the City Council was evenly divided, with nine members of each race. Their salaries were set by the charter at $8,800: thus was preserved the Progressive concept of the part-time, civically oriented legislator.

Atlanta developed a vital neighborhood organizational movement

even before the charter was revised. Interstate highway 20 was completed in the early 1960s, consuming acres of private property in the name
of the public welfare. Plans for the completion of the freeway network
met determined opposition on the part of neighborhood organizations
formed in response to the threat. Their resistance prevented construction of the I-485 highway project, even after much of the property had
been acquired by the state. Once formed, these organizations became
involved in other issues. Mayor Jackson institutionalized them as Neighborhood Planning Units. I talked to Joanne McGeorge, a political scientist from Detroit who served in the mayor's office as a faculty intern. She
felt that the neighborhood organizations were very promising.

> I think its going to be increasingly effective in terms of really getting some
> kind of grass roots participation. And they're going to be taken more and
> more seriously. . . . There's more and more talk about the loss of community
> in cities. In effect, this is really a way of people feeling a sense of community,
> of loyalty to a neighborhood, yet identifying as an Atlantan.

Ms. McGeorge told me that she had visited a physician early in her
stay in Atlanta; when she told where she worked, the doctor asked, "Are
you the token white in the mayor's office?" The senior members of the
office were about evenly divided racially; but white Atlanta had not seen
blacks in significant City Hall positions before, so they assumed that the
office had become all black.

The conspicuousness of the Jackson administration created a different
problem, which was explained by Davey Gibson, the commissioner of
development and human resources, himself a black.

> Blacks and other minorities, because of the black political power, see it as
> an oasis—the best thing that's happening. Consequently, they come literally
> in droves and identify with the city, rather than other areas. . . . Minorities
> and the have-nots see a much more responsive government to their needs and
> wishes than ever before in their lifetime; consequently they continue to
> come, and that puts an additional pressure on the city.

But the nonpartisan politics of Atlanta, like most nonpartisan electoral systems, remained chaotic. I learned that Mayor Jackson had
considered endorsing a slate of candidates for the 1977 municipal elections. This might have focused attention upon issues defined in a joint
platform; and successful candidates would at least have owed the mayor
gratitude for his coattail power. Mayor Jackson decided against such an
elementary move toward harmonizing the efforts of the city legislature
and executive because of accusations that he was attempting to build

personal political power and had exploited the new charter to that end. When no party organization exists to screen potential candidates, personal ambitions and factional rivalries combine to create confusion. In 1977 several black candidates, and sometimes more than one white, offered themselves in each district. Joanne McGeorge explained.

This is where you see the factionalism in the black community, between some of the black organizations, to some extent between established organizations and the remnants of the civil rights movement, who are fighting desperately to maintain some kind of leadership role. Getting people out in the street is not as important now, because you've got a black mayor, you've got some black councilmen—how do they somehow retain a position that they have fought hard for and given a lot for? They're being passed by to some extent.

With no party organizations to pose issues for decision by the electorate, is there some other factor that imposes order on the chaos of private ambitions? In Atlanta that factor is so obvious that it may be taken for granted. Just as, in partisan systems, the voter is most likely to know and be guided by the candidate's party affiliation, in Atlanta the voter is certain to know the candidate's race. Dr. Clarence Bacote, professor of history emeritus at Morehouse College, has systematically compared the vote of black and white precincts, showing the dramatic influence of the candidate's race on the voting decision. His figures also show that the most crucial elections—such as the first election of Maynard Jackson— are determined by a "crossover" vote—voters who support a candidate not of their own race. Jackson's slender margin of victory came from his support in the white community. That support increased as Jackson demonstrated responsible leadership, but he was barred by the Charter from seeking a third term.

National media attention to the role of race in the 1981 Atlanta mayoralty election simply drew attention to the situation that had long existed. Both candidates were aware of the importance of the racial crossover vote and made extraordinary efforts to woo it, which practically canceled each other. Andrew Young's victory came from his successful activation of the black majority.

Maynard Jackson was elected as the first black mayor of Atlanta in time to head a governmental structure that had been considerably modernized, but that very modernization had been accomplished by a state legislature which retained the power to determine much of Atlanta's future. Several Atlanta Guardians pointed out that the Georgia legislature retains a rural outlook and flavor. No matter how responsive the

Atlanta government seemed, it could tackle the intractable urban problems, like housing and transportation, only with outside help. Significant help came from the federal government in the late 1970s; several Atlantans served in Jimmy Carter's White House. Ronald Reagan was no particular friend of Atlanta, nor of any other city.

Atlanta's Shining Towers

The Atlanta I visited was a city riding a crest of confidence. The sense of being involved in work that mattered pervaded the mayor's office. The downtown gleamed with new buildings, including the seventy-floor Peachtree Plaza, the world's tallest hotel. Thirty-six major new buildings were constructed in central Atlanta between 1960 and 1970. After a slowdown due to economic recession, building continued anew in the late 1970s. Most of this development was coordinated by a privately financed, nonprofit association, Central Atlanta Progress (CAP), which traces its origins to a predecessor founded in 1941. Dan Sweat, CAP's president, explained its purposes.

> While I work for private business, we carry out the public purpose. We're the interface, the catalyst, the mechanism between public and business collectively; between private business in its civic planning interest, and the public sector.

The activities of CAP have reached far beyond the traditional provision of a table holding scale models of the downtown buildings. CAP was active in reaching a truce with the neighborhood organizations regarding the further development of freeways. It established coordinating links between business and the planners of the MARTA subway. CAP also worked to modify the practice of "redlining," the designation of entire areas in which banks refuse to write mortgages or make home-improvement loans, on the basis that the neighborhood is decaying: the perfect self-fulfilling prophecy. Dan Sweat described CAP's activities colorfully.

> I maintain that redlining is not a conspiracy; it's a condition that results as a result of a number of things. And so we set out to identify these things and reduce them or eliminate them. . . . We found out that there are loan officers that live out in Red Oak, Georgia, in the suburbs, who come down, they sit in their offices and process loans and they get the hell out before dark —out of the city. They assume that, in the city, everything's bad. We took bank presidents out, board chairmen, out into the neighborhoods, showed

them neighborhoods they had never seen before; opened their eyes. And we took loan officers and appraisers into these neighborhoods to show them what a lot of young people were doing just by using their credit cards to buy lumber on. We got a very active thing going.

Perceiving the need to bring middle-class residents back to the downtown area, CAP formed in 1976 a mortgage consortium with a commitment of $62.5 million to be devoted to the rehabilitation of once elegant but badly decayed neighborhoods. CAP did not apply the label of "gentrification" to this attempt to attract middle- and upper-middle-class residents back to the central city. Dan Sweat felt that the returnees would be of both races.

A lot of people were pushed out of Atlanta or fled Atlanta because of the black expansion, [but] there's no doubt in my mind that there's no problem with having a racial mix now in this city. If you're talking about middle and upper income, we've got a very strong middle and upper economic class of blacks in the city, probably the likes of which you're never going to see anywhere else. Economic barriers were broken down, legal barriers were broken down, and they can afford to buy nice homes. They are moving out into the suburban areas. . . . Eventually, I think, you won't see the [pattern of] black or white—black in the city, white outside.

But the conception of downtown Atlanta as a home for corporate offices, a convention center with myriad hotels to serve the tourist trade, and some homes for upper-income families, left an important gap in providing employment. Davey Gibson described that gap.

Atlanta is going to be heavily dependent on the tourist trade. . . . We're going to have a big gap here unless somehow we can get a hold of it. I think we're going to have a lot of service jobs and we're going to have a lot of white-collar jobs, but we're not going to have the industrial base in between.

Thus, while the alliance blossomed between Atlanta's black politicians and its white business leaders, not all problems were within the competence of that alliance. Elsewhere in Atlanta, I learned more about such problems.

The Atlanta School Solution

In the five years before 1973, the Atlanta public schools lost seventeen thousand pupils, nearly all white. In 1963 the system was 55 per cent white; by 1973, when the city's population included a slight black majority, the schools were 80 per cent black. At his comfortable home in northwest Atlanta, I interviewed former Morehouse College President Benjamin Mays, then eighty-three, who was reelected as president of the Atlanta school board in 1977. Dr. Mays commented poignantly on the phenomenon of white flight.

> If you have a share of nothing but black folks in the city, and all the white folks out in the suburbs, you are killing the city. . . . They've got to see that we've got to get together, and white folks have got to stop running from black folks, and black folks have got to stop running from white folks. If you don't do that, then the city is going to decay, and its going to hurt all of us. . . . The reason why I'm so much concerned about black people and white people living together is my experience at the turn of the century. Everything that I have seen that is totally black, everything, is disregarded by city government, disregarded by state government, and disregarded by federal government. And, in the American mind, if it's black it isn't good. And if you've got a good black—he's an accident.

At least on the surface, the school integration compromise reached in Atlanta in 1973 disagreed with the principles Dr. Mays articulated four years later. Nathan Glazer has summarized the settlement succinctly.

> In Atlanta, there has been a strong black political presence. . . . Local black leaders preferred not to press ahead for a full desegregation, with its attendant problems in the way of greater white flight, racial disturbances and tension, the loss of the black identity of certain schools of which the black community was proud, and the like. The local black leaders were ready to accept a settlement in which black schools remained and in which the number of black administrators in the school system was increased. This led to disagreement between the local chapter of the NAACP and the national NAACP, which wished to press ahead for full integration by whatever measures necessary, which, of course, would call for busing.

The 1973 arrangement required the busing of only three thousand out of the system's ninety-five thousand students and left 83 of the 114 schools all black, while making more certain the black administration of black schools. Dr. Mays told me that the trend towards white flight from the schools was becoming stabilized, if not reversed; the system enrolled four hundred pupils in 1977 that had been in private schools in the county in 1976. He did not believe in the efficacy of compulsory school assignment, because of its interference with liberty, the traditional American freedom of movement; families should be free to select whatever neighborhood they could afford and to enroll their children in the school they found to be the best. He argued that schools of quality will attract serious students, regardless of race. As examples, he cited several formerly all-black colleges and college programs that had become thoroughly integrated through the voluntary application of white students. He was prepared to take a long-range view of Atlanta's future.

I received a more immediate view of the school system from a forty-year-old corporation lawyer, graduate of an Atlanta public high school, when I interviewed him at his office in the Georgia Savings Bank building.

> If you had told me five years ago that I wouldn't have my children in the public schools, I'd have told you that you were crazy; I was absolutely committed to them. We moved into a district where there was an excellent public school; highest test scores in the community, and so on. Then the First Circuit Court of Appeals ordered that all the faculties be apportioned on the basis of race; and 66 per cent of the teachers were black in the system and the rest were white, so every school had to have a faculty composed that way. And they then just simply destroyed every sense of "faculty," because they just uprooted the people who'd been there twenty years or more and moved them to another school. . . . The [1973] plan provided that you could have schools that were predominantly white; they beat back the concept of racial balance in every school. But the plan provided for the voluntary busing of black children into white schools. And the black middle class, and upper class, on the whole were very happy with their schools, so they didn't volunteer. The people who volunteered were the poor, the downtrodden, from the most deprived neighborhoods of Atlanta. So you had the irony of the poorest black kids going to school with the-middle-class-and-above white kids. . . . The black kids are very rough and tumble, and many of them have a vocabulary that would shock an army sergeant. . . . Even our most liberal friends pulled their children out; their children were becoming racial bigots, because they were equating blackness with these qualities they saw in the children they were going to school with.

This statement emphasized an important reality. When working-class Italians in Boston or Poles in Chicago resist the encroachments of black expansion upon their traditional neighborhoods, it is easy to assume that racial bigotry is the cause. In fact, there are differences within races on the basis of income, education, and occupation; these differences are cultural, and they result in different values and manners.

Beyond Race: Divisions in Atlanta's Black Community

An Atlanta political activist explained racial migration in the area of Atlanta, which is principally located in Fulton County.

De Kalb County was historically the bedroom community of Atlanta. The really high-rent district of Atlanta is Northwest; but De Kalb had the highest per capita income, the most college graduates; and now the De Kalb population has increased to over half a million people. Rockdale was predominantly agricultural. . . . Low-income blacks live near the city boundary; then, out a little bit further, moderate-income blacks—all homeowners; and then some of the people who lived in South De Kalb [County] who don't like the black encroachment have moved to Rockdale. . . . Atlanta has the largest number of black millionaires in the United States, the largest totally funded and owned black insurance company in the world, the largest black bank. The wealthy blacks in Atlanta don't want the poor blacks around them.

In the mayor's office, Joanne McGeorge told me that one could not expect the intellectual community surrounding Atlanta's five black colleges to interact very much with working-class blacks, except in special circumstances.

They will unify on any issue that is obviously racial; where race overrides all other things, there will be unity. In an election time, if its going to be advantageous to make some issue a racial issue, the candidate's going to do so. But [race] isn't quite that critical otherwise.

The civil rights revolution made unified political action possible; its full success will be achieved, if ever, when unified political action on the basis of race is no longer necessary. In the meantime, it is erroneous to assume that black voters constitute a monolithic group, sharing common values and perceptions and supporting like policies. The kinds of differences that can exist were demonstrated in Atlanta when I talked to two black members of the state legislature, Lottie Watkins and Julian Bond.

Lottie Watkins is an energetic grandmother who has built her insurance and property-management firm, Lottie Watkins Enterprises, into a business with a monthly income of a third of a million dollars. She resigned her job as a bank clerk in 1960 to found her business in a single room; two decades later, she was appointed to the board of directors of that same (white-owned) bank. Even before founding her own business, Mrs. Watkins was active in community affairs. She served along with Martin Luther King, Sr., as an informal adviser to the civil rights activists who were then college students, including Julian Bond; she helped organize financing for the Voter Education Project; she rose through the ranks of Atlanta business and professional organizations; in 1975 she became a member of the steering committee that advised Jimmy Carter during his quest for the Democratic presidential nomination. She ran first in a field of thirteen candidates in the primary election to win a seat in the lower house of the Georgia legislature.

Mrs. Watkins's ideas about political issues are strongly influenced by her own experiences. She recalled her father's employment by the Works Progress Administration during the New Deal and hoped that Carter's welfare reform would expand the role of the government as employer. She added,

> I think it would help if he would just get rid of food stamps, because there's a lot of fraud in the food stamp business. I have been places, like right across the street at the service station, and the guy has had to turn people around who want to sell food stamps. And when I go to the market, the person in front of me will have steaks and things in her basket, because she has food stamps, and I don't.

As a property manager, Lottie Watkins dealt with both the Departments of Health, Education, and Welfare (as it then was called) and of Housing and Urban Development in arranging for the housing of welfare recipients. She felt that the requirements for the quality of living accommodations were established by HUD without relation to the qualifications for the receipt of welfare, determined by HEW. She felt that HUD should be removed from the picture, so that HEW could concentrate on the individual, determining housing needs as part of considering the person's total situation.

> There are a lot of little girls having babies. They're at home with their mothers. But since they know about the program, they go down and they apply. And then they get an apartment; it's very plush, because everything has to be A-1 [to meet HUD's requirements]. And she gets this fabulous apartment and dishwasher, stove, refrigerator and carpet for she and her child; then she gets a welfare check.

Similarly, Mrs. Watkins favored a teen-age differential in the minimum wage.

> I have a little grandson who will be fifteen next year. When he gets to be sixteen, he can work at Six Flags [Over Georgia, a local amusement park]. So they have to pay him the minimum wage. But Sammy's not qualified. . . . I just can't see my grandson making as much as a man who has a family —when a man comes in to work who has three or four children, he has to start with this amount of money.

Lottie Watkins, the daughter of an itinerant musician, has achieved financial security through hard work and political influence through service to the community. Her attitudes toward political questions are pragmatic; her values are those of a Christian individualist. Julian Bond is younger than Mrs. Watkins by more than a generation. The grandson of a minister and son of a college president, Bond and his sister as children were plaintiffs in the suit that integrated the public schools of Lincoln, Pennsylvania. The family moved to Atlanta in 1957; Bond's role as a civil rights activist began soon afterwards. Julian Bond told me where he lived from 1940 to 1945, the first five years of his life.

> Fort Valley, Georgia, a midget town down south of Macon, a little college town and a farming town. The college was Fort Valley State College—which was then Fort Valley State College For Negroes. It's now just Fort Valley State College, but it's still for Negroes.

That ironic statement summed up much recent Southern history: Atlanta is not all of the South; an accomplished legal revolution in the field of civil rights does not remake society; every step on the road to equality reveals the distance yet to be traveled. Julian Bond's political interests have gone far beyond matters of race to encompass sweeping analyses of American society. I began our conversation by asking him to name the most important issues facing the nation.

> The largest one is economic. The distribution of wealth and income, the distribution of income which in turn can lead to the distribution of wealth. That's the biggest single problem: this imbalance between a relatively small but extremely affluent group at one end of the spectrum, and a comparatively small but almost poverty-stricken group at the other. And then this larger group in the center which helps subsidize these other two. . . . The country has got to find some way to guarantee employment for the able-bodied, while it guarantees a better than subsistence existence for those who cannot fit into the job market. There's a difference between will-not and cannot. There are a lot of cannots, and larger numbers of will-nots.

Bond feels that the long-range solution can only be some system that, for want of a better word before the solution is designed, we would have to call socialism. He is able to talk about long-range solutions when he speaks on college campuses, an activity that provides a major share of his income; as a Georgia senator, his concern is to protect the gains that have been made in and for Atlanta.

Julian Bond's concern for long-range national solutions contrasts sharply with Lottie Watkins's reactions to the political issues she sees exemplified in her daily life. Taken together, these two Georgia legislators show that a common characteristic—membership in the black race

—need not determine a broad range of other attitudes. The fact that they are black, and legislators, and in Georgia, suggests that the day may yet come when all issues in Southern politics are no longer reducible to race.

Houston: Politics Absorbed by Economics

It is hard to imagine a city with a more secure economic future, at least for the next few decades, than Houston. The deregulation of energy prices has unleashed a drive for domestic production of oil. Twenty-nine of the thirty largest oil companies are headquartered there; Houston is the center of the worldwide industry that supports the exploration and drilling for petroleum; its oil companies are expanding their involvement with the extraction of coal and other energy sources; Houston is the center of the petro-chemical manufacturing industry. As world energy supplies shrink, Houston grows, for its business is to find and extract the remaining fossil fuels.

The new urgency of energy production—traditionally a "boom or bust" industry—is grafted onto the Texas frontier outlook. In Atlanta, citizens are differentiated by race; in Houston, by race and by dollars. In other cities, the most difficult questions came at the end of the interviews, when I inquired about the respondents' income and net worth. There was no reticence on such matters in Houston. I could imagine the oilmen of downtown Houston wearing golden tags displaying their current net worth as a kind of proof of manhood. Yet, in the shadows of the stunning new skyscrapers the oilmen work in, lie the unpaved streets of Houston's extensive downtown slum—where, in 1978, twenty-five thousand persons were unemployed.

While Houston's economic future seems assured, its political future is less certain. Statistically, the city is in fine shape—with high average incomes, low unemployment, and no restrictions on further growth through annexation. But the already annexed wealthy suburban districts affect the statistics, which hide the plight of minorities. Houston's population of nearly two million is 26 per cent black and 12 per cent Chicano. Surrounded by instant wealth, the poor of Houston present a stark contrast. Even before the Reagan administration's attack upon welfare, Texas welfare payments provided only $40 a month per child. Many of the slum homes are without heat, and cold snaps can come in winter—while the summer temperatures average ninety-two degrees, with humidity of over 90 per cent; Houston was built on a bayou, and it is annually plagued by floods. The air-conditioning that makes the high-rise office buildings habitable is seldom available to the poor.

In the Houston I visited, city government was a minimal presence. This resulted from rapid growth, a boom-town psychology, and the lack of resources: taxes were low, planning was nonexistent, and it seemed that Houstonians had grown accustomed to the results, although many of its newer residents came from cities with much higher levels of municipal service. The structure of Houston government—a "strong" mayor/council form, rather than the council/manager form usual to Texas—contributed to its minimal performance. Some thirty department heads reported directly to the mayor; they were (and are) removable by the mayor. Nearly every other city employee was protected in his job by a zealous Civil Service Commission. It was as impossible to reward initiative or energy displayed by a city bureaucrat as to fire an incompetent. Furthermore, city budgets were prepared on an incremental basis; any mayor had trouble assessing the performance of city departments, much less influencing their direction. City costs increased, but less work was accomplished; streets fell into disrepair, garbage lay uncollected, and new suburbs hired private security forces.

Private Wealth, but Not for Public Purposes

Houston is probably the fastest growing city in the United States. Since 1976, journalists have printed the estimate that it grows by a thousand persons a month. Each day, one hundred ninety automobiles are newly registered, joining the traffic crush on the freeway system, which was largely designed twenty years ago. The poorly maintained bus system carries only one hundred eighty thousand persons daily. Planning has begun for a rail system, but it has made little progress. Growth by annexation has stretched city services dangerously thin; the annexation of the Clear Lake City region, near the Lyndon B. Johnson Space Center, in 1977, added some twenty-five thousand residents, but not a single policeman or fireman. The crime rate soars; the Houston police department was ranked third in the nation by the U. S. Department of Justice in terms of race and community relations. In 1979 the response rate to emergency calls was twenty-six minutes. In 1977 I interviewed a member of the Houston City Council who was the chief attorney for a major manufacturing firm. At that time, all eight Council members were elected by a city-wide vote. He gave his judgment bluntly. "There is no 'urban crisis' in Houston. We have eighteen- or nineteen-million-dollar surpluses in our budget every year."

But this was not a unanimous judgment. I spoke with an engineer who designs petro-chemical plants about the demands that cities must serve. He had an engineer's concept of cities in general, and he included Houston.

You can't force people to live in a neighborhood that is deteriorating. So, they're going to move out, and then you have one of these fringes around the central core. . . . Cities are very complex. You've got all the transportation problems, with a push to the suburbs; and all this assumes that you're going to have to build roads, sewers; and supply water, natural gas, electricity; and you're basically just leaving a core and having somebody else worry about it. And I think the citizenry needs to realize that this is basically their city, and they need to worry about it.

Most cities would be delighted if they could have Houston's "problems." One of those problems is which outlying area to annex next; most cities in the Northeast and Midwest have no chance of increasing the tax base through annexation. Another is simply keeping up: extending city services to the rapidly growing population; it is largely an affluent new population, with the ability to pay for the extended services. Houston vibrates with vital energy, although the vitality is expressed in the private sector. It seemed to me that there were relatively few citizens to "worry about" their city. I modified that opinion after the 1981 election.

The Houston Schools

Although the popular image of Texas is of the Western frontier, Houston is, historically, a Southern city. Public accommodations were integrated peacefully between 1960 and 1965, leaving the "private clubs" (established to circumvent the state prohibition, which lasted until 1971, against selling liquor by the drink) as the centers of segregated social life for the white middle class. Efforts to achieve the racial integration of the public schools began in 1960. It was opposed by a segregationist majority on the school board until 1969; "freedom of choice" was their mode for achieving integration. In 1970 a federal court substituted "zoning, pairing, and student transfers." In that year, 26 per cent of black students attended integrated schools, and 10 per cent of the district's eligible children were in private schools. White flight from integrated school districts was well established.

When I visited Houston in 1977, it was considered newsworthy that Hispanics remained the fastest growing ethnic group among the pupils of the Houston Independent School district. The district was judged the seventh largest in the nation; its 207,000 students were reported to consist of 44 per cent blacks, 22.8 per cent Hispanics, and 33.2 per cent "whites, Asians, and American Indians." The 1977 figures represented a tripling of the Mexican-American school population since the 1950s. The superintendant reported that school facilities were strained in the East End, where the Hispanic population is concentrated; that "moving patterns have stabilized"; and that some white families were moving back into the Montrose and West University districts.

I spoke to the president of one of Houston's leading independent oil exploration firms about American traditions. When he replied that all are summed up in the word "freedom," I asked about equality.

> I think we have maintained the equality end of it. I think on the civil rights issue we have moved too rapidly. I think that there would have been less strain and less abuse and less hard feelings if it had been done gradually. . . . There's just as much animosity in some localities today as ten years ago. And all because they started moving children, putting the blacks in areas where there were solid whites, and moving whites into areas where it was solid blacks. What they should have done was started with the lower grades, with the first grade, put them all together, and moved them up a year at a time. There would never have been any trouble. But the blacks wanted to move too fast, and I think it was a grave mistake. And I think some of them realize that, too.

I do not think that this Guardian was willfully ignorant of the decade of determined resistance that had prevented any orderly plan for the integration of Houston's schools. Like other Houston industrialists, his daily life is filled with concern for projects and properties distributed around the world. He need not look down from his office window upon the slum below.

The few white returnees to the Houston school district of 1977 did not become a flood. Litigation concerning racial segregation in the district continued. In 1980 federal officials proposed a busing plan that would combine the Houston district with suburban districts, carrying students outward from the central core. Theoretically, the distances could be as much as forty miles. The Houston industrialists I conversed with were sincere in their individualism: they see this nation as providing unique opportunity. But Houston economic elites have not taken careful thought about the assurance of equal opportunity in the public schools. A solution imposed by external authority will be resisted as an interference with liberty; but any reasoned discussion of freedom includes the discussion of responsibility.

Political Reform and Houston's Future

The Houston I visited seemed to have absorbed politics into economics. With notable exceptions like Judge Woodrow Seals, the Guardians I interviewed led me to conclude that the economic elite of Houston is remarkably coterminous with the political leadership. Business values certainly dominated the city's legislature. Market forces have determined the city's development: the downtown area contains no green vistas or other pleasant outdoor spaces. The harsh lines of the great air-conditioned office buildings were interspersed only by parking lots and the rubble preceding the construction of the next office building. There were elaborate commercial developments along the freeway loop beyond the downtown. The most impressive is the Galleria, a shopping center with ice-skating rink, restaurants, and boutiques, all under a single roof hung with chandeliers. Civic pride and accomplishment were on view in the Civic Center, with its striking concert hall and the Alley Theater. I thought the attitude of Houston was summed up well by the same engineer who told me that the citizenry should realize that the city is theirs. "I don't begrudge the millionaires their millions. The American idea is based on equal *opportunity;* there's no guarantee of success."

In the storefront office of Frumencio Reyes, a Mexican-American attorney, I heard a similar declaration. Reyes began life as a migratory worker, attended college at night for ten years, and graduated from law school at age thirty-one, hoping to work through the judicial system to improve the lot of his people. (He waved his hand at a stack of files on the desk. "Of course," he said, "if you have ten million dollars worth of cases, you get a million dollars in fees—that's the system.") Reyes believes passionately in the value of education as the provider of equal opportunity. And he feels confident that when the needed education is made available, his people will need no special favors.

We have not had Chicanos or blacks admitted into law school, medical school, graduate schools. We have very few Chicano lawyers proportionate to the population which we represent. We deserve that chance, of having our own. . . . All we need is ten years or twenty years to come up to parity with the rest of our brothers—white, black, yellow, you name it. Once we do that, we are on an equal setting, and then we can take on anything that comes about. . . . If you don't know how the system works, and you're not in there working with the system, and make the system work for you, the system is rotten. And that might call for a disturbance. But if you know how to work within the system, and make the system work for you, or work for the people you represent, then its beautiful.

Reyes told me of a suit based on the 1965 Civil Rights Act which would charge the city of Houston with discrimination because its system of at-large Council districts denied representation to minorities. Only one black had been able to win election through the system, and no other minorities were represented. That suit was eventually successful. The 1980 Council had five at-large members and nine elected by districts. Although regarded as part-time politicians, the Council members were paid $24,000 annually and had a staff of at least two persons each. The districts elected two women, two additional blacks, and the first Chicano in Houston's history, state legislator Ben Reyes, a close friend but no relation of Frumencio Reyes, who explained the impact of the new Council.

> The at-large districts are for the Chamber of Commerce types, they can spend up to $100,000 per campaign to get the prestige. But they don't do a damn thing; just like the at-large districts before, they aren't accountable to anybody. District elections are making a tremendous difference. For the first time, we're getting an accounting of monies spent by district; Ben Reyes's district is getting a new library; there are new sewers and lighting in inner-city neighborhoods that have never had them before. The two black districts are getting funds for projects that have been on the books for ten or fifteen years—they're actually getting *done*. The new Civic Center is a $650 million project that is a joint venture of the three races—Chicanos and blacks as builders and architects, not just as hourly workers; the same is true for the new terminal "C" at the airport. . . . If you wait long enough and keep plugging along, it finally makes a difference.

Frumencio Reyes himself had been appointed to the Housing Authority, which was newly active in the inner city. He reported with pride that two neighborhoods "behind the bayou" were getting concrete retaining walls, after fifteen years of effort. At last there was a chance of containing the annual flood.

Thus, like San Francisco, Houston has remade its system of municipal representation. San Francisco's citizens adopted district elections voluntarily and revoked them voluntarily. Houston bowed to the federal court. Houston's new system will not prove to be a panacea, but it does offer entrance into the city's decision-making process to the underclass who have been frozen out. According to Reyes, gaining access to the political system will be prelude to attaining more equal educational opportunity, with its promise of better jobs. He suggests that middle-class blacks and Chicanos in Houston will be as dedicated to middle-class values, including the work ethic, as the established black middle class of Atlanta.

Hope for the revitalization of Houston's executive branch came with the November, 1981, election of thirty-five-year-old City Controller Kathy Whitmire as mayor. Her predecessor, Jim McConn, was admired as "a nice man," and he had built political bridges to the minority communities, but his administrative skills were negligible. One of McConn's key aides was investigated for extortion, irregularities in tax assessment were uncovered, and his opponents decried poor street maintenance—"potholes" became a rallying cry for the opposition. In the general election, Mayor McConn placed fourth in a field of fifteen candidates. Incumbent McConn was forcefully backed by the Houston establishment; his rejection indicated voter impatience with decaying city conditions. According to a *Houston Post* reporter,

> There are two kinds of Houstonians. The natives and the newcomers. Rightly or wrongly, the natives remember the good old days before the foreigners arrived. The newcomers—again, rightly or wrongly—look longingly at how good things were back home. In comparison, present-day Houston seems an abomination.
> They needed someone to blame, and McConn was the convenient target.

The candidates in the runoff election were Kathy Whitmire and Harris County Sherrif Jack Heard, sixty-three. Embracing fiscal conservatism and promising an administrative reorganization which would bring "business methods" into City Hall, Kathy Whitmire retained a base of white, middle-class support, while her openness to social liberalism won her the bulk of endorsements from black political leaders and significant support from Chicano leaders. Attacks against Whitmire for being female and enjoying the endorsement of the Gay Political Caucus backfired, and she won with 62.4 per cent of the largest vote ever cast in a Houston municipal election.

At the same time, all incumbent Council candidates seeking reelection were returned to office. Mayor McConn was held responsible for

Houston's administrative shortcomings, but the city legislature was not. The future effectiveness of Houston government depended on whether Whitmire's reorganization would make the "strong mayor" strong in fact. In March 1982 Mayor Whitmire appointed Houston's first black police chief—Lee Patrick Brown, the Atlanta public safety commissioner who led the investigation of youth murders. If Kathy Whitmire should succeed in applying principles of business management at City Hall which would increase the city's responsiveness to citizen needs, local nominations and elections might no longer be so dependent upon Houston's business leaders.

Eventually, the tendency of Houston's economics to swallow up its politics may be contained.

Chicago: Mayor Daley's Legacy

Mayor Richard J. Daley's image was established for a generation of young Americans during the 1968 Democratic national convention. Daley's police smashed demonstrators' heads (although with no fatalities), while Daley refused any compromise within the convention itself. While Daley's actions showed his disagreement with the peace movement, they were almost completely irrelevant to an understanding of his achievements and shortcomings as mayor.

When I visited Chicago in the fall of 1977, its political activists were still recovering from the sudden death of Mayor Daley the previous December. Although Michael Bilandic had taken office as mayor, I found that, when people used the phrase "the Mayor," they referred to Daley. To discuss politics in Chicago that fall was to discuss Daley. Yet I looked elsewhere to support my growing comprehension of the man.

According to one sensitive analysis of the mayor's achievements, his work in and for the political organization he led for twenty-one years is the surest guide to his moral character.

> The political values he honored were the right to a livelihood, security, a place to turn if you get into a jam, and a sense of continuity with the past and the future. He felt these values could survive in the city only if they were secured by the apparatus of the strong and territorial institution he led.

What Richard Daley did was to preserve, not quite as in a museum, the last example of the American big-city political organization. Elsewhere, the use of capital-intensive public relations methods—mostly television—which can be hired for the occasion replaced ward and precinct personnel as the channel of communication with voters, just as the impersonal procedures of the city bureaucracy replaced the warm contact with City Hall that the precinct captain claimed. Daley deliberately kept alive the much more expensive, but very human, network through which permanent party personnel ease the delivery of city services and ask only the citizen's vote in return. In the Madisonian measurement of constituency size, this is the ultimate decentralization, for a precinct captain serves, at most, about five hundred voters. But three thousand precinct captains are gathered into fifty ward organizations, with the ward committeeman controlling patronage positions in the structure of city, county, and state government, along with contacts in local private enterprise. Ample rewards are available for the precinct captains who produce the vote. While each committeeman is relatively independent, his connections with city government are reviewed by the mayor, and his partisan success is reviewed by the Cook County Democratic chairman. Both those offices were filled by Richard J. Daley. In Daley's Chicago, nearly every member of the organization felt that he worked under the watchful eye of the mayor, who controlled access to the favors of the city as well as any advancement in the hierarchy of the party. There were many in Daley's Chicago who felt that Daley was in a far better position to discover and implement the civic good than any other mayor in the nation. Chicago was "the city that works."

Chicago worked at a cost. Daley financed the organization out of the process of renewing the city itself; for the organization controlled such matters as zoning, public subsidies, building codes, and the property tax; it also planned new civic buildings and awarded contracts. The Loop was renewed, creating a building boom for the construction workers: union support for Daley. Daley won the use of state taxes to support courts, jails, and welfare, keeping city taxes at a reasonable level, even while downtown property values increased: business support for Daley. Daley maintained peace with the city workers, avoiding the disruptive strikes in rapid transit, police forces, and among service workers that plagued other cities: citizen support for Daley. And Daley kept the budget balanced, making regular payments on the city's debt: banking support for Daley.

There was a major flaw in this long list of civic accomplishments. Mayor Daley did not tackle the big issues. His support for the war in Vietnam was the instinctive support for a Democratic national administration. His passivity before the civil rights movement and his subtle dissociation from the school board's efforts to racially integrate the schools were much more calculated. The traditional base of the organization had been the inner wards near the Chicago River, containing a third of the city's voters. While only two of the inner wards had a black majority at the end of World War II, ten were black by 1963. Cautiously, Daley began to "play to the white audience on racial issues." He turned his organizational powers to the outer, white-majority wards. Without withdrawing support from the inner wards, he channeled resources to the use of the newly appointed ward leaders of the outer city. As white voters moved out from the inner wards, the machine was in place to welcome them. The black vote for organization candidates declined only slightly, and the organization carried the outer wards. At the time of his death, Richard Daley had succeeded in making the machine potentially effective, for the first time in its history, on a city-wide basis.

Mayor Daley and the Guardians

Nobody I talked to in Chicago was neutral on the subject of Mayor Daley. Political activists either admired or despised him, and this attitude was echoed in their opinion of his organization; but nobody expected the machine to change very much. Leon Despres, who served as a "reform" (anti-organization) alderman from 1955 to 1975, was quoted earlier in the chapter, charging that the Daley machine was determined "to keep the lid on blacks." I asked Mr. Despres what changes the death of Mayor Daley might bring.

> You see, the basic fact about this area of the city and the county is that it's run by a very powerful machine that depends on political patronage, and that exists principally for the purpose of making a living off of politics. . . . They were quite well satisfied to have Daley be the party chairman, because he followed their interests, he protected them, he cheerfully tolerated corruption, he kept his own image relatively untainted, and he was able to command the interest as a public figure so that he could be reelected as mayor. When he died, there was no one ready to fulfill this double role of being mayor and party chairman, so they elected another party chairman, of course, and they elected [Michael Bilandic] a caretaker mayor. This mayor is essentially a front for the ward committeemen, for the men who make up the political party. He doesn't have any independent strength, except the legal power of his office, and he doesn't have the desire or taste to use independent strength.

Two convictions lay behind what Leon Despres told me. The first was the traditional Progressive belief that those who serve the city should do so from a sense of duty, rather than the expectation of a financial reward. The second was the sense of profound tragedy concerning the racial situation in Chicago: Mayor Daley's power was great enough to have done something to ameliorate racial conflict, but he chose not to do so; after Daley, no individual would have the authority to direct the organization to any higher purpose, so the chance had been lost.

Others were not so ready to blame Richard Daley for sins of omission. In their pleasant home in Evanston, I interviewed a corporation lawyer and his wife, who, as the alumni representative of her college, interviews prospective students in the Chicago area. When they told me that Chicago had maintained peace during the troubled 1960s, I asked about the charge that Daley had bypassed the race issue. The attorney answered,

> There may be something to that, but I think that if there weren't something more than bypassing, something more affirmative, that he would have had more problems—

His wife interrupted.

> I think he very much bypassed the black people because of sheer power, and the following he had which permitted him to pull strings wherever he wanted to pull them.

Her husband completed the thought.

> He controlled things very tightly, down to the lowest political level. That's going to break down now.

Earlier, this couple told me that only four of Chicago's many high schools truly prepare students for college entrance, and that they chose to remain in Evanston so their children will have contact in the schools with minorities, including the stable and established, "not really low class" black community of Evanston, about 17 per cent of the suburb's population.

Despite acknowledging the problems he was unable to solve, the Chicago Guardians were largely persuaded that Daley's Chicago was indeed the city that worked. I spoke to Pastora San Juan Cafferty, a faculty member of the University of Chicago, who had served three years on a regional transportation commission after her appointment by Mayor Daley. Professor Cafferty told me that, in contrast to Atlanta and Boston, where I found a conviction that the process of decay had been reversed, Chicago had never been as badly threatened.

I think that some of the things that Atlanta and Boston are discovering, we've been doing all along. . . . There's a lot of hard work being done in Chicago to preserve the city, and a lot of commitment to the city by people who live in the suburbs—our bankers, for example. The commitment to the city by the banking interests here is phenomenal. And it goes beyond just underwriting bond issues. It goes into real estate development, and a lot of activity in civic functions. . . . Very high-paid executives actually sit in on committees; they don't send their third vice-president, they go themselves. A lot of that was the mayor, who would get on the 'phone and call you himself. That personal touch—of saying, "You know, I really need you"— does a lot. And I'm not sure that that kind of personalism is true in many other cities. Maybe because of the turnover: its one thing to be mayor for twenty-one years; its another thing to be mayor for three or four years. . . .

There is no public apathy in this town. Everybody's got strong opinions; they care. . . . I know we do not have an alienated city.

In 1979, when a deficit was discovered and Chicago lost its premiere bond rating, the bankers did not prove to be so friendly.

The clearest description of the sources of Richard Daley's influence was given to me in the office of the commissioner for consumer affairs by its then incumbent, Jane Byrne. I asked about problems in the transition from Daley to Bilandic (and promised not to quote her answer).

I think the situation is very poor right now. There's a lot of divisiveness and a lot of backbiting. We had concentrated power before, which in my judgment was good; we had the same [party] chairman, who was [also] the mayor. He was powerful enough, as chairman, and loved enough by the people as mayor, that he could tell people "No." And they knew a "no," no matter how many times they came back, would remain "no." Whereas, today, the chairman is the County Board, and the mayor is the mayor. The mayor [Bilandic] has no political base whatsoever, none. He is not a [ward] committeeman. He is not anything in the party; nothing. So he is, in my judgment, being pushed by a lot of people who are in the party, and I would hate to see it go back to the situation that it was before Mayor Daley took over, where you had the gray wolves of the Council ordering around a weak mayor.

Jane Byrne saw the issue starkly. The structure of the party organization was geographically based. The ward committeemen—and the aldermen—tended to be spokesmen for the status quo, the established local interests, although they presided over the precinct captains, who gave ordinary citizens a sense of access to the power structure. Mayor Daley, elected by the people of Chicago, was the legitimate spokesman of the general civic interest. County Chairman Daley held ultimate power— their placement on the party ticket for endorsement by the party faithful —over the ward committeemen, and a comparable influence over the fortunes of aldermen. By combining these two sources of power, Daley was able to implement his own particular vision of the public good, over the objections of the local and particular interests.

Commissioner Byrne gave me a vivid example of Daley's authority at work.

> One time, on a very hard decision early in the game, there was a lot of pressure going on about a supermarket chain that we were revoking a license on. And, as I said, he [Daley] had his ear to the ground. And I was really getting wet left and right, and I didn't know from whence it was coming. I just thought I was doing my job. And then one day, he said, "Come here." And I said, "What?" And he said, "It's a big piece of the pie. I don't take a cut. I know you don't. Get it in here today. That's it; I'm shutting it off." And that was it; that's how it was. And I never forgot that. And [the idea of] the piece of the pie is something that now you start to see, I think, in many decisions.

Commissioner Byrne said that an ordinance to regulate the conversion of apartment houses along the North Shore into condominiums, which threatened to drive many people from their accustomed homes, was then being delayed because of opposition by real estate interests in league with certain aldermen. She then showed me a picture of her daughter with John Kennedy, explaining that she had done campaign work for Kennedy. When her husband, an aviator, was killed, the Kennedys introduced her to Mayor Daley, who gave her a job, coached her, and eventually made her co-chairman of the Cook County Democratic Committee, and a member of the Democratic National Committee. I had no inkling that Jane Byrne would one day, as mayor, attempt to restore the legacy of Richard J. Daley.

The Troubles of Mayor Byrne

The Cook County Democratic Committee removed Jane Byrne from her post after Mayor Daley's death. When, in 1978, Byrne accused Mayor Bilandic of "greasing" a taxicab rate increase ("a piece of the pie"), Bilandic removed her from her office. She announced her candidacy against Bilandic in the Democratic primary. Bilandic had the support of the party organization and of the city's establishment. That winter, seven feet of snow fell on Chicago, and the city's efforts to remove it—to unclog the streets, free trapped automobiles, and restore normal traffic—became hopelessly tangled. Voters felt that the situation would have been kept in control by Mayor Daley. Byrne won the February, 1979, primary election by 51 per cent, lined up organization support with conciliatory telephone calls, and easily defeated a Republican opponent in the general election.

The troubles began when Mayor Byrne took office. She shares with Daley an Irish upbringing, but her personality is far more volatile. Having learned her politics at the master's side, she was determined to keep the party organization in operation and to utilize it. Since she lacked a party power base, she needed desperately to expand her public support. Whereas Daley delayed action on looming problems, intervening only when invited by the conflicting parties, Mayor Byrne sought public confrontations. City workers' unions had trusted Daley and sealed agreements with a handshake; Byrne promised true collective bargaining during her campaign. The transit workers, already comparatively well paid, went on strike late in 1979; the strike stranded a million commuters. No sooner was that strike settled than city firemen voted to strike. Meanwhile, an emergency loan from the state had to be arranged to prevent the bankruptcy of Chicago's public schools. An unsuspected deficit turned up in the city's budget; some of the cost of operating the machine, hidden by Daley, was uncovered by the accountants.

In 1980 national attention turned to Mayor Byrne's operations in national politics. After a brief flirtation with supporting the reelection of Jimmy Carter, she endorsed the candidacy of Senator Edward Kennedy, brother of the man who brought her into politics. Both Byrne and Kennedy were booed at the Saint Patrick's Day parade. Kennedy lost the primary election in Illinois.

But the machine has little influence over the voter's choice between glamorous candidates for state and national office. The organization is interested in more obscure positions, like ward committeeman and county assessor, the incumbents of which can dispense jobs. A more important challenge to Byrne was the victory for the office of Cook County state attorney of then state Senator Richard Daley, son of the legendary mayor. The younger Daley was perfectly positioned for an election contest with Jane Byrne in 1983.

In 1977 Jane Byrne expressed her fears of "the gray wolves" of the local and particular interest taking control of the city's policy. As mayor, she lacked Daley's command of the organization and could not privately curb the power of the ward leaders. But her dramatic public activities began to seem more effective. In 1981 she moved into a crime-plagued public-housing project, establishing a second city residence, with the full protection of the city police. The neighborhood crime rate declined dramatically, and opponents conceded that she had made a master stroke. If her gesture were followed by real efforts to ameliorate racial conflict, she could begin to repair the most grievous flaw in Daley's record.

Despite the attractions of studying the nation's last Democratic machine in the throes of change, I found in Chicago that the future of cities is hardly in control of local governmental institutions, whatever their design. I learned from other Chicago Guardians something about the power of corporations and the need to formulate larger constituencies.

The Deacons

Norman Ross, vice-president for public affairs of Chicago's First National Bank, described another aspect of Mayor Daley's influence. According to Ross, Daley's authority was often exercised silently.

> It always seemed to me that a good part of the mayor's power lay in the minds of people who would say, "Oh, we shouldn't do that; Mayor Daley wouldn't like it." Well, maybe he didn't even know what they were talking about. They made assumptions [about] what he wanted or didn't want. And he sat there like a Buddha and just nodded, and you ended up by doing all kinds of things or not doing all kinds of things because you perceived—not necessarily on the basis of any concrete evidence—that it was what he would want or wouldn't want.

Norman Ross was an active member of a nonprofit, semi-private organization called Chicago United. Its functions are comparable to those performed in Atlanta by Central Atlanta Progress: to coordinate the efforts of corporations that seek to serve the civic welfare. But there are important differences. Chicago United is not involved in planning construction projects; Chicago United began in the turmoil of the late 1960s, when white economic elites sought to reach out to aid (or at least calm) the black community. Central Atlanta Progress, also made up of white corporate elites, originated long before the 1960s; in 1977 it was consolidating a cautious alliance with Atlanta's black political elite.

The corporate urban affairs directors who serve on the committees of Chicago United have taken the name of "Deacons." The term originated in 1968, when Norman Ross attended a banker's meeting addressed by black activist Jesse Jackson. When Ross identified himself in response to Jackson's query, Jackson replied, "You're just a deacon. I want to talk to power."

Significantly, Chicago United was formed outside the city's political process; its formation was not blessed by Mayor Daley. And the organization was well aware that any of the projects it advanced that would impinge upon the political process would require Daley's blessing, which was not always forthcoming. In one instance, the organization thought it had a promise of two seats on the school board, but Daley did not deliver.

Norman Ross is the grandson of an English whaling captain who married into the Hawaiian royal family and established the largest privately owned ranch on the islands. Ross was raised as an Episcopalean and at one time considered entering the ministry. Having inherited comfortable wealth, Ross was working as a newspaper columnist and radio commentator when the assassination of Martin Luther King (which brought riots and destruction to Chicago) made him want to become personally involved in efforts to reform society, rather than serving merely as an observer. The bank created his position to serve that wish. Although he had known many frustrations, Ross told me that he was participating in one of the most encouraging developments of American capitalism.

> I see a very encouraging development in corporations around the country —people in jobs like mine, public affairs, urban affairs, community affairs, whatever you want to call it—whose job it is not to put on a show for their company outside, not to brag about what their company does, but to act as an early warning system . . . to learn what people are perceiving as their needs and wants, and bring back to your corporation what some of those things are, so that we can take action to meet the legitimate among those needs, to the extent that we are capable of doing so, rather than being surprised when there are eruptions in various communities.

There are limits to what private enterprise can do, as Ross would acknowledge. He quoted an academic friend as saying that half the black preachers he knew were trying to start businesses, and half the white business leaders were trying to save black souls. Each should be left to what he could do best. He reported that Chicago United had taken an interest in Chicago's public schools—businesses are interested in the education of their potential employees—but had been able to accomplish little more than improving the schools' purchasing system. When they expressed an interest in plans for racial integration, business was accused of wanting to run the schools.

While individual firms may engage in enlightened corporate philanthropy, their example need not enlighten their competitors; and philanthropy that consumes profit unreasonably must be abandoned. Ross assured me that his bank had never engaged in redlining—the denial of loans in neighborhoods labeled as decaying—and that he regarded the practice as reprehensible. None of the Guardian bankers I interviewed in six cities reported that their banks engaged in redlining; but all were familiar with competitors who did so. Redlining by banks and insurance companies remains one of the business practices most detrimental to the survival of neighborhoods within large American cities.

The Neighborhoods Go National

In 1972, two thousand persons met in Chicago to found a new organization called the National Training and Information Center, which became the logistical support arm for a group called National People's Action (NPA). Although the group's populist title suggests the widest possible constituency, its slogan, from the beginning, has been "Neighborhoods First." It is an umbrella organization formed to coordinate the national efforts of the many local community organization movements that grew out of the turbulent 1960s. It is headed by Gale Cincotta, a charismatic mother of six.

I visited the group's headquarters in a decayed Chicago neighborhood. There I talked to Ted Wysocki, who dropped out of political science graduate study at the University of Chicago to become the organization's communications director. Among his tasks was to edit a lively monthly tabloid, *Disclosure*, which reports the activities of member organizations in various cities and advertises upcoming activities of National People's Action. National conventions are held at least twice a year. During the 1970s they were usually held in Washington; federal officials were invited for "dialogue" in the knowledge that speeches prepared for interested groups have a way of becoming policy. NPA also organizes demonstrations and confrontations with private business, such as conventions of the the National Bankers Association.

Ted Wysocki explained the "ripple effect" created by the conversion of existing apartments into condominiums along the North Shore. This increase in housing costs for well-to-do Chicagoans, with no increase in the supply of housing, applied pressure downward throughout the housing market, increasing the cost for everyone. Then we discussed the accomplishments of his organization.

The first target of NPA was the trend toward disinvestment by financial institutions in the central cities, of which mortgage redlining was the primary example. Chicago had an ordinance which prohibited the deposit of city or county funds in banks that practiced redlining, but few cities had followed the example. Neighborhood organizers who complained to branch bank managers were told that policies were set in home offices. The practices of state-chartered banks were regulated by state legislatures, with uneven results. National action was required. NPA's efforts on the issue culminated at a national convention in Washington in 1975, which featured testimony by neighborhood activists— "young, old, black and white, from neighborhoods as far east as Providence and as far west as Oakland"—before the Senate Banking Committee. The result was the Home Mortgage Disclosure Act of 1975, which required banks to publish reports of the extent of their loans in urban neighborhoods. Ted Wysocki discussed its impact.

> Once the Disclosure Act was passed, the record started getting better. . . . If they knew they were going to have to make public their record, well they were going to make damn sure that it was going to look better. And we've had bankers who have admitted that, if the law wasn't there, they weren't sure whether they would have improved their record in terms of community loans. . . . But you still have a major national institution, like the First National Bank [of Chicago]; while they may be giving some increasing new loans to the portfolio in the city, they are also at the same time making very speculative loans abroad. If urban loans were bad risks, what kind of loans are they making overseas?

Disclosure began carrying reports of the extent of major banks' overseas investments, with records of their defaults—"the redlining of America." And it turned its attention to insurance companies, which practice redlining by non-renewing policies, and refusing to write new ones, in whole areas bounded by postal zone zip codes. This required confrontations with corporate presidents and demonstrations at stockholders' meetings; but insurance companies did reach agreements with NPA to modify their practices. NPA prepared a "People's Platform: Neighborhoods First" which was forcefully presented to a regional meeting of the Democratic Platform Committee in 1976. The organization watched over the transition from Ford to Carter with impatience. When the Carter administration developed the Urban Development Assistance Grant (UDAG) as a showpiece of urban policy, *Disclosure* chronicled neighborhood dismay in city after city where UDAGs were used to finance the construction of hotels—hotels which displaced housing, and, once complete, supplied only menial jobs for city residents. It monitored the increases in interest rates and the development of "rollover" and "shared appreciation" mortgages. Gale Cincotta and her followers demonstrated at the 1979 convention of the National Bankers Association in New Orleans and at its 1980 convention in Chicago, where the demonstrators were kept well away from the convention hall, apparently on the order of Mayor Jane Byrne. The year's bright spot was the renewal of the Home Mortgage Disclosure Act.

NPA respresentatives attended the 1980 Democratic convention and found it full of empty rhetoric. When Ronald Reagan was inaugurated, *Disclosure* announced that NPA was waiting for the new administration to demonstrate the content behind its slogans, such as "reindustrialization" and "free enterprise zones." The wait lasted only a few months. By the summer of 1981, the organization decided that it could no longer serve urban interests through representations to federal agencies. Under the Reagan administration, the only hope would be to bring urban needs forcefully to the attention of corporations. NPA arranged a summit meeting with the Business Roundtable, an umbrella association of leading corporations. In the language of pluralism, a meeting was arranged between peak organizations representing corporate power and neighborhood need. NPA announced its strategy change:

> For NPA and its local affiliates, the era of public assistance, no matter how well justified, is over, period. Maybe, according to some, the era of the Great Society, with its social and economic programs, was really more of a methadone for the symptoms than a cure for the causes of urban decay. Either way, the responsibility for urban revitalization . . . now lies with the corporate sector.

The initial June meeting took place only after NPA organized a mass demonstration at the Business Roundtable's Washington headquarters in April. Its main result was that members of the Business Roundtable directorate agreed to arrange contacts between member corporations and NPA neighborhood affiliates seeking corporate assistance in the realms of fuel assistance and weatherization, job training, and neighborhood reinvestment.

The Cities and Reagan's "New Federalism"

When he visited the America of Andrew Jackson, Count Alexis de Tocqueville described individualism as the force that could erode the fabric of democratic society. He also described those American institutions that ameliorate the effects of individualism. Among them was local self-government, particularly as practiced in the New England township.

> The Americans have combated by free institutions the tendency of equality to keep men asunder, and they have subdued it. . . . It is difficult to draw a man out of his own circle to interest him in the destiny of the state, because he does not clearly understand what influence the destiny of the state can have upon his own lot. But if it be proposed to make a road cross the end of his estate, he will see at a glance that there is a connection between this small public affair and his greatest private affairs; he will discover, without its being shown him, the close tie which unites private to general interest.

The closest contemporary event to the one Tocqueville describes would be the construction of a freeway in a city neighborhood. The threat of further freeway construction stimulated the neighborhood organization movement in Atlanta; and the abrupt end in mid-air of San Francisco's Embarcadero Freeway is a monument to the awakening of the civic aesthetic sense. Although the American political landscape has changed dramatically since Tocqueville wrote, and New England has substituted representative gatherings for meetings of all town residents, I wondered if it could still be true that involvement in local government leads citizens away from a concentration on self-interest and accustoms them to seeking the public good.

The answer was clear in Chicago. Involvement in community politics enlarges the mind and spirit of an impoverished Ted Wysocki, as well as a millionaire like Norman Ross; local politics can have a kind of liberating impact upon its practitioners. The quest for power—power to serve a good cause—casts its mystic spell for a Jane Byrne.

However, most persons who work in and for cities, from street sweepers and policemen to city councilmen, do not do so for spiritual improvement. They expect pay; and if their compensation is not increased automatically, they are bound to seek an increase through any available means. In the last decade and a half, unionized city workers have discovered their unequal advantage in collective bargaining: employees and their families constitute such a substantial voting block within the city that they can threaten city officials who do not grant union demands with retribution at the polls. Because of his total control of the party organization, Mayor Daley was immune to such threats; Jane Byrne has not established such immunity. This is hardly to argue that Daley's machine was the champion of the civic good. Local politics is the same as self-interest for Chicago's ward leaders, who make a living from it. And their income comes from advancing the cause of established local interests.

In San Francisco the voters would not tolerate the minor corruption that supports the machine in Chicago; yet San Francisco voters are not willing to pay a decent salary to neighborhood representatives.

Although their areas are much smaller, technological advance coupled with economic and ethnic diversity make large American cities—a New York or a Chicago—comparable, as entities embodying the eternal problems of human governance, to the thirteen states of 1787. Chicago's experience affirms the argument Madison made in the pages of *The Federalist*. The larger the constituency that is served by a responsible political institution, the more certain is the public good to be defined and accomplished. The machine under Mayor Daley had the potential for that accomplishment, since Daley centralized in his person the representative and administrative functions of the entire city. The smaller the constituency, the more certain are established, narrow interests to prevail; this was the tendency of ward politics, over which Daley had an effective veto power.

Although a Chicago may be compared with the thirteen states of 1787 as political systems, contemporary Chicago is but a small part of the national economic structure. This reality limits the scope of action of Chicago or any other city. Ultimately, Daley's Chicago worked because the county and state shared with city taxpayers the costs of its operation.

Cities cannot control their own destinies. They are the focal point of many conflicting forces—social, economic, ideological, constitutional, even meteorological—that are beyond their ability to comprehend, much less influence. To cite one example, the movement to convert apartments into condominiums, which increases housing costs while keeping the supply constant, was inspired by the Tax Reform Act of 1969, which limited the use of "fast depreciation" methods by the owners of newly constructed rental units. Congress did not intend thereby to exacerbate the urban housing problem, but that was the result.

Neither cities nor states dare provide too many costly services for their destitute residents, nor demand too many taxes for any other purpose. Businesses and individuals are free to seek their fortunes in political jurisdictions with less burdensome taxation. Madison's argument for the efficacy of the large constituency in the extended republic was a political argument; the modern economic argument is equally compelling. Ours is a single national economy: its regulation for the public good can be conducted only on a national basis.

Lyndon Johnson's War on Poverty legislation attempted to alleviate the inequities produced by the social and economic systems on the basis of theories about local participation and social change which were not national in scope. The programs it established soon became the preserves of narrowly based bureaucracies responsive to specialized clienteles, and the beneficiaries of those programs were quickly perceived as being ouside the individualist ethic—getting unearned benefits—and thus the proper targets of resentment.

The answer to the problem of unelected officials managing governmental programs with narrow constituencies is not found in an expansion of the electoral process. Ample state experience in the election of subsidiary officials demonstrates the folly of burdening the electorate with additional choices while establishing bureaucracies headed by independently elected chiefs. The problem lies in the narrowness of the constituencies represented by administrative agencies. The Reagan administration draws upon this argument to defend its determination to condense the categorical grants now made to cities and other specific governmental agencies into block grants which will be awarded to states. The states in turn are to allocate resources within the broad categories of health, education, emergency, and social and community services. Congressmen and mayors with experience of state legislatures argue that real needs will be ignored by the states. At a hearing of the House Manpower and Housing Subcommittee, Budget Director David Stockman was told by Congressman Harold Washington of Illinois that the block grant procedure would lead to urban disaster. "The cities are going to blow up on us," Washington charged.

Stockman responded,

As of 1981, I don't believe a case can be sustained that we of the federal government have it all over the states. Those who serve here and those who serve there are elected by the same people. . . . We are going to have to stop accommodating the literally hundreds of groups at the local level who want their special pipeline to Washington.

The concept of a "special pipeline" is precisely the phenomenon of the government agency operating in cooperation with a narrow clientele, outside of public view and immune from responsibility to the electorate. Any number of such relationships could be described. One which the Reagan administration determined to abolish was the federal funding of organizations providing legal aid to the poor. The amount of tax money spent on such aid (which arguably serves the ideal of making all citizens, regardless of wealth, equal in their access to the legal system) is insignificant compared to the budgetary sums provided for the procurement of new military hardware by the Reagan administration. Yet Pentagon practices in the procurement of weapons systems provide a stellar example of the government agency operating in cooperation with a few private firms, well outside the public view. One man's pipeline is another's safeguard for the national security.

Budget Director Stockman's assertion that the states ought to be as competent as the national government to allocate resources gathered through federal taxes denies the wisdom of Madison's belief that the public good is most likely to be served in the extended republic. Mayors who feared that cities would be shortchanged in the allocation of support funds by the states based their fears upon experience; the smaller the constituency, the more likely are established interests to dominate the substance of policy. The wholesale award of federal revenues to states in the form of black grants would encourage the formation of cozy relationships between narrow interests and state legislators and agencies. Such relationships currently existing, contrary to the public interest, would become newly powerful when reinforced with federal funds.

Because of the constitutional requirement for districts of equal population, rural and suburban legislators outvote city representatives in most state legislatures. But there is a "city interest" which is regional or national in scope, independent of state boundaries. Most big-city mayors, particularly in the Northeast, would argue that the preservation of their cities against the market forces that threaten to denude them of industry and managerial talent is a task central to the public good.

An opportunity was given the Reagan administration that had been denied its predecessors; but the opportunity has been missed. That opportunity was to take stock of the relationships between the levels of government that constitute American federalism; to determine which governments are most competent to perform particular functions; and to match funding and democratic responsibility with the level of government where that particular competence lies. This implies assuring that, in the performance of their assigned reponsibilites, governments below the national level will function as somewhat smaller inclusive republics.

The legacy of the New Deal, and particularly of the 1960s reform legislation, is a federal relationship that is increasingly confused. A straightforward theory of federalism is stated in the Constitution's tenth amendment—powers not delegated to the United States, nor prohibited to the states, are reserved to the states, or to the people. The involvement of federal agencies in the traditional functions of state and local government, and the financing of local activities by federal grants, have made a shambles of that theory. In the famous metaphor of Morton Grodzins, American federalism is no longer like a layer cake, with each level of government making its own decisions (and each capable of culinary integrity). Rather, it is like a marble cake, with the tendrils of federal influence reaching throughout the batter. Decisions concerning a particular purpose or function of government are made at all levels of government. Federal, state, and local agencies perform overlapping functions, often with contradictory intentions.

President Reagan's proposal for a "New Federalism" is an attempt to restore the tenth amendment's theory of federalism without considering the two problems of determining competence and assuring responsibility. Nobody can argue for the continuing cozy relationships between government agencies and narrow interests summarized in the phrase, "a special pipeline to Washington." But the proposed trade-off between Washington assuming responsibility for medical care for the elderly, while the states acquire total responsibility for welfare, is a betrayal of Madison's principle of the extended republic. The national government would assume a program that, despite its financial troubles, has a numerous and vocal clientele. The most vulnerable clients—dependent children—would be assigned to the mercies of state political systems. Yet the parents of those dependent children are employed, or locked into minimal jobs, because of the operation of the national economic system. Transfer payments made to the poor are an important element of the national economy, and their adjustment constitutes regulation of that economy. When Reagan's proposal becomes fully implemented, states offering humane support for poor families would endanger their solvency by attracting the poor from less charitable states and driving taxpaying individuals and corporations beyond their borders. Ours is a single economy, and there are no legal restrictions upon movement within it.

The title "New Federalism" was originally attached to a proposal developed by then White House aide Daniel P. Moynihan and presented by Richard Nixon in 1969. Its purposes were to nationalize the welfare system, establish a uniform minimum level of support, and assure continued incentives for the working poor to work ever harder. In return for accepting the nationalization of welfare, the proposal offered revenue sharing to the states. Congress passed revenue sharing but defeated the Family Assistance Plan. The intention of Reagan's New Federalism is precisely the opposite of the Nixon proposal of the same name. Rather than dealing with poverty as a national problem, Reagan's proposal removes poverty from the national agenda.

Reagan's proposed New Federalism, together with the other administration efforts to decentralize the administration and finance of social programs, constitute the abandonment of the cities to forces they cannot withstand. Guardians in both Chicago and Boston expressed their fears for the future of the Snowbelt cities. Unless some federal policy is developed to rescue the older cities of the Northeast—to renew their industries and catch up on the deferred maintenance of their urban infrastructures—the same forces that have so far drawn industries and the middle classes to the suburbs will draw them away from the region entirely. Yet in Houston a bank economist assured me that rising energy prices would make the Eastern cities, with their developed public transportation systems, newly viable.

> I think that this country has got such tremendous investments in the infrastructures of its Northern cities that it can't afford to walk away from them. As energy becomes more and more expensive . . . I think we may very well see a movement back to the big cities that have the transportation that works in place.

The nation can ill afford, he said, to finance rapid transit systems for Houston and Dallas and Phoenix and Los Angeles. Realities of this kind were not recognized in the Reagan campaign, nor have they been addressed by the Reagan administration. Their orderly consideration could lead to a proposed national urban policy based upon the assets and needs of different regions. Such a policy could be instituted only in response to the broadest national constituency, following the lead of a president and a political party. Partisan leadership alone can set an agenda that formulates a national constituency for a particular policy; it is the only process that sustains a search for the public good.

CHAPTER FIVE

Recognizing Limits:
The Environment and
International Influence

If we are to be one nation in any respect, it clearly ought to be in respect to other nations.

—*James Madison, 1788*

My journey to six cities sought persons who are the contemporary equivalent of Madison's "wise patriots," those properly charged with adapting our laws and institutions to social change. One does not locate patriots by asking people to accept or reject the label; the word has an archaic sound for some; others would find the label embarrassing, since it has found its most frequent recent usage in the harangues of the far Right. One of the thirty statements I posed did seek a summary judgment, and that judgment was nearly unanimous. All but six of the persons performing the card-sort exercise agreed with the statement, "America is among the most successful societies of all human history."

This fact must be considered in light of the widespread Guardian belief that government is no longer trusted. If America has been historically successful, but the government's legitimacy is now in question, how is that past success explained, and does it provide future guidelines? At issue is whether political influentials regard American history as a kind of evolutionary process—a clear road from which we have recently detoured, but a path that can be regained—or whether contemporary problems are seen as unprecedented, requiring solutions that the past may not suggest.

I argue in this chapter that there has been a conscious or unconscious assumption of omnipotence, and thus of infinite possibilities, in two related areas—natural resources and international relations. In both areas, a sense of the finite reality is only now dawning. I found the Guardians unified on a few of these issues, and in advance of public opinion; on other issues, they were divided. When the Guardians are unable to agree on policies that accept the nature of these limitations, one can hardly expect an incumbent conservative administration to do so.

The Tradition of Abundance

In 1829 Count Alexis de Tocqueville visited the United States. In a first attempt to formulate his impressions of this vast land, Tocqueville wrote to his friend Chabrol,

> America finds itself, for the present, in a physical situation so happy that the interest of the individual is never opposed to the interest of the whole. . . . The whole world here seems a malleable substance that man turns and fashions to his pleasure; an immense field, whose smallest part only has yet been traversed, is here open to industry. Not a man but may reasonably hope to gain the comforts of life; not one who does not know that with love of work his future is certain.
>
> Thus, in this happy country nothing draws the restless human spirit toward political passions; everything, on the other hand, draws it toward an activity that has nothing dangerous for the state. . . . Nothing is easier than to enrich oneself in America.

Tocqueville wrote at the beginning of the flamboyant Western expansion and development that characterized the nineteenth century. His initial insight, that the American success story depended in large measure upon the abundance of natural resources, did not become a major theme of Tocqueville's *Democracy in America*, although natural abundance undergirded the restless enterprise and equality of social relations which Tocqueville found the most striking aspects of the society. If, as Tocqueville suggests, natural abundance makes American individualism possible, a major national challenge will be to adapt individualist values to the reality of limited resources.

The Guardians generally credited American success to institutions

and traditions—individualism, the Constitution, or free economic enterprise. The single exception was the vice-president of a management
consultant firm with headquarters on highway 128 outside Boston.

> I don't think we have achieved what we have solely or even principally
> because of intellectual, physical, and moral superiority. I think we just had
> the good luck to be dumped into a relatively unexploited piece of territory
> that had extraordinary natural resources and natural advantages. On the
> other hand, we have taken advantage of it, and done something significant
> with it. So we deserve I think some credit for having taken advantage of an
> opportunity, but we can't claim credit for having created the opportunity.
> If you transported the population of the USA to India, and you transported
> three hundred million Indians to the USA today, I don't think we'd do very
> well in India. I think we'd starve just like the Indians are starving.

The presence of seemingly inexhaustible natural resources, coupled
with the ability to exploit them, has been central to the American
consciousness. Abundance resulted from the application of technology
to the environment. The interaction between the experience and the
expectation of abundance shaped the American character. The confidence that, in Tocqueville's phrase, "with love of work his future is
certain" gave hope to the man of modest means and turned his attention
to self-advancement, rather than collective political action. The reality
of abundance meant that those at the top of the economic order could
yield a share to those below, without losing much of their own. Thus,
as already noted, the inherent conflict between the ideals of liberty and
equality could be overlooked. In the words of historian David Potter,
"democracy paced the growth of our abundance, and abundance broadened the base of our democracy."

The Recognition of Limits

Those who have experienced the growth of the environmentalist
movement in the last decade and a half may assume that exploitative
capitalism held sway unchallenged before the first Friends of the Earth
gathered to plan resistance. Actually, John Wesley Powell proposed the
conservation of the forest lands as early as 1878, and attempts to conserve or preserve nature's bounty began a generation later, with the
efforts of the Progressives. Conservation was obscured by the total involvement of the two world wars, and it was a minor theme of the New

Deal, compared to the search for economic recovery. But the environmental movement was revived in the 1960s. It achieved dramatic public support when Americans landed on the moon and looked back at the beautiful and vulnerable Spaceship Earth.

The political influentials I conversed with are aware of environmental problems and of the energy crunch. When, at the beginning of the initial interviews, I asked them to name the most important issues facing the nation, 40 per cent mentioned energy and environmental issues; but the realization that resources are finite and growth has limits is a recent addition to the American consciousness, and it has not replaced attitudes established earlier.

The recognition of the globe's status as an ecosystem came at the same time that American importation of raw materials reached unprecedented heights. The presumption of inexhaustible natural resources became clearly untenable. The federal government added the protection of the environment to its list of responsibilities, and organizations were founded that approached the task of environmental preservation with the fervor of a newly found faith. Before long, these organizations were charged with desiring principally to "protect the playgrounds of the rich," of seeking to preserve the status quo by denying to the economically disadvantaged a share in America's historic abundance. Resentment was strongest in the Western states, which saw Congress as usurping local control over the development of resources. Malcolm Wallop, Republican senator from Wyoming, complained that the Easterners lack understanding.

> People don't understand the scale of the West. Their conceptions are colored by photos of the Grand Tetons taken from far off. They think of the Rocky Mountains as being about the same size as [New York City's] Central Park, and they assume that the Rockies are manicured and cared for in exactly the same way.

Similar resentments have been expressed by Interior Secretary James Watt, who formerly served the forces seeking development of the public lands as head of a Colorado legal organization. Watt claims that Westerners have suffered through drought and blizzard to maintain the stewardship of their lands; Washington should not direct the disposition of those lands. But Watt's principle was contradicted when he insisted on leasing oil drilling rights off the California coast, despite the outraged and bipartisan protests of Californians.

President Jimmy Carter sought to utilize some of the environmentalists' moral fervor when he proposed conservation measures intended to achieve energy independence. Because of the need to sacrifice achieved standards of comfort, he labeled this response to the energy crisis the "moral equivalent of war." And his initial energy proposals were profoundly influenced by those who would emphasize conservation in place of increased energy production and economic growth. When President Carter's initial energy proposals were the subject of heated public debate, Indiana Senator Richard Lugar discussed the failure of Carter's clarion call to win converts to the conservationist cause.

> The question is not often raised at this point, but ought to be: there are a lot of people who are opposed to growth, not on the basis that they believe we would run out of resources, but simply because, as a matter of lifestyle, they like smaller cars, smaller houses; they would rather live in cities than in suburbs; they have different lifestyles that they would like to impose upon other people. . . . They claim that the pursuit of growth is likely to have environmental hazards. . . . I'm not suggesting that we shouldn't be thoughtful about that, but I think often the environmental issue is raised more because they believe that a lot of Americans are overly indulged, spoiled, wasteful, and they would like to see them disciplined by the state, if possible, because they don't feel the marketplace will do it rapidly enough or thoroughly enough.

In this conception, environmentalists would optimize the freedom to enjoy their own preferred lifestyles, at the expense of the liberty of others and of opportunity for all. The conflict between values was stated in very concrete terms by respondents in Houston. I spoke to leaders of the oil industry who are involved on a daily basis with the contest between environmental protection and the race for energy production. Among the most thoughtful was Robert Herring, president of the Houston Natural Gas Co., a multinational corporation with petroleum, coal, and related interests.

> To say that we've got to raise the capital in this country and charge the American people for the use of the capital to go back and rebuild everything we've ever built, and at the same time try to build new job-creating programs and serve the needs of the country, is ridiculous. The American people can't pay this price. . . . What we need—I've been preaching this to every senator and congressman I can get ahold of—is a grandfather clause that says that everything built up to this date, unless it violates the most extreme standards of environmental protection, will be left alone. But from this point on, we'll build with the cleanest technology available. For example, in Illinois the other day, I saw this little power plant that originally cost $89 million. The scrubber

that the EPA [Environmental Protection Agency] has demanded be built—now, this plant has a remaining life of about eleven years on its depreciation schedule—the scrubber's cost is $241 million. The scrubber's no good without the plant. So you've got to amortize the whole damn thing in an eleven year span, and expect the consumer to pay the electric rates that will have to come out of that. . . . It's wonderful to clean up the air and clean up the water, but it must be at a pace that American industry can stand and still meet the needs of the country, and that the American people can afford to pay for.

In this case, the investment to install equipment that would eliminate pollutants from the smokestack of the power plant would be nearly triple the original cost of the entire plant. Environmental protection involves trade-offs between values—a clean environment versus the costs of that cleansing, the maintenance of achieved comfort for some versus the provision of new opportunities for others. Not surprisingly, the persons I talked to were divided on these matters. When I posed the statement, "Groups like the Sierra Club exaggerate the threat to nature," 38 per cent agreed, 54 per cent disagreed, and 8 per cent were neutral or undecided. The reactions to this statement were very similar to the responses to a statement about the presumed error of President Carter's initial energy proposal in emphasizing conservation rather than production. The latter statement elicited 39 per cent agreement and 48 per cent disagreement, with 13 per cent undecided.

The occupational difference in these attitudes is striking. Practicing attorneys (mainly corporation lawyers) see justice in the claims of the environmentalists which the businesspersons and industrialists do not credit. This difference has a partial explanation. The industrialists include a large component of Houston oilmen, while the corporate lawyers are predominantly from Chicago, Boston, Washington, and Atlanta. With one exception, I did not interview the attorneys who represent the Houston industrialists I talked with. But the general point holds good. When values, as well as interests, are in conflict, extraordinary political exertions are required to define and sustain a vision of the public good. The Environmental Protection Agency was launched with such an enthusiastic fanfare that environmentalists could feel secure in their victory. By 1980 it was regarded by business as only another intrusive bureaucracy. In 1981 President Reagan appointed Anne Gorsuch of Colorado as its head. She was regarded as a caretaker to supervise the winding down of the agency and its concerns. Early in 1981 she accepted an 18 per cent cut in the agency's budget; in November, however, she resisted further cuts.

Energy and the Fragmentation of Politics

When a president, with the backing of his party, defines the public good in relation to a particular issue, an agenda for public debate is set, and the contending forces in that debate include, in their strategic planning, an assessment of the likely force of presidential and partisan positions upon general public opinion. The presidential definition sets a bench mark against which the claims of special interests may be measured by all participants in the policy process. In the absence of a firm presidential definition, the debate is dominated by whichever participants shout the loudest. Usually it is impossible to distinguish one shout from another in the cacophony of lobbyists, Congressional committees, and government agencies. Varied interests attempt to enlist public opinion to support their own positions. Government agencies assert their authority over one or another aspect of the issue, seeking to expand their own authority while repelling the assaults of competing agencies upon their jurisdictions. Congressional maneuvers become so complex that interested members of the public can hardly follow developments. Politics becomes fragmented; the actors in a fragmented politics cannot be held accountable by the electorate, or anyone else, for the results of their actions. The much discussed "energy crisis" has been such an issue. Its sorry history presents a picture of interest-group liberalism run amuck. And, since domestic energy policy is profoundly influenced by, even as it influences, foreign relations, the fragmentation of the political process assures that James Madison's simple maxim at the head of this chapter is violated. We are not one nation in respect to other nations.

Frustrated by the outcome of the Yom Kippur war of October, 1973, Arab states that were members of the Organization of Petroleum Exporting Countries (OPEC) imposed an embargo on oil shipments and quadrupled the price of crude oil when the shipments resumed.

After a period of stalemate between Secretary of State Kissinger and Secretary of the Treasury William Simon, Richard Nixon proclaimed his response under the title "Project Independence." The term *energy crisis* was itself a very important part of the package, implying that we were suddenly at that point in the history of our body politic where we would either get well or die. . . . [D]espite all the hullabaloo in President Nixon's response, the administration was unable to put together an energy package until 1975, and then Congress changed the bill in several important particulars in the process of passing it. Consequently, we not only failed to gain independence but also failed to achieve any noticeable conservation of energy or expansion of domestic production.

President Gerald Ford was determined to lessen American dependence upon foreign oil and felt that the price mechanism was the best means. He proposed the deregulation of prices for domestically produced oil and a high tax on gasoline to limit consumption. The Democratic Congress rejected these proposals, in the name of shielding the poor from high petroleum costs, but imposed a fuel-consumption efficiency requirement upon automobile manufacturers. Assured that gas prices would be held down, the public indulged in a three year orgy (1976–1979) of buying full-sized cars and disdained Detroit's compact and even "down-sized" models. Increasingly, the earlier shortage of fuel was blamed on the oil companies, not the Arabs or the Persians. The chance for orderly adjustment to the realities of the world energy market was lost.

President Carter failed to develop a coherent program in advance of his campaign and inauguration; a number of activists from the ecology movement were appointed to relevant federal posts; their energy proposals predictably emphasized conservation over production, but the retention of price controls prevented use of the price mechanism as a means of conservation, while inhibiting domestic production. Carter's campaign had done nothing toward establishing the public support for energy conservation that could counterbalance the outraged response of special interests. This outrage easily submerged any latent concept of the public good.

The process of developing policy to achieve energy independence involved eleven Congressional committees or subcommittees, eight cabinet departments, and four independent regulatory agencies. President Carter's wish to consolidate all such efforts in a single Department of Energy (DOE) is understandable. But the creation of a new department did not change political realities; the same divisions existed within it, and environmentalists complained that the functions transferred from the Department of the Interior to DOE received less sympathetic attention.

In his 1976 campaign, Jimmy Carter promised the deregulation of natural gas; he withdrew from that promise after inauguration, enraging the petroleum industry, which Carter apparently felt was a fine enemy.

In October of 1977, he described the oil companies as executing "the biggest ripoff in history." By March, 1978, Carter felt that a phased deregulation of natural gas prices was necessary to create production stimulus, but its chances in the Senate were so slim that the White House, in a reversal of the textbook pattern, entertained bankers and the executives of gas-consuming industries to persuade them in turn to pressure senators to pass the bill. Then, in 1979, Carter adopted the program of "conservation by price" that had been proposed by Gerald Ford but rejected by Congress, deregulating oil prices, but imposing a windfall profits tax upon oil producers. Finally, by 1980, a gas rationing plan was on standby, a synthetic fuels program was authorized (which would provide federal subsidies for already wealthy corporations), and higher gasoline prices were indeed stimulating conservation, while Detroit began to produce the small cars it had previously been unable to market.

The inception of the energy "crisis" found American government entrenched in its usual habits: intervening piecemeal in the operations of private industry, often in response to industry's wishes, with no ability seriously to coordinate the efforts of diverse governmental agencies. Along with Presidents Ford and Carter, Congress failed to confront the issue through the formulation of a single, consistent vision of what the public interest requires in the form of energy policy.

The strongest Guardian statement against the Carter administration's attempts to emphasize conservation came from a bank economist in Houston.

> If you take an economy and you direct it toward conservation, I think you do something to the inventiveness and the excitement of doing business. If what you do is you give them incentives to go out and find new forms of energy or to develop new sources for oil and natural gas, you create an atmosphere in the economy that will get you to the same place as far as energy savings or cutting down on your oil imports. But you create a robust and moving economy, and a sense of moving ahead rather than a sense of trying to stop where you are—that's kind of a zero-growth economy. I wouldn't want to live in that kind of world.

This statement foreshadowed Republican praises of free enterprise sung during the 1980 presidential campaign. Energy policies resulted naturally from Reagan's ideology: the restoration of market forces through the deregulation of energy prices and the easing of controls upon environmental damage, along with stimulants to investment.

Marching under the banner of Adam Smith, the administration promised to restore the profit motive as the energizer of the public welfare;
several of its members seemed to regard the profit motive as meriting
restoration for its own sake. This was the corollary, in economics, to the
politician's attachment to Madisonian checks and balances, forgetting
Madison's specification of the public good as the purpose of institutions
and policies. As a moral philosopher, Adam Smith had recommended
unfettered free trade as a means to the end of achieving general human
welfare. If experience shows that the means fails to achieve its end, one
would suppose that Smith would be among the first to abandon it.

In the modern world, market forces do not inevitably yield results that
are socially acceptable. The deregulation of energy prices brings huge
profits to the sunbelt states, which produce energy. Those increased
prices are largely paid by the Northeast, which consumes energy to keep
warm when the snow falls. Accelerated depreciation schedules for new
industrial construction, coupled with greater defense spending, encourage industrial development in the Southwest, further draining capital
and competent personnel away from the established cities of the Northeast. This leaves the nation with a double burden: to care for those left
behind in the decaying cities, and to finance the construction of urban
infrastructures to support burgeoning growth in the sunbelt.

Planning, Corporations, and the National Purpose

James Madison was very clear in his understanding that the definition
and achievement of the public good were the great purposes of government. Analytically, two steps are involved: definition and accomplishment. The first may be primarily a political matter; the second an
administrative one. It may be more clear to us than it was to Madison
that the two steps are inevitably linked and that the institutions and
procedures involved in each step influence, if they do not actually determine, the other. Modern presidents have found that, even if a unified
vision of the national purpose (or public good) could be achieved, it
could not be implemented throughout the sprawling bureaucracy.

When market forces in contemporary economies have proven unable
to produce a socially acceptable adjustment, governments have turned
to one form or another of national planning. Yet imperial planning in

the form of English mercantilism helped stimulate the American colonies' revolt; the suspicion of government as the principal threat to liberty in economic as well as social affairs is central to our tradition. The earliest modern attempts at national planning were undertaken by socialist governments, and the concept is still associated with socialism, despite national planning by as capitalistic a nation as France was before electing socialist President François Mitterrand in 1981. In times of economic crisis or military threat, the United States has gingerly approached the planning concept, adopted those portions of it which seem appropriate to the emergency, and discovered that the results are inadequate. Invoking the anti-government tradition, opponents of the planning concept then announce that experience has again demonstrated its failure.

The first New Deal attempt at comprehensive national planning was the National Recovery Administration. Although it attempted to coordinate the production of five hundred industries, the NRA made no provision for economic expansion or for manpower policy. Its inadequacy was demonstrated even before its unconstitutionality was determined. In the later New Deal, President Roosevelt's instinctual preference for coordinated and comprehensive policy gave way to the pattern of partial planning, piecemeal government intervention, and fragmented authority characteristic of interest-group liberalism.

Price controls inhibited inflation during World War II, while miracles of production (and waste) were accomplished, along with an increased living standard at home. But neither manpower nor incomes policies were effectively determined. Fears of a postwar recession stimulated careful thought about true national economic planning, but the postwar boom calmed such fears, and the only significant result of the eventual Employment Act of 1946 was the creation of the President's Council of Economic Advisers.

Harry Truman's attention was absorbed by foreign affairs, and Dwight Eisenhower's administration soon abandoned any notion of dismantling New Deal structures. John Kennedy found that the White House, on its own, could not inject the energy needed to "get America moving." Lyndon Johnson utilized national shock at Kennedy's assassination to pass the Great Society legislation, which sought economic and social equality well beyond the New Deal's emphasis on equal opportunity. But Johnson saw his well-intentioned programs founder on the rock of implementation. Richard Nixon attempted to make the bureaucracy responsive to White House control, but lacked the moral vision that could have given direction to that control. His example stimulated dedication in his helpers, but it did not develop judgment, or even respect for the law.

Jimmy Carter claimed the possession of a moral vision in his 1976 election campaign; but the vision was essentially private, so it little influenced his public conduct after his inauguration. As an outsider, he promised to bring the bureaucracy to heel. He established two new cabinet departments. He approached each policy question as an engineer confronting a new design, unable to make the connections between problems and policies that could eventuate in an overarching concept of the public good. He increased the size of the staff intended to maintain liaison with Congress, but communicated little with that staff. His most trusted White House aides had helped him win election but were relatively innocent of the skills required for governing. Carter's chief counsel, Lloyd Cutler, complained that the presidential task has been rendered impossible by the Madisonian separation of powers; indeed, the "imperial presidency" of Johnson and Nixon, with its potential for both good and evil, lay in shambles.

From this hasty historical account, it should be clear that the cautious approaches of the American government toward the concept of national planning, and its hasty retreats, have left an ambiguous legacy. That ambiguity was reflected by the persons I interviewed. Nearly all pointed out that the phrase "national planning" raises a spectre of socialism within the business community which renders its serious discussion difficult. Whether or not the respondent favored national planning varied according to his or her occupation.

A clear example of the impact of occupation on attitudes toward planning was supplied by a divisional director of the World Bank. He told me that the existence of a national plan was a prerequisite for discussions with the governments of lesser developed nations; he is aware of the possibilities and limitations of the process. He added that the United States has so far been able to tolerate the "slippage" that results from the belated adjustments of the market system, but that day may be drawing to a close. While planning is a fact of life in the rest of the world, he said, the American government fails to plan comprehensively because the political system is sensitive to the political pressures for piecemeal intervention. The result is governmental activity that is uncoordinated and often contradictory.

Several respondents had experiences with urban planners that colored their attitude toward the possibility of national planning. One of these was Thomas Wagner, an attorney then serving as administrative assistant to Senator Adlai Stevenson of Illinois.

> I share some of the reservations others have about planners getting too much control. Because they become fascinated with their own plans, and sometimes they're oblivious to political reality and unwilling to bend and compromise the way they should. . . . We don't have to set up as elaborate a mechanism as is sometimes suggested. We get bogged down oftentimes just setting up that mechanism, and never get beyond that. So planners produce plans that nobody ever takes a damn look at. And, if you see that at the local level, I think you'd see it even more so at the federal level.

If I asked about "indicative planning," or "goal setting," or "centralized forecasting," the respondents were favorably inclined. The respondent bearing the greatest responsibilities in the area was W. Michael Blumenthal, then the secretary of the treasury. I sat on a Chippendale sofa beneath an oil portrait of Alexander Hamilton while the secretary delivered an answer that was in keeping with Hamilton's conviction that government practices should reinforce the endeavors of private business.

> Planning's a dirty word. All businesses do it; in fact, no respectable company worth its salt would be without a three-year plan, or a five-year plan, or a financial plan, or a business plan. But business-government planning is somehow equated in the minds of many businessmen as socialism. I've never thought that that's the case; it depends on what kind of planning you do. . . . To set some targets, to think through—as we're beginning to do in a kind of informal way; you know, what resources you have available, what the priorities are and what you want to allocate them to, and how you use the tax system, and how you use other methods or incentives in order to maximize your chances—I think that makes sense. And I would be in favor of more forecasting and planning of that kind, than has been done in the past.

In July of 1979 President Carter conferred with distinguished citizens at Camp David; came down to announce that the national problem was a crisis of confidence on the part of the people; and then reorganized his cabinet. Secretary Blumenthal returned to private life.

I heard an opinion like Blumenthal's from the legislative branch, when I interviewed an economist on the staff of the Senate Budget Committee whom I have called Ralph Holland.

> The planning process helps to make things more orderly, it helps to set explicit goals, so you can know whether you succeed or fail; it gives you something to measure by. On the other hand, I would hate to get locked into [rigidly defined] goals. . . . The Humphrey-Hawkins bill, in its original form,

insisted on a 3 per cent unemployment rate for adults, and then defined "adults" rather liberally. That might be unfeasible, given the present structure of the labor force. . . . You're going to be faced with this awful choice between doing something you knew was literally going to accelerate inflation, and failing to meet your unemployment goals. Given the nature of our political system, a certain amount of flexibility is very important. . . . So, a certain modesty in planning is called for.

When final action came on the Humphrey-Hawkins bill in 1978, these conflicting purposes were enacted into law. The bill established as goals the reduction of unemployment to three per cent and of inflation to zero per cent in five years. The mechanisms established to achieve these fanciful goals were modest indeed. The original bill had been a bold proposal for national planning to assure full employment; like its predecessor of 1946, the final bill was little more than an expression of good intentions. In 1978, however, the intentions were probably incompatible. Congressman Hawkins charged in 1980 that President Carter had violated the law nine times in failing to set the required goals and submit the plans needed to implement them.

I spoke to another economist who is on the staff of a major bank in Houston. He found the use of tax incentives to stimulate investment a useful device; but he said that the greatest problem is uncertainty.

The best way that you can encourage investment in this country would be through more stable economic policies. If businessmen knew what was going to be happening in the future, they could plan into the future. . . . If the government would announce the we are going to increase the money supply at 4 per cent over the next ten years, that would be a much healthier development for capital investment than any type of tax credit, or whatever other little gimmick you want to think up. . . . [Planning along such lines would be of enormous benefit], but let's don't get into the specific production decisions being made by the individual firms. It [planning] has become an emotional word.

These respondents conceded the need for greater coordination, at the national level, of government policies, particularly including economic policy. Nearly all of them balked at the word "planning," hastening to say that the concept was frightening to others, but not to themselves, provided that no coercion would be involved, and the goal would be cooperation between government and the private sector, rather than an attempt by government to dictate private decisions normally made in response to market forces. (In the jargon of economists, macroeconomics is perforce the concern of government; microeconomics is not; disagreement comes over where the boundary is to be drawn between the two.) Conceding the need for centralized cooperation, the respondents raised questions of implementation. The central thrust of those questions was that the federal government, as presently organized, is incapable of performing such a coordinating function.

I spoke to the director of the staff that supports the work of the Atlanta City Council, who himself prepared the city's fiscal plan. He supposed that this experience should have made him an advocate of central economic planning, but he felt that the size and complexity of the federal government would prevent the accomplishment of such a task.

> It's such a long and treacherous road for a policy to take, from point A at the top, down to the various points that it has to follow, to wind up with some kind of implementation. And I'm not sure, when it comes out of that layer of bureaucracy, that it ever resembles what it was when it started out. . . . I think in general we're on the down-trend scale of consolidation of government and government activity.

In Boston I interviewed the officer in charge of investments for a group of banks. He told me that planning is central to his work; much of his time is spent in imagining the shape of the future. I asked about the possibility for indicative planning by the federal government.

> I view that as a virtually impossible goal to achieve, because of the nature of the beast. The beast being essentially a committee. And you can design that committee anyway you want to, but it is essentially a committee. . . . I find it hard to believe that you can ever get a group of people in Washington to agree on a goal. They'll agree on motherhood and God; but beyond that what can they possibly agree on?

The respondents in Washington had, if anything, less faith in the capacities of the national government than those in other cities. When I asked Fletcher Bradley, the attorney who represents indigent clients before federal agencies, about the possibility of centralized planning and goal-setting by the federal government, he looked at me with open mouth and amazed eyebrows stretching toward his hairline. "Do you mean *this* federal government??"

California Congressman Leon Panetta's response was both more restrained and more detailed.

> The question I have is whether a centralized planning mechanism is going to be the answer to it, or whether it's just going to create another bureaucracy, that will then do all the planning and develop a whole employment base

and not produce anything. I'm for the end you speak to, but I'm not so sure I'm for creating another mechanism to implement it, because we have so many damn mechanisms now. Essentially, the Office of Management and Budget was supposed to do that; essentially every department is supposed to do that; essentially the Congress is supposed to do that, according to the Budget Act. . . . I would prefer to see us try to twist arms to make sure everybody does what they were supposed to do in the first place.

The Guardians favor greater coordination of economic policy on the national level but do not know how it might be accomplished. But they were unanimous in opposing the most Draconian government measures to control inflation. I asked when wage and price controls are justified; the respondents replied that such policies may be needed in time of total war, but they are not feasible at other times. The response of Treasury Secretary Blumenthal was typical.

I think wage and price controls are only justified in periods of national emergency, because they don't work. We've had plenty of experience with efforts to make them work in periods other than wartime, and they have generally failed. . . . So it would only be in the most dire emergency, and then you have to have a full-blown control mechanism.

This was a striking difference between the policy attitudes of these political influentials and general public opinion. The Guardians had closely observed such attempts at economic intervention as President Nixon's wage-price controls of 1971–74 and found them a failure. As the pace of inflation continued, the Gallup Poll asked citizens if such controls should be reestablished. Fifty per cent of the respondents answered affirmatively, with 39 per cent opposed and 11 per cent undecided. While the values of the Guardians are those of the general political culture, elite attitudes toward specific policies are more likely than those of mass publics to have a reasoned foundation.

The Reagan administration's emphasis upon supply-side economics is nothing less than a form of national planning that is intended to stimulate economic growth and production while keeping most decisions as to the purpose of that growth in the private sector. For those purposes to remain socially acceptable, one must have faith in the charitable impulses of the decision-makers of a thousand corporations.

The Guardians I interviewed are the leaders, or at least active members, of the organizations that dominate the landscape of contemporary society. While these include a range of charitable and voluntary enterprises, the principle mode of organization for business purposes is the corporation. Norman Ross of Chicago coordinates the charitable enterprises of a large corporation; for most of the Guardians, social improvement involves enlisting the aid or regulating the activities, rather than challenging the existence, of corporations. The belief that most ills of modern society stem from the corporate form of economic organization remains the conviction of a minority in academia. The belief has not won even a toehold among the Guardian class, with the possible exception of those few who can at least contemplate a socialist society, like Julian Bond.

How does one fashion national policy based on a recognition of the place and power of the corporation? The 1980 Republican platform provides one example. The basic thrust of the platform, as of President Reagan's economic program, is to reduce taxes upon individuals and corporations. This is the principle of supply-side economics. Once the dead hand of confiscatory tax rates is removed, increased incentives will lead to investment, economic growth, increased productivity, full employment, and the control of inflation. But the general stimulation of incentives by cutting tax rates is not seen as a substitute for specific tax reductions designed to encourage particular activities. In its first thirty-six pages, the platform proposes eighteen different "tax incentives." These specific tax reductions are the mechanisms for accomplishing a vast range of purposes, from saving the family farm (by reducing federal estate and gift taxes on family farm property—p. 36) through preserving urban neighborhoods (by making charitable contributions deductible whether the taxpayer itemizes deductions or not—p. 21) to the revitalization of central cities (by the establishment of "enterprise zones" where taxes and regulations are lessened—p. 22). Tax policies are also counted on to assure a supply of affordable housing, protect independent businesses from predatory conglomerates, and help middle-class students attend college (through tax credits for tuition payments).

Taken together, these proposals to benefit particular interests sully the Republican claim to serve the general good. They also represent a partnership between the federal government and private enterprises. Whoever has his taxes reduced is being subsidized by those who have insufficient influence to win a tax reduction. This pattern is hardly new; the tax code has long been a crazy-quilt of special exemptions and loopholes. The Republican platform merely proposed adding some new swatches to the quilt. The adjustment of tax rates on a selective basis allows government to subsidize particular endeavors without actually transferring funds. Thus the Republicans remain true to their promise to "get government off the backs of the people" and maintain the fiction that the public and private sectors of society are carefully separated from each other.

Tax policy is established politically over the decades. It does not reflect a judgment about national priorities at any given time. And it is never adequate to meet the crises created by large corporations which, by threatening sudden and acute unemployment, can blackmail Congress into awarding loan guarantees (and for an instant revealing the phony division between the public and private sectors). Its loan guarantee restored the Lockheed Corporation to prosperity; the outcome of the loan guarantee for the Chrysler Corporation is so far less encouraging.

The decay of American cities, particularly in the Northeast, shows that, in default of something like national planning, the structure of tax incentives as a substitute for an acknowledged partnership between business and government leads eventually to disaster.

An acknowledged partnership has been proposed by Felix Rohatyn, the New York financier who, as head of the Municipal Assistance Corporation, brought New York City back from the brink of bankruptcy. *Newsweek* magazine touted his proposals as the only new ideas put forward by a member of the Democratic party and the basis for rallying the Democratic party to propose viable alternatives to Reagan's policies. Rohatyn proposed that national planning establish certain priorities, among which would be the preservation of Northeastern cities, in part through the renovation to meet foreign competition of the heavy industries located therein: steel, automobiles, rubber, and the like. The vehicle would be a Reconstruction Finance Corporation established by Congress, its bonds guaranteed by the government, to become a source of equity capital for business renovation and the renewal of urban amenities. Rohatyn argues that the new RFC (loosely modeled on that established by the New Deal) would have the financial clout necessary to influence management decisions and win important concessions from unions. Its bonds would also be an effective means of recycling surplus dollars held by the OPEC nations. He argues further that his plan would allow the people of the nation to share equally in both the sacrifices and rewards of adapting to the economic realities of the world.

My interviews with the Guardians indicate that Rohatyn's plan would meet resistance from the very stratum of political influentials whose support is essential for its acceptance. The Guardians are hostile to the concept of national planning; the Rohatyn scheme could perhaps avoid that label and win greater acceptance simply as a means for publicly guaranteed industrial investment. Although the tax laws create hidden partnerships between government and particular enterprises, open partnerships would seem to threaten traditional liberties. Such fears would be accentuated by the dedication of so many Guardians to individualist values.

Yet a long view of economic history suggests that the increasing centralization of capitalism is inevitable. In America, the last century and a half produced the change from single-product, single-family firms to multiproduct, multinational corporations. The next step of centralization—already well advanced in Japan—is a form of state capitalism based on national planning and the governmental provision of finance capital for selected industries.

In default of national planning, Congress has been the federal investment banker, providing loan guarantees to Lockheed and Chrysler to save the jobs of voters. This is the pathway to "lemon socialism"—the nationalization of failing enterprises, involving public solvency in that failure. Contrast the Japanese pattern of financing innovative ventures, such as the manufacture of industrial robots.

If the economic policies of the Reagan administration continue to reduce inflation and interest rates at the cost of increased unemployment, public clamor for new interventions will become overwhelming. Yet the dominant figures in the administration are precisely those for whom the concept of "planning" is anathema. Therefore, should the administration launch any attempt to coordinate the economic efforts of the federal government, with or without the cooperation of the private sector, that effort will not be called "national planning."

Human Rights and the Limits of Nature

The proper role of the United States within the family of nations has been an unsettled question since the national foundation. Jefferson wrote that a "decent regard for the opinions of mankind" required that the reasons for the separation from England be set forth in the Declaration of Independence. (The need to attract allies, who had no reason to settle a quarrel so the colonies could rejoin the mother country, was just as compelling a motive.) Jefferson's assertion of the right of peoples to replace governments that failed to protect individual liberties was capable of universal application; from the beginning, there was disagreement over the appropriate American role as the champion of the principle. Should America provide a successful democratic example, which other nations would be free to imitate, or should America intervene actively to support democratic forces in other nations?

Initial claims that the American democratic mission required overseas intervention overlooked the weakness of the new nation and the pretentiousness of any claim to status as a world power. In 1793 John Adams wrote a despairing note to his son:

> The Anti-Federal party, by their ox feasts and their civic feasts, their King-killing toasts, their perpetual insolence and billings-gate against all the nations and governments of Europe, their everlasting, brutal cry of tyranny, despots, and combinations against liberty, etc., etc., etc., have probably irritated, offended, and provoked all the crowned heads of Europe at last; and a little more of this indelicacy and indecency may involve us in a war with all the world.

The War of 1812 demonstrated national weakness as well as invincibility. The United States could not defeat a major European power; neither could its vast area and diffused population be conquered by an invading force. Jackson's victory at New Orleans followed the signing of the peace treaty but was hailed as proof of democratic superiority; the national mission was focused upon the conquering of the continent, behind the barely recognized protective screen of the British navy. National unity, and the end of chattel slavery, was achieved by force in the 1860s. The national flirtation with imperialism came in the 1890s, and the norm of isolationism (setting the democratic example) was broken "to make the world safe for democracy" in 1917. But the peace was lost, isolationism triumphed, and the stage was set for the further confrontation of nations that began in the late 1930s.

Victory over the Axis powers, at the cost of bleeding the British Empire, thrust the United States onto the world stage to perform a role it had trouble defining for itself, just when the monopoly of atomic weaponry gave factual support to the traditional assumption of American invincibility. Political defeat of Henry Wallace and others who proposed closer communication with Soviet Russia assured the statement of the American mission in negative terms: opposition to the spread of "Godless communism." This impulse led to intervention in the Korean conflict that was crowned with modest success and to intervention in Vietnam that was a military and political disaster. Meanwhile, the realization grew that a bipolar picture of the world was inadequate; that not all nations could be classified as allies of either East or West; and that American support for oppressive regimes in the name of opposing communism could lead to the embarrassing denial of her founding principles. The capture and holding hostage of fifty-two Americans at the Teheran embassy demonstrated the inability of any nation to determine the outcome of events in another.

As noted in chapter two, many Guardians welcomed the Carter administration's emphasis on the centrality of human rights for the American stance in international relations. That chapter also reviewed the simultaneous adherence to liberty and equality, pointing out that the expectation of continuing natural abundance has inhibited the inherent conflict between these two aspects of the democratic creed. Among the Guardians, the most firmly established value is that of liberty: human rights are seen as guarantees against interference by government in personal freedoms such as speech, press, religion, and assembly. This is the human rights tradition of the liberal thinkers of the seventeenth, eighteenth, and nineteenth centuries: Locke, Jefferson, John Stuart Mill, and their followers.

Such a conception of human rights is a luxury affordable by societies that provide the needs of subsistence for most of their populations. In the less developed nations, human rights have primarily a materialistic significance. Provision of the basic necessities of life is the leading preoccupation. As the maintenance of customary American affluence requires the increasing importation of basic materials, the emerging nations are bound to seek ever higher prices for their exported materials, aware that nature's bounty is finite, and that their nation's share can only be sold once. The formation and operation of OPEC was but an extreme example, made possible by world economic conditions, of a predictable reaction. Nations not blessed with petroleum reserves could only wait for some other precious mineral to become the center of world attention.

The absence of a definition of human rights in the United Nations Charter led to the 1948 "Universal Declaration of Human Rights and Fundamental Freedoms," which has been described as "providing a connecting link between different concepts of human rights in different parts of the world." The Universal Declaration, which has never been adopted by the United States because of doubts about the propriety of superceding the U.S. Constitution, lists rights as defined in both the liberal and materialist traditions, without attempting a synthesis. Thus the conflict between liberty and equality (defined as seeking an equality of condition) is projected on a worldwide arena.

Before his inauguration, Ronald Reagan dramatized a concern for more certain relations with Latin America by meeting Mexican President Lopez Portillo at a border city for talks. News accounts of the meeting's purpose said little or nothing about the inability of Americans to agree with other nations on the definition of human rights. Instead, the discovery of large oil fields in Mexico was portrayed as making our neighbor important in a way it had never been before. The decision of the Reagan administration to send military advisers to El Salvador seemed to demonstrate a determination to view Third World nations primarily as arenas for conflict in a bipolar world.

In the fall of 1981, a summit conference was held in Mexico between representatives of the industrial Northern Hemisphere nations and the developing nations of the south. In advance of the meeting, President Reagan declared that the key to solving world economic problems lies in free trade between private enterprises. Foreign leaders preoccupied by developing national plans to avert famine among their people were predictably unimpressed. The perception seemed inevitable that capital-rich America was incapable of understanding the constraints imposed by economic scarcity upon the developing nations. At the Cancun Conference itself, Reagan indicated that the United States would be willing to participate in "world negotiations," provided their focus would be on economic development, rather than the redistribution of wealth, and that no new international bureaucracy would be created. President Reagan proclaimed himself well pleased with the progress made at the talks.

The Panama Canal: Guardian Approval, Public Dismay

As it is with other aspects of foreign affairs, the American public seems less sensitive to the nuances of relationships with the Third World than are "attentive elites" like the Guardians. This contrast was shown dramatically by 1977 attitudes toward the Panama Canal treaties. At a time when the Harris Poll showed that the public opposed the treaties by a margin of 51 per cent to 26 per cent, with the remainder undecided, only 3 of my 117 respondents opposed them.

A third of of those respondents supporting the Panama Canal treaties did so on the basis of principle; two-thirds did so for practical or strategic reasons. An example of the first kind of reaction came from Pastora Cafferty, a Chicago academic who grew up in Cuba.

It amazes me that most people don't know that we don't own Panama. One thing that's true of the United States is that it is the most ignorant nation, internationally, for a nation of its sophistication and education. . . . There's a lot to be said for power, in that you don't have to know these things, because you're the one that's in charge. On the other hand, it makes for some rather unreal national attitudes about international affairs.

The Washington editor I have named Daniel Randolph offered a balanced account of the practical reasons for approval of the treaties.

I'm persuaded that it's the most practical and prudent course for this country to take. . . . In the first place, I don't at all see any historical basis for the claim that we have sovereignty in the Canal Zone, which in fact is simply not the case, under the terms of the 1903 treaty. I'm persuaded that the present regime in Panama, notwithstanding its drawbacks, is about as reasonable a regime as we are likely to have in the foreseeable future to negotiate a realistic treaty with. I'm persuaded by what I read about its declining commercial and military importance. And I really can understand, in what is obviously a sort of postcolonial world, the sensitivity of the Panamanians to the peculiar features of the Canal Zone.

This disagreement between general public opinion and that of the Guardians suggests a partial explanation for the confirmation of the treaties by the U.S. Senate. Opinion polls do not measure the intensity of opinion or probe very deeply into the informational background from which individual members of the public draw their opinions. The senators I asked about the treaties called themselves undecided, as the issue was yet to be voted on by the Senate. Senator Lugar remarked upon the intensity of opposition to the treaty in Indiana; at public gatherings, questioners demanded to know his position on that issue before any other could be discussed. In Maryland, Paul Sarbanes did not find a comparable preoccupation with the question. When the issue came before the Senate, Lugar voted with many of his fellow Republicans against ratification, while Sarbanes voted for it, in conjunction with most of the Democrats.

The Canal issue was of long standing. Treaty negotiations had been conducted by several administrations of both parties, so that those who pay attention to noncrisis developments in foreign affairs were well informed on the issue. Attentive elites were well equipped to bring their opinions to bear, and public opinion soon accepted the treaty, once it was ratified. But not all questions in foreign affairs are of such long standing, and most administrations assume that their freedom of action will be impaired if attentive elites are fully informed of developing international situations by sources independent of the government. The Reagan administration has proved to be no exception to this rule.

Defense Needs, Arms Limitation, and Soviet Intentions

The Guardians did not support Carter's human rights stance on the basis of abstract justice alone. There was an undertone of relief that this emphasis was the appropriate counterweight to the influence of the Soviet Union upon the Third World nations. Several Guardians pointed out that the policy could never live up to its potential, for its implementation meant that many regimes with little regard for human rights would continue as allies, and that the United States would never be able to persuade major powers, such as Russia in its treatment of Jews, to change their habits. Among the Guardians, awareness of the less developed nations' role in international relations (the so-called North-South conflict) has not replaced concern for the tensions between East and West characteristic of the cold war. Rather, opinions on nearly every aspect of international affairs are influenced by attitudes toward the contest between communism and the free world; or, more precisely, between Soviet Russia and the United States.

The Guardians were about equally divided between "hawks," who fear the intentions of the Soviet Union and would increase defense expenditures in anticipation of trouble, and "doves," who, while they hardly see Russian intentions as benign, argue that increasing American military capacities will only escalate the arms race and make the situation less stable. Dovish attitudes were more likely to be expressed by those who live outside Washington and work in occupations not associated with the defense industry. The dovish position was best articulated by Thomas Atkins, the Boston NAACP attorney.

Maintaining a nuclear superiority over the Soviet Union commits us to their schedule of production, commits us to their priorities as between defense expenditures and domestic priorities. And I just think this country ought to be operated on the basis of our priorities, not somebody in the Kremlin. . . . At some point, whether the next month or the next year, if it appears that there is in fact a real danger that we face an attack, either from Russia or from Tanzania, you address that problem. You try to anticipate. But to keep count of the number of silos they've got and the number of mobile missiles they have and say, "If they've got twelve, we've got to have thirteen," is a policy which favors only generals, admirals, and other commanders, and defense contractors—people who benefit from war. The country does not benefit from war; wars happen to kill people and other living things.

Atkins's statement, which was far from calling for unilateral disarmament, came as close to a pacifist comment as any made by the Guardians. The most thorough and articulate argument from the hawkish viewpoint came, not surprisingly, from Melvin Laird, secretary of defense under President Nixon.

The Soviet Union is moving in the direction of a massive military build-up, seeking to have a superior position in the world, and will deal from a superior position certainly by 1983 or 1984. They're using a greater proportion of their gross national product then ever before. When [the proportion of] their gross national product [devoted to military expenditures] was at 14 per cent, everyone in the intelligence community and a lot of our foreign policy experts were saying that, because of the economic pressures from consumer goods industries, they would be forced in the opposite direction. In the last three years, they've gone from 14 per cent of the gross national product to 17 per cent of the gross national product, and that's an agreed-upon figure now with everyone in the intelligence community. They're moving in the opposite direction. They're building a superior navy, a superior air force, and a superior ground combat capability. . . . The Soviets are in the position where they're building this great strength for political reasons. And, because of their system they're able to do it.

In our defense budget, we're spending about 6 per cent of our gross national product; but of that 6 per cent, 60 per cent goes to personnel costs. . . . [The Soviets] are spending much more than we are, but of that 17 per cent of their gross national product, only 22 per cent goes into personnel costs.

This case for increased defense expenditure was made on the assumption that American security in the broadest terms requires some kind of parity of strength with the Soviet Union. But Laird shied away from discussing particular weapons systems, such as the B-1 bomber and the cruise missile, seeming content with presidential decisions on such matters made on the basis of information available to the president at the time.

In 1977 I asked most of the Guardians if they expected atomic weapons to be used within their lifetimes. No other question induced such a moment of solemnity into the interviews. All the respondents fervently prayed that they would not. Several mentioned the possibility of nuclear usage by terrorists or smaller nations. But all argued that, whatever Russia's ultimate aims, her leaders are essentially rational. None expected nuclear war to be launched by either of the superpowers, although Melvin Laird mentioned the possibility of nuclear blackmail. "I expect nuclear weapons to be used as a political weapon, not as a weapon of war. I think that's the Soviet position."

In the years following, evidence accumulated of an arms build-up—both nuclear and conventional—by the Soviet Union. Jimmy Carter issued a presidential directive based on assuming Russia's willingness to fight a "limited" nuclear war. And the Reagan administration took office with verbal six-guns blazing against the Russians.

The case for suspicion of Russian intentions was put more dramatically by Senator Malcolm Wallop, Republican of Wyoming, who discussed the complexities of achieving "nuclear superiority" over the Soviet Union.

> A first-strike exchange between Russia and the United States is estimated by even the most dovish people to be somewhere in the neighborhood of twelve million Russians and one hundred million Americans. So, you know, we've got more numbers, but that's not a very good exchange. . . . They have underground shelters. They're capable of putting about 80 per cent of their wartime manufacturing capability in a very protected locations, within a very few hours. We're not. . . . They have another thing that isn't often commented upon in the American press. With all their stationary missile silos, they have multiple firing capabilities. Our missile silos have single warheads. They can shoot off two or three from the same silo in a matter of hours.

In Boston, John Winthrop Sears had a similar opinion of the Soviet Union's ambitions, coupled with high hopes for the efficacy of a strategic arms limitation treaty.

> If we're going to junk the B-1 [bomber] and then junk the cruise missile, then may God have mercy on our souls, because out there in the rest of the world, what they understand is not moralizing.

Sears described the successes of the Washington naval disarmament treaty of 1921 in contrast to the then current SALT negotiations, and argued that the American stance in the SALT negotiations was unlikely to produce a favorable result.

> But [successful] arms limitation talks would at least put a cap on something. I'm afraid that the one thing that was quintessential to the success of [the] Washington [naval limitation] treaty was that there was no power

which had an immediate ambition to dominate and govern the civilized part of the planet. And that isn't the situation now. The Soviets have constantly evidenced a desire to control much more of the world's land area than they already do; that's the central fact of international relationships, as far as I can see.

When the Carter administration produced the SALT II treaty, considerations of the kind voiced by Malcolm Wallop were repeated by many senators as they resisted a vote on its ratification. Once again, the Carter administration had failed to communicate its sense of the complex factors that restrain national action in relation to other nations. By that time, President Carter admitted that Russian aggression in Afghanistan made necessary a reassessment of Russian intentions. In the 1980 campaign, however, Carter depicted the SALT II treaty as an achievement of statecraft endangered by warmonger Reagan, ignoring the opposition to its ratification by so many senators, including leading Democrats like Georgia's Sam Nunn.

Walter Pincus, the Washington journalist whose reporting about the neutron bomb made that weapon the sudden center of national attention, gave me an account of the arms contest that was little related to hardware.

> I go back to leadership. If you have somebody running your government in whom the public has faith, he doesn't have to prove [nuclear] superiority, or parity. It all depends on what the people believe their leaders are capable of doing. In the case of the Soviets, it all depends on how they perceive our reaction to whatever they do. What you really want is not the Soviets to be fearful that we have terrible weapons, and will destroy them; we've got those already. What you want the Soviets to realize is that there are severe limits beyond which they cannot go; and that we have leadership that can rally the country behind it to prevent them from doing things they shouldn't be doing and that we don't want them to do. And that's deterrence. Deterrence is a state of mind. And it depends as much on attitudes towards people as it does on weapons and capabilities.

Early foreign affairs initiatives of the Reagan administration, such as establishing a symbolic presence in El Salvador and the aircraft skirmish in the Bay of Sidra on the coast of Libya seemed calculated to demonstrate that whatever "nerve" the United States lost because of defeat in Vietnam had been recovered. Libya had claimed the Bay of Sidra as part of its territorial waters as an "historic bay," and the Carter administration did not dispute that claim. But Reagan sent the fleet to conduct maneuvers there. Such unilateral actions, which specify geopolitical boundaries and then patrol them, undercut legitimate international efforts like the United Nations Conference on the Law of the Sea, and they tend to nurture assumptions of American impotence because the sovereign nations interfered with are less than major powers. During the discussion of the Bay of Sidra incident and a similar event off the coast of North Korea, when a missile was apparently fired at an American plane, no Reagan spokesmen pointed out that Russia shares our interest in maintaining naval maneuvering rights and thus would not support Libya in its confrontation with the U.S. fleet.

The administration and the defense establishment had not adopted Walter Pincus's understanding of deterrence, however. The Pentagon's shopping list of military hardware was soon delivered to the White House, and, even as the Libyan planes flamed down, Defense Secretary Weinberger battled Budget Director Stockman for funding. Few stories about presumed "hit squads" dispatched to Washington by Libya's dictator, Muammar Kaddafi, the following December, mentioned the incident in the Bay of Sidra.

The basic question about defense spending had not been addressed by candidates Reagan and Carter during the 1980 campaign: the purpose for which defense spending is to be used. In all the talk about MX missiles, mobile striking forces, and presidential directives, there was little admission that the capabilities of weapons systems tend to determine strategic planning, and that studies of cost effectiveness (the updated version of the "more bang for a buck" argument common in the early days of nuclear stockpiling) give little guidance as to the kinds of battles that may actually be averted, if they have been adequately prepared for. Candidate Reagan promised to increase defense spending, citing reasons like those given to me by Melvin Laird in 1977. He did endorse specific weapons systems. But he did not indicate a vision of the purpose of increased defense spending—the priorities that should be addressed first, the allocation of funds between research and development as opposed to production, the balance between nuclear forces and conventional military capabilities. The administration could not claim a "mandate" for particular details of defense spending proposals; but the proposals made in mid-1981 were described as defining the American defense posture through the end of the century.

The Reagan budget called for steady increases in defense spending—for a total greater than the proposed decrease in domestic programs—and thus a risk of following Lyndon Johnson's path of stimulating inflation through a defense build-up without new tax revenues. The abandonment of the "shell game" scheme for shuffling hundreds of MX missiles between thousands of launching areas scattered over the American West revealed a healthy recognition that the much discussed "window of vulnerability"—when Soviet missiles of the late 1980s can theoretically penetrate hardened silos—can never be reliably sealed off. But the variety of other weapons systems suggested no other recognition of limits: every technological possibility was to be explored, every strategic option prepared for; and the B-1 bomber, abandoned by Carter, was now to be built.

Senator John Tower, who chaired the 1980 Republican Platform Committee, explained on national television that defense-spending increases are required to demonstrate our "national will" to the Soviet Union. He made this statement at a time when Russia was bogged down in its invasion of Afghanistan.

When the administration had announced its determination to support the government of El Salvador against the "communist" guerrillas, its justification for the policy was attacked by the press, and the administration was unable to confine debate to its own version of reality. The administration was apparently forced to scale down the amount of military assistance it had planned to send into Central America. Then, overtures made to Argentina as the adminstration attempted to enlist Latin allies for a confrontation with Nicaragua were blamed for contributing to the miscalculations which led to war over the Falkland Islands.

By 1982 the Reagan foreign policy was clearly being formulated by men who feel they understand the operation of the international system and are confident that international realities will yield to unilateral manipulation by the United States. Far from admitting that any nation is hard pressed to influence the behavior of another nation when that nation does not choose to be influenced (despite the failure of President Reagan's invasion eve telephone call to President Galitieri of Argentina), the aggressive stance of the administration seemed to exhibit all the moral self-confidence that had characterized Lyndon Johnson's "best and brightest" advisers during the escalation of the Vietnam war.

There were many signs that the insistence of the administration on viewing the world through thirty-year-old lenses would prove inadequate. Ideological and material conflict between the United States and the Soviet Union was only one aspect of the international situation. Furthermore, the United States could not impose its understanding of the world on other nations. Our attempts to rehabilitate the combatants after World War II had succeeded, and now we were faced with challenges to our once vaunted technological and industrial superiority by Japan and by Western Europe. Our attempt to assign all nations to the status of either pro- or anti-communist would not provide an adequate guide for the conduct of international affairs.

But the Soviet Union had not suddenly become a friend, and its arms build-up was real. The nuclear arms race had been stimulated by the attempts of both sides to deal from strength before negotiating limits upon their production. The Reagan administration announced its willingness to negotiate a "meaningful" arms limitation treaty, but only after developing a military position of undeniable superiority. Yet the established Pentagon practices of weapons procurement, emphasizing high technology, high cost, and optimistic estimates of the requirements for maintenance, promised increasing costs without greater combat utility. The search for "superiority," or even a budgetary demonstration to Russia of the strength of national will, promised only a spiraling escalation of the arms race, coupled with economic despair at home.

Like the regulation of nuclear power plants, the procurement of defense weapons systems is a technical question of great complexity which most citizens despair of understanding. (The citizens of Nevada and Utah did awaken to the threat to their environment posed by the looming construction of the MX missile complex.) Despite its growing staff, Congress itself is hampered in its efforts to oversee such administrative agencies by its lack of scientific advice that is independent of those agencies. While the accident at Three Mile Island suddenly broadened the constituency concerned with the decisions of the Nuclear Regulatory Agency, public attention soon passed on to other matters. I have reported the tendency of the Guardians to defer to the expertise of government officials on highly technical matters. The result is that the normal involvement of the constitutional structure in determining the public good, subject to an after-the-fact judgment by the voters, does not operate. If the policies and practices of the Defense Department succeed in fomenting the very nuclear war they are intended to prevent, the voter's judgment will come too late.

Prior to the belated withdrawal of American forces from Vietnam, the nation had never experienced a losing war; that the War of 1812 had been a stalemate was obscured by Andrew Jackson's victory at New Orleans. Disaster in Vietnam, coupled with the protracted holding of hostages by Iran, confirmed that neither American scientific technology nor its political institutions guarantee a particular portion of international prestige or influence. Yet the sense of an historical mission persists, and the question of whether the American nation should exert international influence directly, or by providing an example for imitation, remains. Rick Stearns, the Boston attorney who would later become a leading campaign strategist for Senator Ted Kennedy, defined the baneful influence of an ideology that can obscure the national interest.

I wouldn't say that American foreign policy should be immoral, but sometimes it has to be amoral. We've tried to introduce ideology under various guises into American foreign policy. I suppose [President Woodrow] Wilson was the first really aggressive attempt by the United States to order the world in its own image. In the cold war we had a philosophy that was less appealing than Carter's because it was a negative philosophy, whereas Carter's is a very positive one, and to that extent a very appealing one. But . . . the purpose of foreign policy is to protect the legitimate interests of this country. . . . I'm not going to say that it doesn't bother me as much as it bothers anyone else that the Jews in the Soviet Union are persecuted and not allowed to emigrate, or that the press in China is not free, or that Idi Amin is an abomination. But I think the purpose of foreign policy is something different than promoting our ideology.

The Guardians and Foreign Policy

The Guardians are clearly members of what political scientists call the "attentive elite" regarding foreign policy: they pay attention to evolving international issues, and their greater information makes them less likely to project personal emotions or senses of inadequacy onto the international stage. In 1977's public debate, the most vocal opponents of the Canal treaty attempted to stimulate public opposition based upon primitive possessive instincts, reinforced by generalized national pride. Historians since Thucydides have questioned the ability of democratic populations to wisely judge international questions when they have no direct experience of the life and needs of other nations.

In the United States, foreign affairs controversies in which opposition leaders seek votes to topple the incumbents have been based on a politics of hindsight. Democrats castigated Republicans for remaining isolationist despite Hitler's early victories; Republicans castigated Democrats for "losing" China to the Communists; the New Right chides the Establishment for "giving away" the Panama Canal. The politics of hindsight ignores any sense of the constraints of the international system which limit what any nation can achieve. (China was never ours to lose.)

On the other hand, incumbent administrations seeking support for policy innovations oversimplify matters by exaggerating the need and overselling the remedy. Harry Truman stimulated the "red scare" to win support for the Marshall Plan; John Kennedy held out high hopes for stability in Latin American as a result of the Alliance for Progress; Lyndon Johnson rang changes on the domino theory as he sent more troops into Vietnam. These tactics also deemphasize or ignore the constraints that operate in the international arena.

That sense of constraints is also at risk when the energies of an energetic executive seek an outlet in foreign adventures, as the president seeks to establish through international affairs a presence that will be useful in domestic politics. Gerald Ford had his *Mayaguez* incident; Lyndon Johnson had his *Pueblo*. Jimmy Carter rightly claimed the Camp David accords between Egypt and Israel as a leading accomplishment of his administration. Such instances seem insignificant compared to the awesome responsibility of presidents to avoid unleashing the nuclear beast with its certain destruction on a global scale. Because the stakes are so high, the need for clearheadedness in the formulation of foreign policy should be obvious. Intellectual clarity is the first requirement. A president should be able to summon the support of a national constituency among an attentive public for foreign policy innovations, without creating the crisis situation that assures a surge of public patriotism and replaces reason with emotion.

The president's political party should be the source of such an attentive public. Unhappily, the political parties have shown themselves largely incapable of operating as responsible policy mechanisms, and most citizens pay attention to foreign questions only when their sense of crisis has been stimulated. New directions in foreign policy are proposed and tested in a dialogue between government and the attentive elites. Intellectual clarity among the Guardians is a necessary, but not sufficient, requirement for a sane foreign policy.

Epilogue
Guardian Values and the
Public Good

*The republican principle demands that the deliberate sense of
the community should govern the conduct of those to whom they
entrust the management of their affairs; but it does not require
an unqualified complaisance to every sudden breeze of passion,
or to every transient impulse which the people may receive from
the arts of men, who flatter their prejudices to betray their interests. It is a just observation, that the people commonly intend
the PUBLIC GOOD. . . . When occasions present themselves,
in which the interests of the people are at variance with their
inclinations, it is the duty of the persons whom they have appointed to be the guardians of those interests, to withstand the
temporary delusion, in order to give them time and opportunity
for more cool and sedate reflection.*

—Alexander Hamilton, 1788

The interpretation of American politics presented in this book is familiar
within the social sciences, but it is rarely discussed in the public media.
The state of public opinion, as measured by modern polling techniques,
is regularly featured in newsmagazines, the daily press, and some television commentaries. These reports are seldom accompanied by discussions of "linkage," the complex process through which public opinion
influences, or fails to influence, the formulation of public policy. Readers
or viewers with curiosity and developed memories may wonder why an

overwhelming public preference, measured by the polls, is never implemented by government. They can turn to reports of the legislative process in Congress or to the statements by "the White House" or "the Pentagon" (remembering that buildings don't actually speak), or they can seek accounts of the operations of what political scientists call "linkage institutions"—the political parties and the organized interest groups. The role of a class of political influentials—the Guardians—is never discussed, although that role is central to the two-way connection between mass opinion and government policy.

The Guardians hold a potential veto power over the program of any administration. Despite President Reagan's legislative victories, resistance grew among the public and among the Guardians, stimulated by economic recession. The winter of 1981 was very similar to the fall of 1977, when a Guardian told me, "the bloom is already off the Carter rose," and described his fear of a succession of one-term presidencies. As 1982 began, one could no longer assume that the 1980 election and its aftermath signaled a revitalization of the political process, a resolution of the value conflicts, or a repair of the institutional flaws, described in the preceding chapters.

Special Interests and the Public Good

The Reagan administration was barely installed before it launched policy proposals intended to reverse established governmental directions, both foreign and domestic. After any election, the winners are likely to grow impatient with opposition leaders whose seats they were unable to challenge, and the 1980 contest was no exception. The victors are tempted to assume that people's judgment is a final act in the political drama, rather than—as the founders intended—a prologue to determining the sense of the community.

The political party as a force for cohesion became newly significant with a Republican majority installed in the Senate. The majority was slender enough to concentrate partisan attention: the Reagan economic program sailed through the Senate with relative ease. The legislation's acceptance in the House depended on renewing the ancient cooperation of Republicans with conservative Democrats. President Reagan's personal lobbying assured that cooperation. It was a display of legislative leadership by the president unlike any since Lyndon Johnson's enactment of his Great Society program. And it stimulated similar, if muted, cries of "executive tyranny" from the opposition—the liberal Democrats who had once supplied the base of Johnson's majority.

A version of Madison's concept of the public good was adopted by the supporters of the Reagan economic program. It supplied the rhetoric to justify the cutback of domestic programs in favor of increased defense spending. Curbing inflation and restoring a strong international posture were defined as the top national priorities. Those opposing domestic program cuts were described as special interests, stimulated by selfish motives to thwart the public good.

President Reagan's most striking use of the concept came in June, 1981, when he asked a skeptical convention of the National Association for the Advancement of Colored People to accept cuts in social programs because his economic program would "lift the whole nation." The time had come, he said, to recognize that the good of the nation was more important than the allocation of special benefits to its various parts.

Two months earlier, Congressman Guy Vander Jagt, chairman of the National Republican Congressional Committee, sent a computerized letter to possible contributors.

> Right now, a coalition of special interest groups and liberal Democrats is on the verge of destroying the President's program to cut both taxes and government spending. . . .
>
> President Reagan has said that Congress must hear "the voice of the average American, not that of special interests or full time lobbyists."
>
> . . . Yet, despite this severe [economic] crisis, union leaders, welfare activists, lobbyists and bureaucrats have joined with liberals in Congress in a deliberate effort to defeat outright President Reagan's program. . . .
>
> Let me give you just one example.
>
> Mr. Reagan wants to cut the food stamp program by weeding out welfare cheaters and removing from eligibility those who are not in real need.
>
> Yet every welfare activist, lobbyist and federal bureaucrat who makes his living off of this program is pressuring Congress to block this cut.

In essence, Congressman Vander Jagt complained that politics was still being conducted. His appeal was to the concept of a plebiscitary executive: the people had awarded their mandate; other elements of the constitutional structure should bow before the will of the people. This concept, developed originally on behalf of Napoleon III, attracted the Nixon White House following the landslide election of 1972; it became an element in the mind-set that nourished the Watergate cover-up. While the authors of the Constitution accepted without question the

concept of the public good, they were under no illusion that its definition would be readily ascertained in a particular set of circumstances,
and they argued that its definition necessarily involved all elements of
the constitutional structure. In the passage heading this epilogue, Alexander Hamilton expresses doubts about the dependability of the people's
judgment that would never pass the lips of a contemporary politician.
However, his phrase about the flattery of prejudices to betray interests
provides the text for an epitaph that any number of liberal commentators would like to write on the Reagan administration.

The phrase "special interests" was also invoked by the Democrats.
When he solicited contributions for the new Fund for a Democratic
Majority, designed in imitation of conservative direct-mail operations,
Senator Edward Kennedy wrote, "We are far behind the special inter-
ests and the New Right, but we can regain lost ground."

These were instances of the pot calling the kettle black. The tendency
of interest-group politics to obscure the public good was firmly established by the New Deal, then accelerated by both Republican and
Democratic administrations. In the absence of an agreed and specific
content for the public good, the term "special interests" was in danger
of becoming no more than a synonym for "my opponents."

Guardian Values and Contemporary Conservatism

The picture of the Republicans as the champions of the interests of
wealth and the Democrats as protectors of the poor reduces the political
contest to striving between rival factions which does not account for the
importance of values in motivating political behavior. The devotion of
the president and his staff to supply-side economics exhibits an element
of sincere faith which is more powerful and certainly more admirable
than a mere adherence to the interests of wealth. (Alexander Hamilton's
desire, as treasury secretary, to wed the wealthy to the new nation
through ties of interest also exhibited admirable motivation.) The cries
of anguish that greeted the publication of Budget Director David Stockman's expressions of doubt concerning the efficacy of supply-side economics can only be understood as the rage directed by the faithful at
an apostate. Unfortunately, the Guardians who establish the content of
the national news portrayed Stockman's trip "to the woodshed" with

President Reagan as a question of whether adolescent misbehavior would be punished, rather than a story casting doubt upon the worth of a national policy.

In the realm of values, there are three elements in contemporary American conservatism that are hard to admire. The first is the tendency for all political questions to be absorbed by economic considerations. Far from a Burkean concern for the diverse elements of an organic society, the compulsive Reaganite concern for marketplace incentives makes all matters of social or legal equality secondary to the pursuit of economic liberty. This tendency is echoed in Guardian attitudes, as was demonstrated in chapter two. Economic freedom seems to be the dominant value of the 1980s, as political equality energized the 1960s. But a substantial group of Guardians (34 per cent) feel that both equal opportunity and legal equality are ideals that are yet to be realized. There is, among the Guardians, a reservoir of public spiritedness that could be called on to support political movements organized beneath equality's banner.

The second deplorable fixture of contemporary conservatism is its marriage of convenience with the kind of coercive individualism that would, with the aid of the state, impose judgments about such matters as abortion upon individuals who do not share the religious faith that prescribes that judgment. Although such proposals contradict the call to "get government off the backs of the people," the New Right ignores the contradiction. Governmental enforcement of moral judgments was a feature of Puritan New England, but the practice is foreign to the American liberal tradition established in the eighteenth century. That only three of my respondents could be counted in the "coercive individualist" category suggests that the liberal tradition is well rooted among political activists. Serious attempts formally to curb civil liberties are likely to simulate such opposition as to damage the influence of New Right spokesmen within the conservative coalition.

The third distressing feature of contemporary conservatism is its stance in foreign relations. Advertising itself as based on "realism," the administration's foreign policy wears the trappings of a moral crusade against communism. In its daily operations, the administration indulges in practices that are both manipulative and secretive—as in the skirmish with Libyan air forces. (Reagan has no monopoly here; systematic lying to the American public concerning foreign affairs was practiced by the Johnson and Nixon administrations; Harry Truman oversold the dangers of communism to win support for the Marshall Plan.) The Guardians accept the assumption that Russia is the natural enemy, and they also tend to yield to the expertise of others in the realm of foreign policy. The free exchange between the government and the attentive elites which could build support for a sane foreign policy is thus inhibited by Guardian attitudes, as well as by the government itself.

I have argued that a renewed concern for Madison's concept of the public good must precede any effort to repair the flaws that have grown into the Madisonian governmental structure. The evocation of a contest between the public good and the evil of special interests by supporters of Reagan's economic policies did not represent that renewed concern, unless one shared the economic faith upon which it was based. It served as a rhetorical flourish in the contest between a determined executive and an opposition party in disarray. The challenge for the Guardians is to accept the concept but to broaden its meaning beyond economic policy. It is imperative to understand American politics as being more than a mere contest between conflicting interests. This is the central, but neglected, legacy of Madison's thought.

Madison insisted that the public good resulted from the joint operation of all elements of government, achieving compromise between conflicting policies and balance between centers of power. The outcome was assured by the superior moral sense of the men placed in positions of authority by the successive refinements of the electoral process. Many of the flaws in modern American government stem from the fact that such a large part of the government—bureaucracies in the executive branch, assistants in the White House, and burgeoning professional staffs to assist Congress—flourishes outside the electoral process, beyond the reach of the sovereign people. And this part of government deals with narrow, specialized constituencies, often organized as interests with a special pipeline to Washington.

Madison's vision of the extended republic must be modernized as the concept of an inclusive republic. Madison depended upon the virtue of the representative to assure his attachment to the public good. If today we find it embarrassing to speak of virtue, we can at least remember that the public interest will be most closely approximated when the legislator (or the administrator) deals with the widest possible range of particular interests.

The Substance of the Public Good

This book began with an invocation of V. O. Key's conclusion that the "beliefs, standards, and competence" of the political influentials determine the health of the American democratic order. The book has been about those influentials—the Guardians. In describing their values, I have developed several arguments about the current state of American institutions and policies. Taken together, these arguments constitute the author's perception of the most pressing public issues and the values that ought to guide their resolution. These arguments also constitute my understanding of the substance of that elusive entity, the public good, for the balance of the 1980s.

Anyone may assert that particular goals constitute the substance of the public good for a particular era. Usually, interested parties seek support for their own desires by appropriating the label. But the public good is inclusive, not exclusive, and I would argue that any definition of the public good or national interest that does not take the six following categories into account is at best a partial definition, and suspect for that reason. In reviewing Guardian beliefs in these six areas, I offer one man's measure of the health of the democratic system.

Preventing nuclear war. Nobody disagrees that the holocaust unleashed by a nuclear exchange between Russia and the United States should be prevented. Survival takes precedence over other goals. While most of the Guardians expressed their belief that neither side will initiate this unwinnable contest, Melvin Laird expressed his fear of nuclear blackmail—the fear that Europeans or others will somehow knuckle under to the Soviet Union because they perceive Moscow as "stronger." Both Laird and Senator Malcolm Wallop expressed anxiety at Moscow's growing ability to launch a first strike that would cripple the American capacity to strike back—the "counter-force strategy." This is the "window of vulnerability" so prominent in pronouncements of the Reagan administration.

The most certain means of preventing a major nuclear conflict (which may also be politically feasible) is to undertake verifiable nuclear disarmament which diminishes the firepower available to both sides. As this is written, the reengagement in arms limitation talks (now labeled START rather than SALT) has just begun. The degree of good faith with which either side will bargain is hard to predict from their initial posturing, although President Reagan's subjection of Russia to verbal punishment for the military rule in Poland hardly encourages mutual trust at the outset. Simultaneously, the administration has planned an unprecedented rearmament. Among its announced purposes is the demonstration of our "national will."

As a class, the Guardians should be among those most likely to focus upon a clearheaded conception of the national interest that recognizes the limited utility of phrases like "the national will." However, I found that the attitudes of some Guardians toward world affairs are most influenced by the experiences of the cold war, while the attitudes of others were more determined by the experience of Vietnam. There was among them no clear balance between the guilty withdrawal from international action taken to be the lesson of Vietnam and the aggressive, often unilateral, assertiveness of the Reagan administration.

Recognizing the limits of international action. The Guardians' eagerness to embrace human rights as a guiding principle in foreign policy was tempered in several cases by their recognition that human rights in other nations (or even our own) are far easier to propose than to guarantee. A few would claim that Reagan is simply being realistic in abandoning the role of human rights champion. On the other hand, many Guardians would argue that to focus foreign policy primarily on the containment of presumed communist ambitions is inadequate and ultimately demeaning.

The Guardians should be at the forefront of those who recognize arrogance and ignorance among policymakers as twin vices that lead to foreign policy disasters. They should take the lead in insisting that international intervention be undertaken with a dash of humility and without high expectations for its efficacy. I found, however, that many of the Guardians I interviewed outside Washington (with notable exceptions, like John Winthrop Sears) disclaim expertise and thus opinions that could guide their actions concerning defense policy and foreign relations. Rather than participating in a dialogue concerning policy innovations, the Guardians are unlikely to assert a unified influence in the realm of foreign policy until some foreign adventure has been publicly recognized as a disaster.

Restoring equality as a national value. The tension between liberty and equality, the two faces of the democratic creed, has energized much of American history. Some ultimate resolution of this tension is as unlikely as it would be undesirable. To recognize why equality has been relegated to its present low estate is the first step toward its restoration. While equality guided political action in the 1960s which has permanently changed social practices and public attitudes, the government programs of the Great Society have foundered and are being reduced or repealed by the Reagan administration. The quest for equality was, in the 1970s, assigned as the task of administrative and judicial bureaucracies which behaved first as bureaucracies, and only secondarily as the champions of equality. Their purposes inevitably clashed with the individualist tradition, which makes Americans suspicious of any personal claim to an unearned benefit.

New conceptions of equality are required which recognize group attributes without violating the positive features of individualism. The Guardians are precisely the class from which such new definitions should emerge. However, the discussion that could lead to a new synthesis of liberty and equality has so far been confined to the courts; and the judicial system, as an institution, is ill equipped to achieve a transcendent understanding that encompasses conflicting values.

Economic revitalization. The Reagan economic policies sacrifice any concern for increasing material equality on the altar of economic liberty —freedom for the rich, supported by hidden partnerships between government and private enterprise operating through the tax code. Enacted and protected by the pressures of business interests, these tax policies have cumulative results of great magnitude. Depreciation rates on capital investment support the movement of industry into the sunbelt, while the Northeastern cities decline. In the name of restoring economic incentives, government protection of the environment and regulation of worker and consumer safety have been curtailed. The Reagan vision of federalism is based on decentralization—the decentralization of administration, but even more of finance. If local needs are not met with local taxes, those needs could not have been genuine. Thus is denied Madison's precept concerning the extended republic.

Economics is the field in which Guardians are most likely to disclaim expertise. Since nobody opposes prosperity, the situation within the ranks of professional economists consists of an agreement on goals but a disagreement on ends. The attitude of the Guardians is like that of the public; but the Guardians' general financial security makes them more patient. That attitude is a watchful waiting, a willingness to test the economic remedies of an administration so overwhelmingly elected. But the Guardians are at least as likely as the general public to demand the modification of policies that demonstrably fail—and a renewed prosperity that clearly benefits the few at the expense of the many is as likely to stimulate the opposition of the wealthy Guardians as that of the Guardians with modest incomes.

The New Deal firmly established the expectation of government intervention to ameliorate the socially unacceptable results of market forces. At the end of 1981, with nine million persons unemployed, the Reagan administration seemed to be tied more firmly than ever to its economic policies. Further dramatic deterioration of the economy would profoundly damage the administration. However, alternative economic policies making creditable promises to revitalize the industrial base, preserve the older cities, and stabilize the dollar were yet to be proposed by the opposition, which embraced at least the principle of increased defense spending.

By the early Spring of 1982, Reagan's budget proposals, with their record deficits, were bogged down in the Congress. There was no majority for the president's program, but no majority support for any alternative. Congressional confusion reflected the lack of clarity concerning economic matters I had found within the Guardian class.

Recognizing the limits of nature. I found a division among the Guardians on environmental questions. The industrialists applauded the lessening of government regulation, while others responded positively to environmentalist arguments. Surely the public good lies in achieving some reasonable balance between developmental needs and the desire for pure air, pure water, and unspoiled wilderness. Yet this balance is approximated through a series of discrete decisions about individual projects, leases, and regulations made after confrontation between the interests involved. The public interest is not always represented.

The Guardians are those most likely to credit the conception of a public interest that is superior to those of the parties directly involved. Indeed, it is in the nature of guardianship to insist upon the stewardship of natural resources for the benefit of generations yet unborn. For a few, this lack of bondage to immediate economic interests takes the often admirable form of arguing that the whales (or other endangered species) should be preserved for their own sake, quite apart from human concerns.

The Guardians perceive the limits of nature at an intellectual level. But the habits of American industry are predicated on abundance, and it is not certain that even Guardians can act upon the perception of limits when their own interests are involved. The lobbyist for an automobile manufacturer told me of his personal crusade against pollution of the airwaves caused by network television programming.

Establishing the inclusive republic. The substance of the public good involves more than the five areas of challenge listed here. Such problems are unlikely to be dealt with in a timely manner unless our institutions are reformed in line with Madison's insistence that the public good is the appropriate end for which institutional means are fashioned. The key to institutional change is found in Madison's discussion of the extended republic and his insistence that representatives not be instructed by narrow, local interests. In our fragmented society, constituencies become ever more narrow and specialized, even when they are widely distributed geographically. Congressmen respond to the single-issue demands of groups that appear to wield the balance of power in otherwise heterogeneous districts. Government agencies provide functional representation to client groups that make demands inconsistent with public needs and general interests. The symbiotic relationship between defense contractors and Pentagon officials supplies the most striking example of narrow constituency service in the executive branch, yet the relationship is shielded from public view by invoking the requirements of national security.

In general, the Guardians I interviewed were remarkably public-spirited men and women, capable of seeing beyond their own immediate concerns toward an enlarged vision encompassing a wide range of issues. But they seldom question institutional practices and hardly ever become involved in institutional reform. With the exception of Boston's Rick Stearns, none were involved in rebuilding the political parties, the institutions traditionally devoted to formulating, even as they respond to, national constituencies. Although several Guardians decried the parties' collapse, only Julian Bond suggested that other institutions may perform the parties' vital functions. He suggested that issue-oriented action groups are coming together to win the use of the party as an umbrella for their joint endeavors. To be truly effective, he said, such groups must become broader in vision and more flexible in their ability to join shifting coalitions.

The presidency is the other institution that is potentially responsive to a national constituency. Yet, reacting to the presumed failure of Great Society programs, Ronald Reagan has led a retreat from the very concept of federal solutions for domestic problems. In 1982 he borrowed the title of one of Richard Nixon's proposals, New Federalism. Reagan's purposes were the opposite of Nixon's. Nixon proposed sharing federal revenues with the states; Reagan slashed federal social programs relentlessly, stating that their continuation should be up to the states. Nixon sought a nationalization of the welfare system; Reagan proposed assigning the problem of poverty to the states, thus not only to dismantle the

legislative principles of Lyndon Johnson's Great Society, but to deny
federal responsibilities that had been assumed by Franklin D. Roosevelt's New Deal. All of this was proposed in the name of expanding
economic liberty and improving the national defense.

It is time for the supporters of equality to remember that there is no
substitute for the hard political labor of building broad constituencies
based on shared public values and the compromise of conflicting interests. With the disintegration of the parties, this process can be success-
fully performed only by modifying existing institutions, or at least changing our habits of operation within those institutions, toward the goal of
achieving the inclusive republic.

The Guardians are the citizens who will undertake that modification,
if it is ever accomplished. Whether their position on issues was liberal
or conservative, I found the Guardians attached to the institutional
status quo. They neither seek nor support its modification. This is surely
the most disturbing sign of ill health in the American political order.

The Guardians' Responsibility

America's Guardian class bears an awesome responsibility. Operating
both within and outside the constitutional framework, since they are
both private citizens and public officials, the Guardians are the intermediaries between forces in both the public and the government that
would derail the quest for the public good. Such forces in government
include the growing pretensions of the plebiscitary executive and the
tendency of bureaucracies to serve narrow constituencies. Such forces in
the public include the burgeoning single-interest pressure groups and
the normal public tendency to ignore questions, particularly in international affairs, that have no immediate impact upon their lives.

The Guardians I interviewed demonstrate the capacity for fulfilling
that responsibility. Contrary to the lament of Melvin Laird and others
that the best people are not being attracted to political life, I found a
remarkable level of sophistication, articulateness, and good will. I also
found a degree of frustration, as various Guardians expressed their dis-
tress at both public apathy and the public loss of trust in government.
Public trust in government will be restored when the public is assured
that government serves the welfare of all, rather than politically favored
particular interests. Policies of the 1960s, emphasizing equality, served
particular racial and economic minorities and soon stimulated resent-

ment. The policies of the 1980s, emphasizing economic liberty for the already wealthy, are now simulating public resentment. The public good lies in defining a synthesis of these conflicting values and changing institutional habits to reflect that synthesis. The loss of trust they lament can only be rectified with the active involvement of the Guardians themselves.

The American system now grants to the public at large a greater role, both in theory and in practice, than was contemplated by the founders. Citizens in many of their states vote directly on public policies through the referendum process. Party voters in presidential primary elections now make decisions that were once determined by a process of deliberation among the party's established leaders. But the decisions of American government were never intended to be made by national plebiscite, and they still are not so made. After the public's electoral choice initiated the process, every element of the constitutional structure was intended to be involved in determining the public good. Supplemental institutions (particularly the national parties) that were not designed into the original structure have developed to enhance the public role in determining the national future. The Guardians should be involved in efforts to strengthen the parties, so that the electorate's voice will be as well informed and as authoritative as possible. But the Guardians should also unite in rejecting any vision of the national election as a plebiscite that determines the details of policy. The more widely involved in seeking solutions to national problems the political activists become, the more certain is the Madisonian process to distill out "the cool and deliberate sense of the community."

The first requirement for performing the Guardians' responsibility is the achievement of intellectual clarity—a clear understanding of the nature of the contemporary world, and a clearer understanding of the meaning of accepted values in the contemporary context. As James Madison said in 1829,

> To the effect of these changes, intellectual, moral, and social, the institutions and laws of the Country must be adapted, and it will require for the task all the wisdom of the wisest patriots.

Appendix
The Guardians: Demography

LOCATION OF THE INTERVIEWS

Atlanta	13
Boston	19
Chicago	18
Houston	21
San Francisco	12
Washington	34

SEX OF THE RESPONDENTS

Male	94
Female	23

RACE OF THE RESPONDENTS

White	103
Black	8
Spanish-surnamed	5
Native American	1

RELIGIOUS AFFILIATION

Protestant		54
Same denomination as in childhood	35	
Different denomination	19	
Catholic		19
Jewish		10
Other (Greek Orthodox, etc.)		6
Agnostic or atheist		3
Data missing		25

AGE IN 1977

Under 30	3
31–40	34
41–50	45
51–65	30
66 or over	5

EDUCATIONAL ATTAINMENT

High School	4
College (B.A. or B.S.)	29
Harvard Law School	13
Other law school	23
Graduate business school	8
Other graduate study	27
Data missing	13

OCCUPATION

Practicing attorney	23
Business and industry	38
(includes lobbyists)	
Journalism	8
television 2	
print 6	
Labor union officials	3
Civic leaders	6
(League of Women Voters,	
downtown association, etc.)	
Elected officials	12
U.S. Senator 4	
U.S. Congressman 2	
Lt. Governor 1	
(O'Neill of Massachusetts)	
State legislators 3	
City councilors 2	
Appointed officials	19
Cabinet or subcabinet officials 3	
(Treasury, State, & Justice Depts.)	
Federal Judge (Woodrow Seals) 1	
Congressional staff 6	
State govt. officials 2	
County officials 2	
City officials (e.g., Commissioner) 5	
Scholar (David Riesman)	1
Spouse interviewed jointly with primary respondent	7
wife 6	
husband 1	

INCOME IN 1976

$19,999 or less	7
$20,000–$39,999	18
$40,008–$59,999	32
$60,000–$99,999	19
$100,000–$149,999	12
$150,000–$249,999	6
$250,000 or more	4
Data missing	19

PARTY IDENTIFICATION

Intense Democrat	23
Mild Democrat	31
Intense Republican	14
Mild Republican	17
Other	1
(Stephen Vargish: "I vote Democratic or Socialist.")	
Leaning independent	13
Determined independent (abhors parties)	3
Data missing	15

Notes

INTRODUCTION

p.3:   *V. O. Key on elite values:* The passage is found in *Public Opinion and American Democracy* (New York: Knopf, 1961), p. 558. Key set a standard for skepticism about the pretensions of scholars, coupled with ironic wit and a respect for the capacities of the average citizen, which is scarce among the current generation of social scientists.

p. 4:   *"One man, one vote":* The standard was applied to state legislatures by the Supreme Court in *Wesberry v. Saunders*, 369 U.S. 186, and *Reynolds v. Sims*, 376 U.S. 1. Both cases were decided in 1964.

p. 5:   *Pluralism and elitism:* The literature devoted to this debate is nearly boundless. C. Wright Mills, *The Power Elite* (New York: Oxford U. Press, 1957) has inspired numerous elaborations, including the works of my colleague, G. William Domhoff. See his *Who Rules America?* (Englewood Cliffs, N.J.: Prentice-Hall, 1967); *The Higher Circles* (New York: Random House, 1970); *Fat Cats and Democrats* (Englewood Cliffs, N.J.: Prentice-Hall, 1972) and *The Bohemian Grove and Other Retreats* (New York: Harper and Row, 1973). Elite theory as a descriptive tool is examined in Kenneth Prewitt and Alan Stone, *The Ruling Elites* (New York: Harper and Row, 1973). Also see Harold D. Lasswell, Daniel Lerner, and C. Easton Rothwell, *The Comparative Study of Elites* (Stanford: Stanford U. Press, 1952).

For the views of a pluralist sociologist, see Arnold M. Rose, *The Power Structure* (New York: Oxford U. Press, 1967). The most comprehensive statement of the pluralist thesis is David B. Truman, *The Governmental Process* (New York: Knopf, 1951). However, the most active spokesman of pluralism among political scientists has been Robert Dahl of Yale. Dahl has developed the theory (*A Preface to Democratic Theory,* 1956, and *After the Revolution,* 1970), described its application to understanding America (*Polyarchy: Participation and Opposition,* 1971), and has used it to inform a classic study of decision-making in New Haven (*Who Governs? Democracy and Power in an American City*, 1961). The argument comes full circle with Domhoff's *Who Really Rules? New Haven and Community Power Reexamined* (1978). Domhoff reexamines Dahl's data and claims to find the tracks of a ruling class that Dahl missed.

p. 6: *David Truman on the system's stability:* The quotation is from the concluding paragraph of Truman's *The Governmental Process*, p. 535. Following his experiences as Provost of Columbia University during the 1960s, Truman in 1971 published a second edition of the book that is less hopeful for the future of the American system.

p. 9: *The political leaders interviewed by David Broder:* The reference is to Broder's *Changing of the Guard: Power and Leadership in America* (New York: Simon and Schuster, 1980). Since Broder and I were fishing in some of the same waters, an overlap in our respondents was inevitable. Eleven of the individuals featured in Broder's book are among those respondents I have called the Guardians.

p. 9: *Open-ended depth interviews:* The interactive nature of open-ended depth interviews, together with the advantages and pitfalls of elite interviewing are analyzed by Lewis Anthony Dexter in *Elite and Specialized Interviewing* (Evanston, Ill.: Northwestern University Press, 1970).

p. 10: *"The new class":* I believe the term was first applied to the United States by David T. Bazelon in *Power in America: the Politics of the New Class* (New York: New American Library, 1964).

PROLOGUE

p. 13: *Epigraph:* The quotation is from Gaillard Hunt, ed., *The Writings of James Madison* (New York: G.P. Putnam's Sons, 1900–1910), vol. IX, p. 360n, quoted in Alexander Landi, "Madison's Political Theory," VI *The Political Science Reviewer* (1976), p. 110.

p. 15: *Several of Reagan's cabinet choices declined appointment:* The process of selecting Regan's cabinet is described in *Newsweek*, January 12, 1981, pp. 27–29. Of the three Reagan favorites who declined, at least one (John Connolly) refused a post that seemed too lacking in influence for Connolly's taste, according to the report.

p. 21: *Boston as the home of the alienated voter:* See Murray B. Levin, *The Alienated Voter: Politics in Boston* (New York: Holt, Rinehart, and Winston, 1960). Levin's account is based on the mayoralty election of 1959, in which John Collins, a relative unknown, defeated John Powers, candidate of the political establishment, by charging him with practicing "power politics." In ten years as mayor, Collins did much for Boston, including the renewal of its dilapidated central area. Essentially, Collins persuaded the economic elite of Boston to invest in the city's restoration. Boston's physical renaissance is described more completely in chapter four, below. For a comprehensive account of Massachusetts politics, see Edgar A. Litt, *The Political Cultures of Massachusetts* (Cambridge: M.I.T. Press, 1965).

p. 26: *Plato's guardians were educated underground:* The quotation is from Harry Jaffa, *Equality and Liberty: Theory and Practice in American Politics* (New York: Oxford University Press, 1965), pp. 129–130.

p. 27: *Their values . . . were confused or contradictory:* For confirming evidence drawn from the Columbia University survey of economic and political elites conducted in 1971 and 1972, see Allen H. Barton, "Fault Lines in American Elite Consensus," *Daedalus*, Summer 1980, pp. 1–24.

CHAPTER ONE

p. 28: *President Reagan's Inaugural Address:* The quotation here was transcribed from a recording. Its punctuation varies from the official version but is, I believe, more faithful to the speech as delivered. I thank my father, Lawrence Lamb, for making the recording.

p. 29: *Only 53.9 per cent participated in the 1980 election:* The turnout figures given here are from Martin Plissner and Warren Mitofsky, "What if They Held an Election and Nobody Came?" *Public Opinion*, February/March, 1981, p. 50. The authors calculate the 1976 turnout at 54.4 per cent but point out that the Census Bureau estimated the voting age population for both 1976 and 1980 on projections of the understated 1970 census. They further note that the most common reason for failing to vote was a failure to register, and that "only" a quarter of the nonvoters polled suggested alienated responses to the political system as the reason for not casting a ballot. The authors do not speculate about reasons voters might have for failing to register, other than a change of residence. It should be remembered that the voting age was twenty-one in nearly every state during the New Deal era; a national voting age of eighteen increases the likelihood of nonvoting. Conversely, local intimidation that prevented black voting in the South has diminished appreciably since then.

p. 30: *The 1980 result marked a rejection of Jimmy Carter:* For the evidence, see Gerald M. Pomper, "The Presidential Election" and Kathleen A.

Frankovic, "Public Opinion Trends," in Pomper et al., *The Election of 1980* (Chatham, N.J.: Chatham House, 1981).

p. 31: *V. O. Key labeled these events "critical elections":* See his seminal article, "A Theory of Critical Elections," 17 *Journal of Politics* (February 1955), pp. 3–18.

p. 32: *Edmund Burke's vision:* Burke was an Irish member of the English Parliament who supported the American claim to independence on the grounds that the Americans sought no more than their traditional rights as Englishmen, thus to preserve the established framework of their life. When he was invited to support the French Revolution in 1789, Burke set forth his philosophy in his great polemic, *Reflections on the Revolution in France* (Chicago: Henry Regnery, 1955; first published, 1790), in which he predicted the violence that would overwhelm France.

p. 33: *President Reagan's speech accepting the nomination:* The excerpts quoted here are from the Republican National Committee, "Acceptance Speech by the Honorable Ronald Reagan . . .", mimeo., August 5, 1980, pp. 1, 5, and 8.

p. 34: *Leaders have shared the values of the general political culture:* The most comprehensive comparison of elite and mass political values in America is being made by Herbert McClosky and his associates. A preliminary report of their findings was made in Dennis Chong, Herbert McClosky, and John Zaller, "Patterns of Support for Democratic and Capitalist Values," a paper prepared for delivery at the 1980 annual meeting of the American Political Science Association. The authors find that adherence to the belief systems of capitalism and democracy is widespread, and has been so since the nation's inception. Among elites, there is a conflict between support for traditional *laissez-faire* capitalism and contemporary welfare capitalism. The dominant belief systems are imperfectly understood by segments of the mass electorate, due to an incomplete process of "social learning," which is responsible for their lower order of sophistication. McClosky's findings with regard to elite values, based on the analysis of multiple attitude surveys of elite respondents, are compatible with my own findings, which are based on depth interviews of a much smaller sample.

p. 35: *Ted Morgan:* The quotation is taken out of sequence from Morgan's *On Becoming an American* (Boston: Houghton Mifflin, 1978) pp. 309, 271–72.

p. 36: *The long tradition of liberal individualism:* Liberalism is here defined as the perception that the individual person is the basis of politics, and that rational design is more to be trusted than tradition in determining the nature of governments. For an account of the English origins of liberalism which stresses its susceptibility to crassness, see C. B. Mac-

Pherson, *The Political Theory of Possessive Individualism: Hobbes to Locke* (Oxford: Oxford University Press, 1962). For the pervasive influence of liberalism in American life and thought, see Louis Hartz, *The Liberal Tradition in America* (New York: Harcourt, Brace, 1955)

p. 38: *Max Lerner on nationalism:* The passage is from Lerner's massive *America as a Civilization* (New York: Simon and Schuster, 1957), p. 903. Lerner's concern was with how the nationalist tradition would adapt itself to the threat of Soviet communism; he was particularly concerned by the contribution of nationalism to the virulence of Senator Joseph McCarthy's witch-hunt.

p. 39: *According to Katz and Lazarsfeld:* The reference is to Elihu Katz and P. F. Lazarsfeld, *Personal Influence* (Glencoe, Ill.: Free Press, 1955). The authors present convincing tests of their hypothesis that the content of the media reach the general public in a two-step process, via the mediating attentive elites.

CHAPTER TWO

p. 42: *John Randolph on liberty and equality (epigraph):* Randolph is quoted in Russell Kirk, *John Randolph of Roanoke* (Indianapolis: Liberty Press, 1978), p. 46.

p. 43: *Minimum-wage laws abridge workers' freedom to make contracts:* This was the majority argument written by Justice George Sutherland in *Adkins v. Children's Hospital,* 261 U.S. 525 (1923). Justices Oliver Wendell Holmes and William Howard Taft both dissented. Minimum-wage legislation won the approval of the Court only in 1937 with *West Coast Hotel Co. v. Parrish,* 300 U.S. 379.

p. 45: *Wilsonian idealism becomes chauvinistic nationalism:* For a persuasive formulation of this argument, see Garry Wills, *Nixon Agonistes* (New York: Signet, 1971), Part IV, and particularly pp. 439–51.

p. 45: *Tocqueville on individualism:* The quotation is from *Democracy in America,* tr. by Henry Reeve (New York: Schocken, 1961), vol. II, p. 120. Americans who lacked Tocqueville's aristocratic bias made the concept of individualism their own, gave it positive connotations, and were soon using it as a label for the uniqueness of the American experiment. Ralph Waldo Emerson, for one, made individualism a central feature of his philosophy.

p. 46: *"Coercive individualism" among partisan activists:* The 1972 study was conducted as part of a larger effort by Richard Hofstetter, reported as *Bias in the News: Network Television Coverage of the 1972 Election Campaign* (Columbus: Ohio State University Press, 1976). For the account of Hofstetter's findings concerning coercive individualism, I am dependent upon John Kessel, *Presidential Campaign Politics* (Homewood, Ill.: Dorsey Press, 1980), pp. 66–73.

p. 53: *Lincoln on individualism:* Quoted from Richard N. Current, ed., *The Political Thought of Abraham Lincoln* (Indianapolis: Bobbs-Merrill, 1967), p. 188.

p. 53: *Garry Wills on the metaphor of the race:* The quotation is from Wills's *Nixon Agonistes,* pp. 223–24. Wills argues that Nixon, by embodying national myths such as individualism, has demonstrated their absurdity and heralded their dissolution (see p. 546). The response suggested by my research is, maybe so, but it won't happen soon.

p. 54: *According to James Tobin:* The quotation is from Tobin's essay, "Reaganomics and Economics," *New York Review of Books,* December 3, 1981, p. 13. Tobin argues that both the Reagan and Thatcher administrations are involved in counterrevolutions against the Keynesian theories and policies instituted thirty-five to forty-five years ago.

p. 55: *The impact of faith in equal opportunity on working people:* In his classic study of fifteen working men in New Haven, Robert E. Lane found that men tend to explain their low incomes as a failure to seize opportunities, particularly educational opportunities. See *Political Ideology* (New York: The Free Press, 1962), chapter 4. Working-class consciousness is examined by Richard Sennett and Jonathan Cobb in *The Hidden Injuries of Class* (New York: Vintage, 1973). They find that working men do not justify their lower status through a rationalization of the individualist ethic, but are torn by internal conflict which generates a hidden rage, because of judging themselves by society's standards. Sennett and Cobb elicited outraged feelings that were largely absent in Lane's respondents.

p. 57: *The legal fiction that treats corporations as individuals:* While the corporation was found to be in some sense the legal equivalent of an individual as early as 1819 in *Dartmouth College v. Woodward,* 4 Wheaton 518, the heyday of extending protection for vested property rights through "substantive due process" came late in the nineteenth century. See any American constitutional law text; for example, Robert F. Cushman, *Cases in Constitutional Law,* 5th ed., (Englewood Cliffs, N.J.: Prentice-Hall, 1979), pp. 257–73.

p. 57: *President Roosevelt's speeches:* The quotations given here are from Basil Rauch, ed., *Franklin D. Roosevelt: Selected Speeches, Messages, Press Conferences, and Letters* (New York: Rinehart, 1957). Samuel I. Rosenman stated that the Commonwealth Club speech was primarily the work of Adolph A Berle, Jr., "as revised by the Brain Trust." Rosenman, *Working with Roosevelt* (London: Rupert Hart-Davis, 1952), p. 165.

p. 63: *The concept of group rights is absurd in American law:* This conclusion is reached after a tightly reasoned analysis by Timothy J. O'Neill, "The Language of Equality in a Constitutional Order," paper prepared for delivery at the 1980 meeting of the American Political Science Association. Abundant source citations are found in the paper. For a persuasive defense of quotas and affirmative action, see John C. Livingston, *Fair Game? Inequality and Affirmative Action* (San Francisco: Freeman, 1979).

p. 63: *The Constitution need not be color-blind:* The phrase "color-blind Constitution" originated in the famous dissent by Justice John Marshall Harlan to the Supreme Court's approval of racial segregation on railroads in *Plessy v. Ferguson,* 163 U.S. 537 (1896). The Bakke case is *Regents of the University of California v. Bakke,* 56 L. Ed. 2d, 98 S. Ct. 3140 (1978).

p. 63: *Brian Weber's claim of discrimination:* The training program was sponsored by Weber's union, so the case is *United Steelworkers of America v. Weber,* 99 S. Ct. 2721 (1979). The issue was treated as one of statutory, rather than constitutional, interpretation, since the Constitution's equal-protection clause is held to require states and their agencies (such as the University of California, in the case of Alan Bakke) to treat persons equally. But it makes no such requirement of private organizations.

p. 64: *Constitutionality of the minority "set-aside" provision:* See *Fullilove v. Klutznick,* 100 S. Ct. 2758 (1980). Marshall's concurring opinion is at p. 2797.

p. 65: *A new understanding that would transcend individualist values:* Some of the theoretical groundwork has been laid by the Harvard philosopher John Rawls. Rawls's massive *A Theory of Justice* (Cambridge: Harvard University Press, 1971) was a summary and culmination of the work of more than a decade. Hailed upon publication as an original work of great power, the book clearly sets forth an alternative to utilitarianism as the basis of justice in society. Justice is defined as that fairness which would result if a community of equals established the nature of the social contract anew. Social and economic inequalities are acceptable if they operate to improve the lot of the least advantaged members of society, and if they are attached to positions and offices that are open to all. Thus Rawls's concept of "equality of fair opportunity" is far removed from the mere notion of "an equal start in the race of life." But Rawls offers revised abstractions to replace the current ones; his principles must be embodied in concrete proposals before they can become the subject of popular discussion. For clear thinking on some of these issues (which is also more readable than Rawls) see John H. Schaar, *Legitimacy in the Modern*

State, (New Brunswick, N.J.: Transaction Books, 1981), chapters 7–10.

CHAPTER THREE

p. 66:   *Epigraph:* The two paragraphs by Madison are taken from *The Federalist,* numbers 45 and 52. Both papers argue that the governmental design most able to define and achieve the public good is the extensive "federated republic."

p. 66:   *John Adams on constitutionalism:* The quotation from Adams, and the comment upon it, are in M. J. Heale, *The Making of American Politics* (London: Longman, 1977), p. 46.

p. 67:   *"Law has flourished on the corpse of philosophy":* The quotation is from Louis Hartz, *The Liberal Tradition in America* (New York: Harcourt, Brace, 1955), p. 10.

p. 67:   The Federalist *"lays down for us a constitutional morality":* The quotation is from Willmoore Kendall and George W. Carey, *The Basic Symbols of the American Political Tradition* (Baton Rouge: Louisiana State University Press, 1970), pp. 141, 142. The authors' claim that the Constitution is a legislative supremacy document gains credence from the detail concerning the powers of Congress in Article I, and the spare phraseology of the remainder. That this was not the single intention of the founders is suggested by the many references to the separation-of-powers principle recorded in Madison's *Notes on the Federal Convention.*

p. 68:   *Lyndon Johnson unbalanced the Constitution:* One plea for the strengthening of Congress in opposition to the executive branch, written during the Lyndon Johnson era, is Lewis Anthony Dexter, " 'Check and Balance' Today: What Does It Mean for Congress and Congressmen?" in Alfred de Grazia, ed., *Congress: The First Branch of Government* (Washington: American Enterprise Institute, 1966), pp. 83–113.

p. 70:   *Liberals praise popular control, while conservatives laud the auxiliary precautions:* For the details of this interpretation, see Martin Diamond, "Conservatives, Liberals, and the Constitution," in Robert A. Goldwin, ed., *Left, Right, and Center* (Chicago: Rand McNally, 1965), pp. 60–86.

p. 70:   *Madison's description of the Senate:* The quotation is from *Federalist* 63. At the conclusion of the paper, Madison predicts that "nothing will be able to maintain even the constitutional authority of the Senate, but such a display of enlightened policy, and attachment to the public good, as will divide with [the House of Representatives] the affections and support of the entire body of the people themselves."

p. 71: *Brock Brower quoting Senator Fulbright:* Brower wrote an extensive profile of then Senator J. William Fulbright which was published in *Life,* May 13, 1966. The essay is reprinted in Brower's book, *Other Loyalties* (New York: Atheneum, 1968), pp. 138–164.

p. 72: *The internal norms of Congress:* That "it is not the striving for reelection that explains the behavior of Capitol Hill, but the quest for personal power within Congress itself" is the thesis of Rochelle Jones and Peter Woll, *The Private World of Congress* (New York: Free Press, 1979). The authors stress the role of staff members who serve as power resources for their bosses but play their own power game, in order to advance their own reputations. The growth and development of the staff is recounted in Harrison W. Fox, Jr., and Susan Webb Hammond, *Congressional Staffs* (New York: Free Press, 1977). Also see Michael J. Malbin, *Congressional Staff and the Future of Representative Government* (New York: Basic Books, 1980).

p. 73: *As Garry Wills makes plain:* The reference is to Wills's *Explaining America: The Federalist* (Garden City, N.Y.: Doubleday, 1981), *passim.* Wills's remarkable book was published after my own (far more cursory) examination of *The Federalist* was completed. He argues that "the political scientists' Madison," depicted as either a champion of pluralism or of governmental paralysis, has been constructed only by overlooking Madison's devotion to an aristocratic vision of the public good, characteristic of the American Enlightenment. I agree.

p. 74: *Separation . . . as conceived by Montesquieu:* Baron Charles Secondat de Montesquieu's *De l'Esprit des Lois* (The Spirit of the Laws) was first published anonymously in 1748 and was immediately successful. Madison explicates Montesquieu's principle of separation and balance in *Federalist* 47.

p. 74: *There is no opposing branch to balance the bureaucracy:* Recent presidents have been frustrated by the loose organization of the executive branch. A secret report to President Lyndon Johnson summarized the situation succinctly: "Top political executives—the President and Cabinet Secretaries—preside over agencies which they never own and only rarely command." Quoted from *The Organization and Management of Great Society Programs, Final Report of the President's Task Force on Governmental Organization,* June 1967, in Richard P. Nathan, *The Plot That Failed: Nixon and the Administrative Presidency* (New York: Wiley, 1975), p. 88. Nathan's book chronicles Nixon's attempt to bring the bureaucracy to heel, which was part of the White House atmosphere that led to Watergate. Watergate, in turn, gave executive reorganization which would provide greater presidential authority a bad name. Jimmy Carter's promise to reform the bureaucracy resulted only in the creation of two more cabinet departments, Energy and Education. The Department of Energy quickly become a cumbersome bureaucracy, in the eyes of its critics, while the Department of Education was Carter's payoff of a campaign promise to the National Education Association. The problem of asserting political leadership over the bureaucracy has been a preoccupation of the Reagan cabinet. According to U.N. Ambassador Jeanne J. Kirkpatrick and Interior Secretary James Watt, frequent cabinet meetings during the initial weeks of the administration renewed their sense of collective purpose and kept cabinet members from being captured by the concerns of the established bureaucrats in their departments. See the interview of Kirkpatrick and Watt in *Public Opinion,* February-March, 1981, pp. 10–12.

p. 77: *An economy of countervailing power:* See John Kenneth Galbraith, *American Capitalism: The Concept of Countervailing Power* (Boston: Houghton Mifflin, 1952), revised in 1956. The book was re-issued in 1980 by M. E. Sharpe, White Plains, N.Y., with a preface in which Galbraith asserts that the analysis remains valid, but that "inflation is assuredly inimical to a socially benign deployment of countervailing power" (p. vii).

p. 77: *The pluralist prescription for American politics:* For a brief account of the vast literature on the topic, see the note to the Introduction headed "Pluralism and elitism."

p. 77: *Authors label their understanding of the Constitution with Madison's name:* Such writings include Charles A. Beard's classic *An Economic Interpretation of the Constitution of the United States* (New York: Macmillan, 1913; many subsequent editions), Robert A. Dahl's more modern, but equally classic *A Preface to Democratic Theory* (Chicago: University of Chicago Press, 1956), and James MacGregor Burns's 1963 call for a responsible party system, *The Deadlock of Democracy* (Englewood-Cliffs, N.J.: Prentice-Hall). In his chapter VI, Beard designates *Federalist* 10 as the core of the political science of the Constitution. Beard sees that famous paper as strictly an economic document, overlooking Madison's listing of noneconomic motives for the formation of factions and his argument that, in an extended republic, the great variety of economic interests will prevent any single interest from dominating, just as the great variety of sects is the best guarantee of religious liberty. In his Part I, Burns labels as "the Madisonian system" that combination of federalism with the "balance of checks" which frustrated the legislative proposals of John F. Kennedy and thus defeated the presumed mandate of an electoral majority. In his chapter 1, Dahl labels as "Madisonian democracy" the inhibition of majorities in favor of particular minorities. For a biting critique of Dahl's misreading of Madison, see the twenty-fifth anniversary review of Dahl's book by Ronald M. Peters, Jr., VII *The Political Science Reviewer* (Fall, 1977), pp. 145–80.

p. 78: *Exalting the group role:* The quoted paragraph is from Theodore J. Lowi, *The End of Liberalism: The Second Republic of the United States* (New York: Norton, 2d ed., 1979), p. 51. Lowi's first edition, in 1969, was subtitled "Ideology, Policy, and the Crisis of Public Authority"; it was presented as a polemical prophecy. Finding that the Republican administrations of Nixon and Ford only continued the practices of Democrats Kennedy and Johnson, Lowi argues in the second edition that interest-group liberalism has now supplanted the traditional constitutional arrangements to the extent that a Second Republic has been established.

p. 81: *Madison's was the world of the American Enlightenment:* The quotation is from Garry Wills, *Explaining America: The Federalist,* p. 268.

p. 82: *"The public interest as means and procedure":* The quoted sentence is from Frank J. Sorauf, "The Conceptual Muddle," in Carl J. Friedrich, ed., *Nomos V: The Public Interest* (New York: Atherton Press, 1962), p. 185. The modest list of three ways in which the phrase "public good" is used follows the lead of Sorauf's essay. Sorauf is among those who, seeking to establish a value-free social science, would ban scholarly use of the term "public interest." But see the other essays in the same volume. C. W. Cassinelli's "The Public Interest in Political Ethics," pp. 44–53, insists upon the need for a concept of the public interest in any consideration of political ethics and finds that it is tied to concepts of the good life and of political responsibilities, as well as rights. For a similar point, see Richard E. Flathman, *Concepts in Social and Political Philosophy* (New York: Macmillan, 1973), pp. 514–32.

p. 82: *Pluralists who oppose the public and private interest:* The dean of contemporary pluralists, David B. Truman, holds that "Assertion[s] of an inclusive 'national' or 'public interest' . . . are part of the data of politics. However, they do not describe any actual or possible political situation within a complex modern nation. . . . [We] do not need to account for a totally inclusive interest, because one does not exist." Truman, *The Governmental Process* (New York: Knopf, 1951), pp. 50–51. Truman quotes Arthur F. Bentley's 1908 book, *The Process of Government,* to the same effect. I suspect that Madison himself would not have defined the public good as a "totally inclusive interest," and the politicians I interviewed who found the concept useful did not specify unanimity as a precondition for the existence of a public interest.

p. 83:   *Those in the approving category were elected officials:* Unfortunately, this question was posed to only thirty-five of the respondents. Nearly all were either practicing attorneys or legislators. The question about the public interest was not asked of federal civil servants. Such persons were too small a subsample among the Guardians for reliable results, in any case. Apologists for bureaucracy have argued that bureaucrats have come to perform representative functions, in many cases in a manner superior to that of elected officials. Peter Woll concludes in *American Bureaucracy* (New York: Norton, 2nd ed., 1977), chapter 6, that the bureaucracy has become a fourth coordinate branch, subject to political checks by the other three. The difficulties of assigning a representative role to bureaucracies are analyzed by Joseph P. Witherspoon, "The Bureaucracy as Representatives," in Pennock and Chapman, eds., *Nomos X: Representation* (New York: Atherton Press, 1968), pp. 229–56. Like Woll, Witherspoon neglects Madison's consideration of constituency size; my argument is that most agencies' client groups form constituencies that are numerically small, narrowly focused, and neglectful of the public interest. That members of Congress conceive of their representative function in a manner congruent with the concept of the public interest is well established in the literature. For one example, Roger H. Davidson has applied the representational categories developed by Wahlke and Eulau to the House of Representatives, finding that 27.6 per cent consider themselves to be "trustees," 19.9 are "delegates," and 50 per cent act as "politicos," combining the two roles. (Senator Richard Lugar's statement about the public interest in the text is a classic rendering of the "trustee" concept.) Davidson, "Congress and the Executive: The Race for Representation," in de Grazia, ed., *Congress: The First Branch of Government,* p. 394. Davidson also finds that the focus of representation is seen as being more national than district-oriented in a significant number of cases. Any congressman who sees himself as the trustee of national interests is perforce guided by a concept of the public good.

p. 85:   *Madison on the advantages of an extended republic:* The point made by David Hume is in his essay "The Idea of a Perfect Commonwealth," published in 1777; reprinted in Henry D. Aiken, ed., *Hume: Essays, Moral and Political* (New York: Macmillan, 1975), p. 385. My account of Madison's argument is drawn from *Federalist* 10 and 51 together. The quotation is from the conclusion of number 10.

p. 86:   *Grant McConnell on constituency size:* The quotation is from *Private Power and American Democracy* (New York: Knopf, 1967), pp. 104–5, 106. McConnell's point about the Senate is on p. 110. The American preference for small organizations and constituencies is described throughout McConnell's book.

p. 88:   *The tradition of small, homogeneous assemblies:* Jane Mansbridge makes the important distinction between two separate democratic traditions and sets of procedures. In "unitary" democracy, participants are united by membership in a community and/or dedication to a cause. This agreement on ends allows the determination of means by consensus in face-to-face meetings in which all participate. In "adversary" democracy, there is no attempt to achieve agreement on ends. The focus is upon formal procedures which lead to a majority decision, with due regard to minority involvement. The classical republicans, Rousseau, and Tocqueville (in his admiration for the New England town) were, and the contemporary communitarians are, theorists of unitary democracy; Madison is a theorist of adversary democracy. See Mansbridge, *Beyond Adversary Democracy* (New York: Basic Books, 1980).

p. 89:   *The* Dred Scott *decision:* The reference is to *Dred Scott v. Sanford,* 19 Howard 393 (1857), which denied citizenship to members of the black race, found the Missouri Compromise unconstitutional, and became yet a further step toward civil war. For a contemporary case study of the complex elements involved in compliance with a Court decision, see William K. Muir, Jr., *Prayer in the Public Schools: Law and Attitude Change* (Chicago: University of Chicago Press, 1967). A collection of articles on similar topics is Theodore L. Becker, ed., *The Impact of Supreme Court Decisions* (New York: Oxford University Press, 1969).

p. 91:   *The judicial movement for school integration:* For an unrelenting attack upon the wisdom and procedure of the courts in establishing school integration through busing, see Lino A. Graglia, *Disaster By Decree: The Supreme Court Decisions on Race and the Schools* (Ithaca: Cornell University Press, 1975).

p. 92:   *The presidency at the center of a mythical understanding:* The literature on individual presidents, presidential campaigns, and the presidential institution is vast. One book that touches on all three is Joseph A. Califano, Jr., *A Presidential Nation* (New York: Norton, 1975). For an account of Nixon's fall which accentuates the mythical force of the pre-Nixon presidency, see Theodore H. White, *Breach of Faith* (New York: Dell, 1976).

p. 93:   *John Taylor on parties:* The quotation is from Taylor's "A Definition of Parties," excerpted in Noble E. Cunningham, Jr., ed., *The Making of the American Party System, 1789–1809* (Englewood Cliffs, N.J.: Prentice-Hall, 1956), p. 21. This compendium of documents thoroughly conveys the flavor of the partisan contest of the era.

p. 94:   *The contrast between Andrew Jackson and his predecessors:* The mode of life in the District of Columbia during the era of the Jeffersonian presidents is described in James Sterling Young, *The Washington Community, 1800–1828* (New York: Harcourt, 1966). The national capital was little more than a frontier outpost; Congress and the executive branch were physically and emotionally separated; representatives were sent to Washington to guard their constituents against the development of real authority by the national government. The social and political environment did not encourage partisanship. In these circumstances, the success of Jefferson is even more remarkable than the failure of Madison.

p. 96: *The disintegration of the party system:* A succinct summary of knowledge about parties and voting before the 1980 election is found in Jeanne J. Kirkpatrick's "Changing Patterns of Electoral Competition," in Anthony King, ed., *The New American Political System* (Washington, D.C.: American Enterprise Institute, 1978), chapter 7. For a short, forceful statement of the thesis offered here, see Everett Carll Ladd, Jr., *Where Have All the Voters Gone?* (New York: Norton, 1978). Ladd earlier published, with the aid of Charles D. Hadley, a more detailed account in *Transformations of the American Party System*, 2nd ed. (New York: Norton, 1977.) The American anti-party tradition, and the effects of reform efforts, are described by Austin Ranney in *Curing the Mischiefs of Faction: Party Reform in America* (Berkeley: University of California Press, 1975). The new textbooks reflect the consensus of political scientists on the question. For one example, see William J. Crotty and Gary C. Jacobson, *American Parties in Decline* (Boston: Little, Brown, 1980).

p. 100: *Uncommitted delegates will "exercise unique influence":* The quotation is from an Associated Press account of the national committee meeting in the *San Francisco Chronicle*, March 27, 1982, p. 1. Symptomatic of the low regard of Californians for party professionals, the story was headlined, "Democrats Give Bosses More Power."

p. 100: *One leader of the New Right:* The reference is to Richard A. Viguerie, *The New Right: We're Ready to Lead* (Falls Church, Va.: The Viguerie Co., 1981), chapter VIII.

CHAPTER FOUR

p. 102: *Epigraphs:* The Jefferson quotation is from his *Notes on Virginia,* cited in Max Beloff, *Thomas Jefferson and American Democracy* (New York: Collier, 1962), p. 82. Beloff points out that the *Notes* were written before Jefferson visited France and observed its revolutionary fervor; his agrarianism was established early and endured long. The Herb

Caen quotation is from his column in the *San Francisco Chronicle and Examiner,* Sunday, March 1, 1981.

p. 109: *Ian Menzies comparing Boston and San Francisco:* The quotations are from "The Two Most Exciting Cities in the Nation?" Boston *Globe,* Sept. 27, 1970, cited in Neal R. Pierce, *The Megastates of America* (New York: Norton, 1972), p. 168.

p. 112: *Robert Wood on decentralization:* Wood is quoted by Neal Pearce in *The Megastates of America, loc. cit.*

p. 115: *"The smartest thing . . . was to murder Harvey Milk":* The quotation is from Charles McCabe's column, *San Francisco Chronicle,* August 14, 1979.

p. 116: *The Board of Supervisors has been "trivialized":* The quotation is from Jerry Burns, "The View from San Francisco," *California Journal,* January, 1980, p. 13.

p. 118: *An estimated $2,000,000 in city services was delivered:* The estimate was made in Eric A. Nordlinger, *Decentralizing the City: a Study of Boston's Little City Halls* (Cambridge: The M.I.T. Press, 1972), p. 287. My account of the program is dependent upon this thorough analysis. Nordlinger finds that the Boston program was the most complete example of this type of decentralization. He concludes that the experiment has proven itself worthy of emulation by other cities.

p. 120: *Racial conflict in the Boston schools:* The story of Darryl Williams is in *Newsweek,* October 19, 1979, p. 79; the figures for white attendance in the Boston public schools and the account of the South Boston high school is from *U. S. News and World Report,* March 31, 1980, p. 66.

p. 121: *Nathan Glazer on San Francisco's Mission District:* The quotation is from *Affirmative Discrimination: Ethnic Inequality and Public Policy* (New York: Basic Books, 1978), p. 104. Throughout his chapter on school busing, Glazer cites Boston and San Francisco as leading examples of the most destructive efforts to achieve equal racial distribution throughout the schools.

p. 122: *A 1973 decision of the U.S. Supreme Court:* The decision was *Keyes v. Denver School District,* 413 U.S. 921.

p. 125: *District elections were needed to satisfy civil rights requirements:* Federal courts have held that Section 5 of the 1965 Civil Rights Act prohibits the use in Southern states of at-large elections for local legislatures that dilute the voting power of racial minorities. See Derrick A. Bell, Jr., *Race Racism and American Law* (Boston: Little, Brown, 1973), pp. 152–158. This federal legislation also led to mixed district and at-large Council seats in Houston; but a lawsuit was required in Houston, and the change was not effective until 1980. The 1965 Act did not apply to Boston or San Francisco.

p. 130: *Nathan Glazer on school integration in Atlanta:* The quotation is from

Affirmative Discrimination, p. 107. For further details on the personalities involved in the compromise, see *Newsweek*, July 30, 1973, pp. 42–43.

p. 135: *When all issues are no longer reducible to race:* The reference here is to the stark conclusion of V. O. Key's classic *Southern Politics* (New York: Knopf, 1949). In the South Key studied, all politics was related to the maintenance of white supremacy.

p. 136: *Mayors had trouble assessing the performance of city departments:* See Paul Burka, "Why Is Houston Falling Apart?" *Texas Monthly,* November 1980, pp. 189 ff., for an historically oriented account of Houston's institutional flaws and the shortcomings of former Mayor McConn.

p. 136: *Annexation has stretched Houston's services dangerously thin:* The figures given here are from "A City's Growing Pains," *Newsweek,* January 14, 1980, p. 45.

p. 137: *Efforts to integrate Houston's schools began in 1960:* The account in this paragraph is condensed from Chandler Davidson, *Biracial Politics* (Baton Rouge: Louisiana State University Press, 1972), pp. 130–34.

p. 138: *Hispanics in the Houston school district:* The figures quoted are from "Hispanics labeled fastest growing HISD ethnic group," *Houston Post,* October 28, 1977, p. 3A.

p. 141: *There are two kinds of Houstonians:* The quotation is from Juan Palomo, "Whitmire, Heard found McConn convenient target," *Houston Post,* November 4, 1981, p. 18A.

p. 142: *Mayor Daley's values:* The quotation is from Ralph Whitehead, Jr., "The Organization Man," *American Scholar,* Summer 1977. For a description of machine operations under Daley, see Milton Rakove, *Don't Make No Waves—Don't Back No Losers* (Bloomington: University of Indiana Press, 1975).

p. 144: *Daley began "to play to the white audience":* The quotation is from Whitehead, op. cit.

p. 150: *The origin of the name of Chicago's "Deacons":* The story is recounted in detail in the pamphlet "Chicago United: Its Origin and Its Opportunities" (Chicago: Chicago United, n.d.), Appendix B.

p. 153: *"The era of public assistance . . . is over":* The quotation is from "NPA Squares Off At Roundtable," *Disclosure,* July-August, 1981, p. 1.

p. 154: *Tocqueville on the tie between local and public interest:* The quotation is from *Democracy in America,* vol. II (New York: Schocken, 1961; first published in English, 1840), pp. 125–26.

p. 155: *Cities cannot control their own destinies:* For the elaboration of this argument, see Paul Peterson, *City Limits,* (Chicago: University of Chicago Press, 1981).

p. 156: *Budget Director Stockman defending block grants:* The quotation is from an Associated Press report in the *San Francisco Chronicle*, April 29, 1981, p. 8.

p. 157: *The Pentagon practices of weapons procurement:* For a description of these practices, see James Fallows, "America's High-Tech Weaponry," *Atlantic Monthly*, May, 1981, pp. 21–33. Also see Fallows's *National Defense* (New York: Random House, 1981).

p. 158: *Morton Grodzins's marble-cake metaphor for federalism:* See Grodzins's "The Federal System" in *Goals for Americans*, President's Commission on National Goals (Englewood Cliffs, N.J.: Prentice-Hall, 1960).

p. 158: *The original New Federalism proposal:* I have written a brief history of President Nixon's proposal for welfare reform, and the interesting treatment it received in Congress, in *The People, Maybe*, 2nd ed. (North Scituate, Massachusetts: Duxbury Press, 1974), pp. 437–50.

CHAPTER FIVE

p. 160: *Epigraph:* The quotation is from *Federalist* 41, in which Madison justifies the assignment of important powers to the federal government, with the power to conduct foreign relations heading the list.

p. 160: *All but six agreed that American has been a successful society:* The six "deviant" responses to this statement came from five women and one man, the most striking sexual difference in the data. The lone male was Judge Woodrow Seals of Houston, who takes a long historical view of American civilization and finds standards in his religion to judge the trend of contemporary affairs. Judge Seals would be near the top of any list of "wise patriots." One other Houstonian joined in disagreement with the statement: Billie Carr, the liberal Democratic County chairperson. The other three women who disagreed were the San Francisco civil rights attorney and feminist, whose ideals of reform established in the 1960s were frustrated in the 1970s; the wife of a native American Washington lawyer (her husband agreed with minor reservations); a Washington attorney with major responsibilities in the American Bar Association; and Pastora Cafferty of Chicago, who served on public boards by appointment of Mayor Daley. None of these women could be excluded from the list of wise patriots. Each in her own way is attempting to repair the faults she finds in American society. However, the subsample involved is too small to form the basis of other than speculative generalizations.

p. 161: *Tocqueville's letter to Chabrol:* Quoted from George Wilson Pierson, *Tocqueville in America* (Garden City, N.Y.: Doubleday, 1959), p. 87;

translated by Pierson. This volume is an abridgement of the author's *Tocqueville and Beaumont in America.*

p. 162: *David Potter on abundance:* The quotation is from David M. Potter, *People of Plenty* (Chicago: University of Chicago Press, 1954; Phoenix paperback, 1966), p. 141. Potter's concern is to demonstrate the effects of abundance on the American national character. The concept of a national character was a stock-in-trade for scholarship in the 1950s. Perhaps such questions came naturally in that more stable era; scholarly preoccupations now are more with divisive themes than unifying ones. I obviously feel that Potter's work continues to be relevant.

p. 166: *Nixon's response to the "energy crisis":* The quotation is from Theodore J. Lowi, *The End of Liberalism* (New York: Norton, 2d ed., 1979), pp. 148–49.

p. 167: *The public indulged in a three-year orgy of buying full-sized cars:* The story of this aspect of the energy policy disaster is told by William Tucker in "The Wreck of the Auto Industry," *Harper's,* November, 1980, pp. 45–60. A year later, Tucker chronicled the impact of price deregulation in "The Energy Crisis is Over!," *Harper's,* November, 1981, pp. 25–36.

p. 167: *President Carter's energy policies:* The outline given here follows the reports on energy in the *Congressional Quarterly Almanac* for 1978 and 1979.

p. 170: *The NRA's inadequacy preceded the determination of its unconstitutionality:* The NRA was struck down by the famous "sick chicken" case, *Schecter Poultry Corp. v. United States.* 295 U.S. 495 (1935).

p. 171: *Madison is blamed for Jimmy Carter's troubles:* See Lloyd Cutler, "To Form a Government," *Foreign Affairs,* vol. 59 (Fall/Winter, 1980/81), pp. 126–43, 421–22. Cutler's argument that a parliamentary system produces able leaders ignores such examples as Asquith and Chamberlain. David Butler and other British scholars have argued that the English system performs best when it behaves most like the American presidential system.

p. 175: *The Gallup Poll asked citizens about price controls:* There were three separate polls. Public approval of the concept of economic controls increased as inflation was recognized as a problem. See the results reported in *Public Opinion* magazine, May/June 1978, p. 25.

p. 177: *Felix Rohatyn's proposals:* The account here is based on his essay, "Reconstructing America," *The New York Review of Books,* March 5, 1981, pp. 16–21. The *Newsweek* cover story on Rohatyn, "The Cities' Mr. Fixit," appeared on May 4, 1981.

p. 178: *A long view of economic history suggests centralization:* For one such long view see Robert L. Heilbroner, "The Demand for the Supply Side," *New York Review of Books,* June 11, 1981, pp. 37–41.

p. 179: *John Adams's despairing note about antimonarchical sentiment:* John
Adams to John Quincy Adams, December 22, 1793. Quoted in Page
Smith, *John Adams*, (Garden City, N.Y.: Doubleday, 1962), p. 845.

p. 180: *The Universal Declaration of Human Rights as "a connecting link":*
The quotation is from J.L. Brierly, *The Law of Nations*, 6th ed. (New
York: Oxford University Press, 1963), p. 294. The Universal Declaration is a resolution, rather than a treaty. It does not bind its members
to any particular behavior.

p. 181: *The Harris Poll measured opposition to the Panama Canal treaties:* The
question asked of a national sample by the Harris organization in
September, 1977, was: "As you know, President Carter asked the U.S.
Senate to vote approval of a new treaty between the U.S. and Panama
that will hand control of the Panama Canal back to Panama by the
year 2000. Would you favor or oppose the U.S. Senate approving this
treaty with Panama?" The question and results are reported in *Public
Opinion*, March/April 1978, p. 33. Surveys at the time revealed that
respondents with greater information about the provisions of the treaty
were more likely to support it. The Guardians were better informed
than the general population; the three respondents who opposed the
treaties were little interested in learning more about them.

p. 187: *Russia shares our interest in maintaining naval maneuvering rights:* My
analysis of the implications of the Bay of Sidra and North Korean
incidents depends on a penetrating study by Bruce D. Larkin, "Con-
tested Access: the Libyan and Korean Incidents of August 1981,"
unpublished ms, October 5, 1981.

EPILOGUE

p. 192: *Epigraph:* The quotation is from *Federalist* 71. Emphasis in the original.

p. 194: *Congressman Vander Jagt writes to possible contributors:* Vander Jagt
to Karl A. Lamb, dated "Wednesday" (April, 1981). This appeal made
no mention of proposed increases in defense spending that could more
than offset the cuts in domestic programs. The letter included a "National Voter Survey" which was "registered in your name with a unique
computerized number. This number will ensure your answers confiden-
tiality and allow the Committee to tabulate and report the results by
congressional district." A five-dollar contribution was asked to process
and tabulate the survey responses and "distribute additional surveys,"
and contributions were solicited for the 1981 GOP Victory Fund to
elect a Republican majority to the House in 1982. I believe that the

technique of including an "opinion survey" in fund solicitation letters was pioneered by radical Right organizations.

p. 195: *David Stockman's apostasy:* The famous article reporting Stockman's expressions of doubt concerning Reaganomics to a Washington reporter is William Greider, "The Education of David Stockman," *Atlantic Monthly,* December 1981, pp. 27–54.

Index